Front Range
Bouldering

Bob Horan

Chockstone Press
Evergreen, Colorado
1989

© 1989 Bob Horan. All rights reserved.

Published and distributed by
Chockstone Press, Inc.
Post Office Box 3505
Evergreen, Colorado 80439

ISBN 0-934641-21-8

Cover photos:
(front) Bob Horan at Carter Lake, Horan collection
(back) Steve Mammen at Horsetooth Reservoir, Horan collection

All uncredited photos by the author.

Preface

Thirty years ago, bouldering was seen as practice climbing – training for the larger world of technical climbing. For many practitioners today, bouldering is firmly established as an end in itself.

John Gill, the most famous pioneer of modern bouldering, saw bouldering as a gymnastic performance, with the outcrops and boulders being the apparatus and each individual problem being a unique performance. For Gill, and for all serious boulderers since, difficulty and style are the equal goals. It has been this philosophy that defines the major difference in outlook between bouldering and rock climbing. As more climbers have accepted bouldering as an alternative to roped climbing, the need for a guidebook has arisen.

Pat Ament's *High Over Boulder* guides, besides describing the longer fifth class routes, also described many of the Boulder, Colorado area problems but without the helpfulness of the topo. Another Ament book, *Master of Rock*, chronicled the story of John Gill and his many bouldering accomplishments. Many of his Colorado problems were described and pictured in this inspiring book.

The idea of a specific bouldering guide to the Colorado Front Range has been tossed around for many years. Because I have been bouldering up and down the Front Range for over a decade, much of the information in this book has been gained directly from experience. Hopefully, this first-hand knowledge allows me to provide route descriptions which even the uninitiated newcomer will find accurate and useful.

No guidebook can be done without the help and support of others. I'd like to thank my family for allowing me the freedom that spurred my interests in climbing and bouldering. I'd also like to thank the people who provided historical background to the many boulder problems this book covers and for their support and contributions to *Front Range Bouldering*: Pat Ament, John Baldwin, Noel Childs, Charlie Fowler, John Gill, Christian Griffith, Tom Henry, Rick Johnson, Steve Mammen, Dennis McCarron, Mike McCarron, Olaf Mitchell, Nancy Prichard, Shane Rymer, Jim Sanders, John Sherman and Mark Wilford.

"The depths of climbing lie in its personal, individualistic aspects. Popular values, dictated by the masses, discourage creativity. Unique individuals are given definitions and to be defined, I think, is to be degraded."

    Pat Ament,
        from a conversation with John Gill in the book *Master of Rock*.

Foreword

by **Christian Griffith**

Bouldering is at the heart of all climbing. Strength, coordination, speed; the mechanics of our craft are all most readily developed in short combinations. In training, endurance and recovery can be greatly enhanced by bouldering, and it is on the short cliffs that the all-important mental parameters of the sport are best honed.

Bouldering is such an effective developmental tool because as an activity it is so flexible. A bouldering session can be exactly tailored to the specific needs of a climber. Long traverses are perfect to build endurance, short powerful dynamic and static moves build strength, perseverance and visualization are developed on problems where the moves are known but they are still a bit too hard; what better mental training tool is there?

While no definition of climbing could be complete without mention of bouldering, it could be more strongly said that bouldering itself defines climbing. Historically, the leading edge of each generation has turned to the boulders for the tools they need to redefine their sport. Viewed simply, the evolution of rock climbing has been the application of increasingly harder boulder moves. In the early days people bouldered for general fitness, and their routes likewise were fitness oriented. Nowadays, problems are sought which mirror specific moves high on routes; this form of practice can be attested to the myriad of "Psycho" simulators found on Flagstaff Mountain.

Though it is a fair appraisal to say that one cannot expect to do hard moves high on a cliff if one cannot do them close to the ground on boulders, bouldering, as much as it is an important proving ground for technical climbing, is still a very unique and important discipline in its own right.

It is again the flexible and manageable aspect of bouldering, its segmentation, that gives it at one time extremely personal and at others very social moments. It is the variety that keeps things interesting. Indeed, personalized circuits of problems can be as great, if not greater, statements of creativity and talent than longer climbing routes.

Creativity and enthusiasm keep bouldering from getting boring. New movements, new eliminates and even new holds can always be found. Bouldering areas always provide a challenge. Ironically, because of the very nature of the activity, it could even be said that the true potential for an area is never fully realized until all its problems have been completely wired.

Residents along the Front Range are fortunate in having one of the world's greatest concentration of boulders to climb and explore. Flagstaff, Morrison and Horsetooth Reservoir, the most popular areas, offer a mix of classic lines and criss-crossed training walls rarely found in other areas. Variations in rock type, hold type, steepness and environment provide climbing and training possibilities for climbers of all abilities under virtually any weather condition.

Contents

Introduction	1
Horsetooth Reservoir	8
Carter Lake Reservoir	54
Mount Sanitas	78
Flagstaff Mountain	86
Eldorado Canyon	132
Morrison Wall	164

Introduction

The Colorado Front Range is graced with high quality bouldering. The diversity of the many small outcroppings and boulder fields found here rival if not surpass the quality and richness of such world class bouldering spots as Fountain Bleu, outside of Paris, France, and the varnished boulders of the Buttermilks, in California. Smooth, polished creekside rocks, extremely overhanging outcrops, short free-standing pinnacles and spires, pebbled and crystaline walls and well-endowed fields of soft sandstone characterize the Front Range bouldering paradise.

The historical roots of modern bouldering are tightly aligned with the Colorado Front Range, providing an inspiration and magic that can't be beat. Since the days when John Gill roamed the slopes of Colorado, establishing testpieces, climbers from all over the world have come to the boulders of Colorado in search of the many classic problems that make this area legendary. What they also find, from the shimmering shores of the Horsetooth Reservoir to the solar collecting, overhanging Morrison Wall, is a refreshing mountainous environment that is rich with rock that challenges all levels of ability.

Introduction — 1

Hitting the hole just right on the Just Right problem (B.1+) on Capstan Rock, Flagstaff.

Jim Sanders

2 — Introduction

In the late '50s and early '60s, before bouldering was accepted by the climbing world as an end in itself, enthusiastic climbers such as Corwin Simmons, Bob Beatty, Prince Willman, Ray Northcutt, Dallas Jackson, Layon Kor, Larry Dalke, and the strong fingered Bob Culp, dedicated time to the boulders of the Front Range.

An energetic beginning boulderer, Pat Ament, emerged on the scene in the early '60s and progressed on the boulders of Flagstaff Mountain to produce some standard-setting bouldering trends.

Meanwhile, John Gill, a mathematics major and driven rock climber, took up training as a gymnast to enhance his acrobatic dexterity, poise, gracefulness, and balance for the rocks. His rope climbing and ring workouts gave him a super human physique which became useful when applied to the strenuous boulder problems he established.

Gill's gymnastic attributes, along with singular discipline and drive, allowed him to single-handedly create new standards in difficulty. Gill saw bouldering as a more severe athletic activity than classical rock climbing, requiring the use of gymnastics, acrobatics, and aeorobatics as techniques to develop. His routes are still respected as top notch bouldering.

In 1967, after spending much time with schooling in the midwest and developing his bouldering skills on many of the area's rocks, Gill decided it was time to expand on his mathematical skills and he began teaching at Colorado State University in Fort Collins. It was during this time that he first began working out on the rocks surrounding Horsetooth Reservoir. Also at this time he was introduced to a strong gymnast named Rich Borgman. Borgman was described by Gill as a superlative climber, and routes such as **Borgman's Bulge** (B.1+) at the Torture Chamber of Spring Canyon Dam attest to Borman's bouldering talents.

Gill and Borgman pushed each other on the sandstone outcrops and boulders that Gill describes as his favorite rock. Gill's testpieces, such as **Torture Chamber Traverse** (B.1), **Sunshine Boulder** (B.1), **Talent Scout** (B.1+), the **Eliminators** (B.1+), the **Pinch Overhang** (B.1+), among others, have remained as monumental standard markers for future generations. The use of little white arrows, painted on by Gill, mark the ways of his most accomplished problems.

In the late '60s, inspired in part by John Gill, Pat Ament pursued bouldering intensely, with Gill's training methods. Expert boulderers such as Paul Hagan, Bob Poling, Eric Varney, and Richard Smith joined Ament in a pushing of the standards on Flagstaff Mountain, with such routes as **Hagan's Wall** (B.1), at Cloud Shadow, the **Poling Pebble** (B.1), on Beer Barrel Rock, **Smith Overhang** (B.1+), at Pratt's Overhang, and the **Eric Varney Direct** (B.1+), up the middle of the Red Wall. Ament, who had a visionary drive to establish new problems, came up with several classics, such as **Right Side of Red Wall** (B.1), **First Overhang** (B.1), **The Consideration** (B.1−), at Cloud Shadow, and the **South Overhang** (B.1), on Capstan Rock. Ament also had a knack for one-arm ascents as he demonstrated on the One-Arm Rocks. Another talented boulderer named Bob Williams, who struct a beautiful balance between static and dynamic techniques, put up such routes as **Double Clutch** (B.1+), on Beer Barrel Rock, and the **Williams Pull** (B.1−) at Cloud Shadow.

In the early 1970s, Gill and Borgman visited Flagstaff and made first try ascents of Smith Overhang, the Right Side of the Red Wall, and several other difficult routes. Gill again left his mark on Flagstaff with first ascents of the

Introduction — 3

Gill Swing (B.2), at Pratt's Overhang Area, and the Gill Direct (B.1), in the Amphitheatre Rocks.

Later Gill traveled down to Eldorado Canyon to put up more problems. The Gill Boulder in the back of the canyon reveal more of his talents.

The mid '70s on Flagstaff brough on more gymnastic talent with the honed Bob Candelaria and the very tall and lean Jim Holloway. Routes such as Face Out (B.1+), on the Great Ridge, Hollow's Way (B.2), on the Notlim Boulder, and Butt Slammer (B.2) are just some of the problems Candelaria powered up. He was also known for his mantle hand stands. Holloway, with his fabulous body span, took a quantum leap in Flagstaff's history with routes like Just Right (B.1+), on Capstan Rock, A.H.R. (B.2), and Lower Bulge Traverse (B.2), on Cloud Shadow, as well as the Stretcher (B.2) on Pratt's Overhang Area. Another strong boulderer during this period was the gracefully strong Dave Breashears, who established, on sight, first try, the Nemesus Standard Route (B.1+), at Torture Chamber on Horsetooth Reservoir, and the thin Shield (B.1+) on the Bastille in Eldorado Canyon.

In the late '70s and throughout the '80s a large number of dedicated and very talented boulderers arrived on the scene. Steve Mammen put up many hard traverses at Horsetooth Reservoir and began developing some difficult problems at Carter Lake, the Kahoonee Roof (B.2), most noteworthy. Mammen also bouldered up the long-standing problems on the right side of the Milton Boulder's west face to come up with Never Say Never (B.2). Another Fort Collins boulderer named Mark Wilford followed in Gill's footsteps and established many hard problems at the Reservoir, notably The Scoop (B.1), Master of Disaster (B.1+), the Cinch (B.2), and Motion Picture Slob (B.1).

Dan Stone made his way up and down the Front Range and established such problems as Dandy Line (B.1+), and Stone Ground (B.1), on Flagstaff. He also left his talented marks at Morrison with Magnum Force (B.1+). Many of the problems around the cave area of the Eldorado's Whales Tail may have been his.

Another well conditioned and naturally talented boulderer name Skip Guerin emerged in the 1980s and applied his skills to the rocks of Flagstaff and Eldorado. Most of his original problems consisted of strenuous or micro thin traverses. Along with Christian Griffith, Guerin made some desperate sitting-start problems on the Red Wall of Flagstaff.

In the 80s, I have also been very active on the boulders. The Distant Dancer (B.1+) and the Masochism Tongo (B.1+), on First Overhang are good, hard problems. In Eldorado, I have found many problems along the Eldorado Creek bed such as Cranbaker (B.1), Psychic Roof (B.1+), Eastern Priest (B.1−), and the Kiss of Life (B.2). On the Milton Boulder I found Micro Sheer (B.2), as well as some steep thin faces on the north face of the Gill Boulder. I have also bouldered out such short but difficult routes on the Whales Tail such as Horangutan (5.12b), and N.E.D. (5.12a). Darius Azin managed to boulder free-solo Amputee Love (5.12b), on the Whales Tail.

Many other active climbers have taken to the boulders with much enthusiasm and have put up problems of good quality and added some color and character to the Front Range. Scott Blunk, Malcolm Daly, Jeff Achey, Harrison Dekker, John Sherman, Charlie Fowler, Rufus Miller, Noel Childs, Olaf Mitchell, among others, have all been active.

ACCESS

All of the areas mentioned in this book are on public land and fall within the jurisdiction of city parks, state parks or federal Bureau of Land Management. All of these agencies have statutes and regulations regarding public access and activities. It is important to become familar with these since they vary somewhat from one area to the other. Eldorado Canyon is the only area that requires an entrance fee. It is $3.00 per vehicle or $25.00 for an annual pass. A $1.00 walk-in fee is required for those not equipped with a vehicle.

There are some areas on the Front Range that were relatively popular bouldering areas in the 1960s but have since become privately owned. As time goes on more and more encroachment will be made by commercial developers. Let's respect the environment that we have set aside for public use, for this is all we may have left. Access problems for climbers are best prevented by a sensitivity to irresponsible behavior. When access problems do arise, the Access Committee of the American Alpine Club can do much to help negotiate, organize, and even litigate closures of climbing areas. In fact, contribution to the AAC Access Fund, a tax-deductable donation, can help finance the actual purchase or preservation of climbing and bouldering areas. Contact them care of the American Alpine Club, Post Office Box 67A25, Los Angeles, CA 90067.

ENVIRONMENTAL CONSIDERATIONS

The areas in this book were set aside for the preservation and enjoyment of the natural environment. Already these areas are feeling the effects of their ever-growing popularity. As loving outdoor participants, it is our duty to help in the preservation of these beautiful areas through removal of the litter we may come across and by staying on the trails or footpaths as much as possible. Many of the bouldering areas described in this book are used and treasured by a diverse public, most of whom do not boulder. Have some consideration and lend a helping hand by keeping these places at least as nice as when you found them.

WEATHER

For the most part, the weather along the Colorado Front Range is good all year round. Since the bouldering is found at a fairly low elevation, if the sun is shining through it is usually warm. If it happens to snow, just wait a few days and if the sun appears it is sure to dry the rocks.

Every winter usually hosts at least one period of extended cold or rain, this occurring in late winter or early spring, if at all. The fall or spring normally has the best weather, although on a nice winter day in Colorado conditions could not be better.

SAFETY

Bouldering usually afflicts injury in the form of pulled tendons and twisted ankles. Avoiding this is very simple. Use a rope that is securely anchored if you feel that there is any chance that you may be hurt if you fall off the rock. Just because some daring climbers choose to free-solo does not mean that it is good for everyone. Warming up and progressing slowly to prevent injury to the joints, tendons or muscles and concentrating on safety is the key to a long life of fun bouldering.

Introduction — 5

Bouldering with a partner inevitably provides incentive to push each other's ability as well as providing the confidence of a good spot. The spotter should stand behind the boulderer while he ascends the problem and be prepared for a possible slip or miss. The role of the spotter is not to catch the falling climber; instead it is to properly realign feet of the falling climber with the landing zone, perhaps also in some small way allowing a gentler landing. When properly done, a spotter and boulderer can work together and take off a little bit of the psychological edge.

ON EQUIPMENT

One of the true pleasures of bouldering is the simplicity of gear needed. A pair of shoes and a chalk bag are usually enough to please most boulderers. At times a top rope may want to be employed for those problems that are too high to be safe. Some of the boulders or outcrops may have a fixed anchor station on its summit; these are marked in the book. If the drawing does not show a fixed anchor you may want to bring an assorted rack of gear and the necessary knowledge to use them.

RATINGS

The following rating system was introduced by John Gill and serves as a general classification for the hardest problems. A plus or minus has been added to the B.1 range for finer tuning.

B.1− is bouldering at 5.11a.
B.1 is bouldering at 5.11 or higher.
B.1+ is bouldering at 5.12.
B.2 is bouldering at 5.13.
B.3 is something that is done once, tried frequently, but is not repeated.
   If it is repeated it drops to B.2.

Often there are problems easier than B.1− and an approximate fifth class rating is given, preceded by a B. For example, a B5.8 would be similar to a 5.8 move on a fifth class route, etcetera.

It is a difficult task to create a consistantly accurate grading scale without an ascent consensus. Usually when a route is completed the first ascentionist will tack on a grade based on his experience with the grading scale and his personal feeling of difficulty within it. This is more or less a suggested grade, and until other climbers repeat that route and a general consensus is gathered, the original grade holds. But after the consensus is made the grade of the route may be pushed up or down.

Many of the grades in this book are only tenative grades because the routes have seen little traffic. A problem can feel harder for some and easier for others. Get a general feel for the grading scale and make your own decision; the grades are only there for general feel for its difficulty, and should not be taken too seriously. After all, you are only as good as you are and comparing can only lead to selfishness.

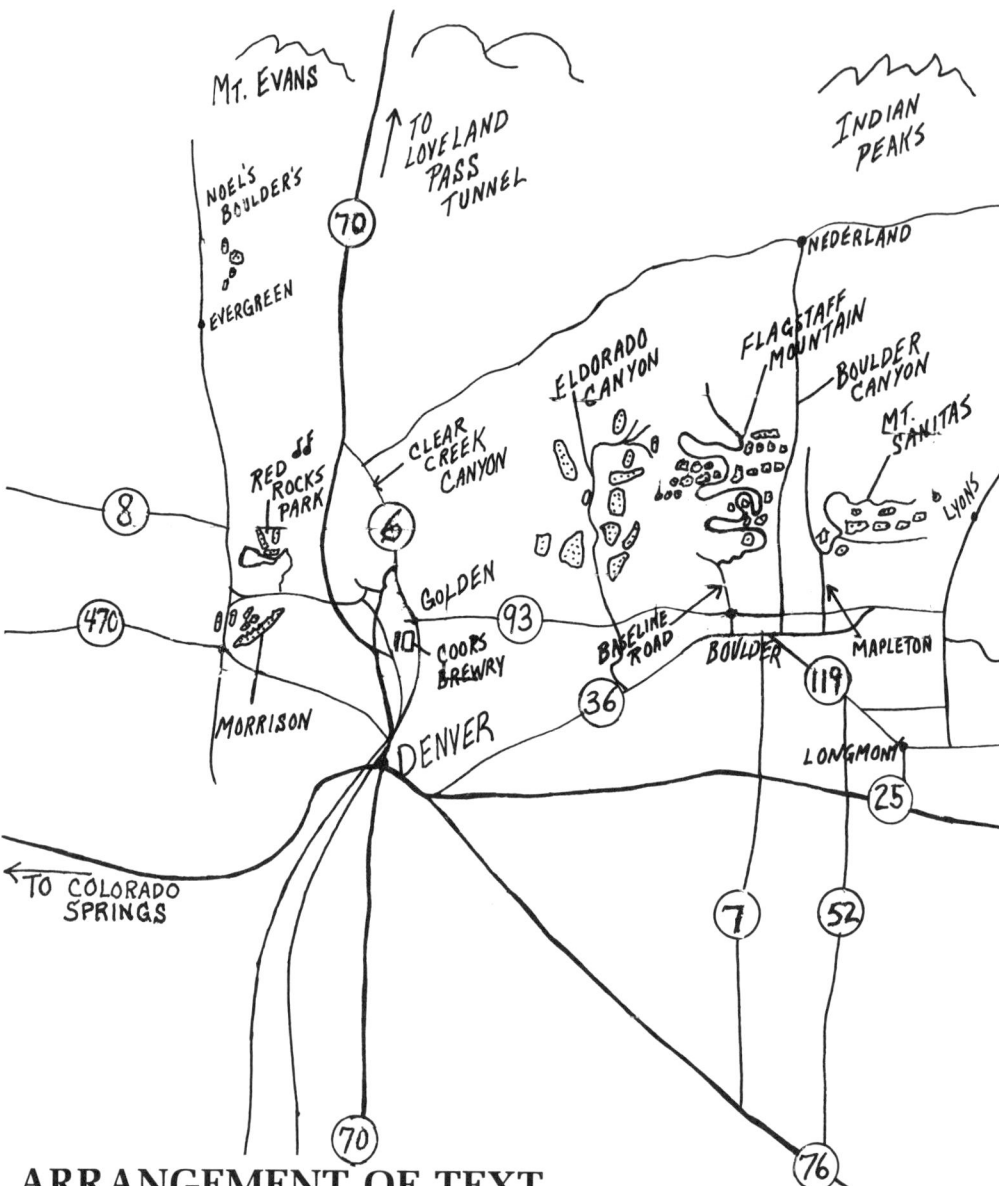

ARRANGEMENT OF TEXT

The areas along the Front Range are described from north to south, Fort Collins to Morrison. The use of the topos should be self-evident; text that accompanies them may reiterate or supplement the information found on the drawings. It will be obvious that many, many problems are not described. Traverses, variations, and eliminates are naturally found everywhere. But by directing the reader to the major features and routes, this book will have provided a glimpse of the great bouldering to be found along the Front Range. Hopefully, your imagination will be spurred to discover your own combination of moves, your own problems, to realize the joys of discovery that is so much the fun of bouldering.

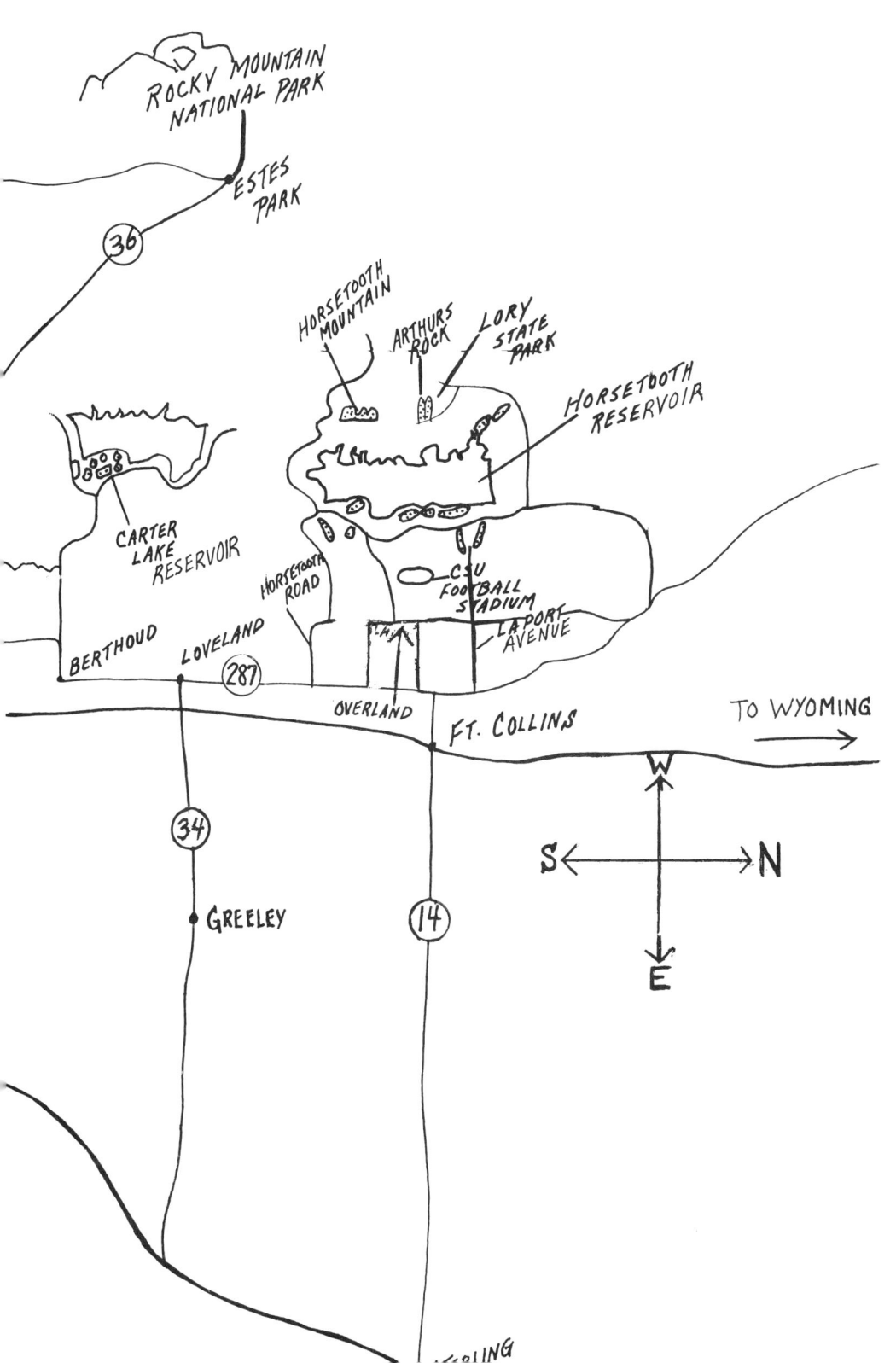

Horsetooth Reservoir

The sandy shores of Horsetooth Reservoir are spotted with some of the best bouldering anywhere. Soft Dakota sandstone can be found from one end of the reservoir to the other, either outcropped from ridges or spread out miraculously amoungst the slopes in boulder form.

Such John Gill legacies as The Torture Chamber, Sunshine Boulder, The Eliminator and Mental Block can be found throughout the slopes that surround this refreshing mountain lake. The abundance of quality rock offers a bouldering paradise for climbers of all abilities.

To reach Horsetooth Reservoir take Interstate 25 to the Fort Collins exit at Highway 14. Head west until you intersect Highway 287, which runs north-south through the center of town. Head south from Highway on 287 until you reach Drake. Follow this west towards the mountains. Drake will turn into Overland at a curve that heads to the north. Continue on this for a few miles until you come to a left at road 42c. Take this west past the Colorado State University football stadium up to the reservoir. At one point the paved road will take a sharp curve to the south. This will lead you to the Marina Area,

Piano Boulder, Duncan's Ridge and Torture Chamber. From that same sharp curve a dirt road heads north to Rotary Park, The Scoop Area, Land of the Overhangs and the North Quarry. All mileage markings were taken from this intersection.

ARETE RIDGE

From the mileage intersection head up the dirt road along the reservoir towards Dixon Dam. On the north side of the dam there is an arete at the start of a ridge that extends up to the north. There are several top-rope problems on this formation, including the 5.11+ arete.

Dennis McCarron (right) lunges up Pinch Overhang (B.1+) while his brother Mike (left) cranks the Corner Lock (B.1), Horsetooth Reservoir.

10 — Horsetooth Reservoir

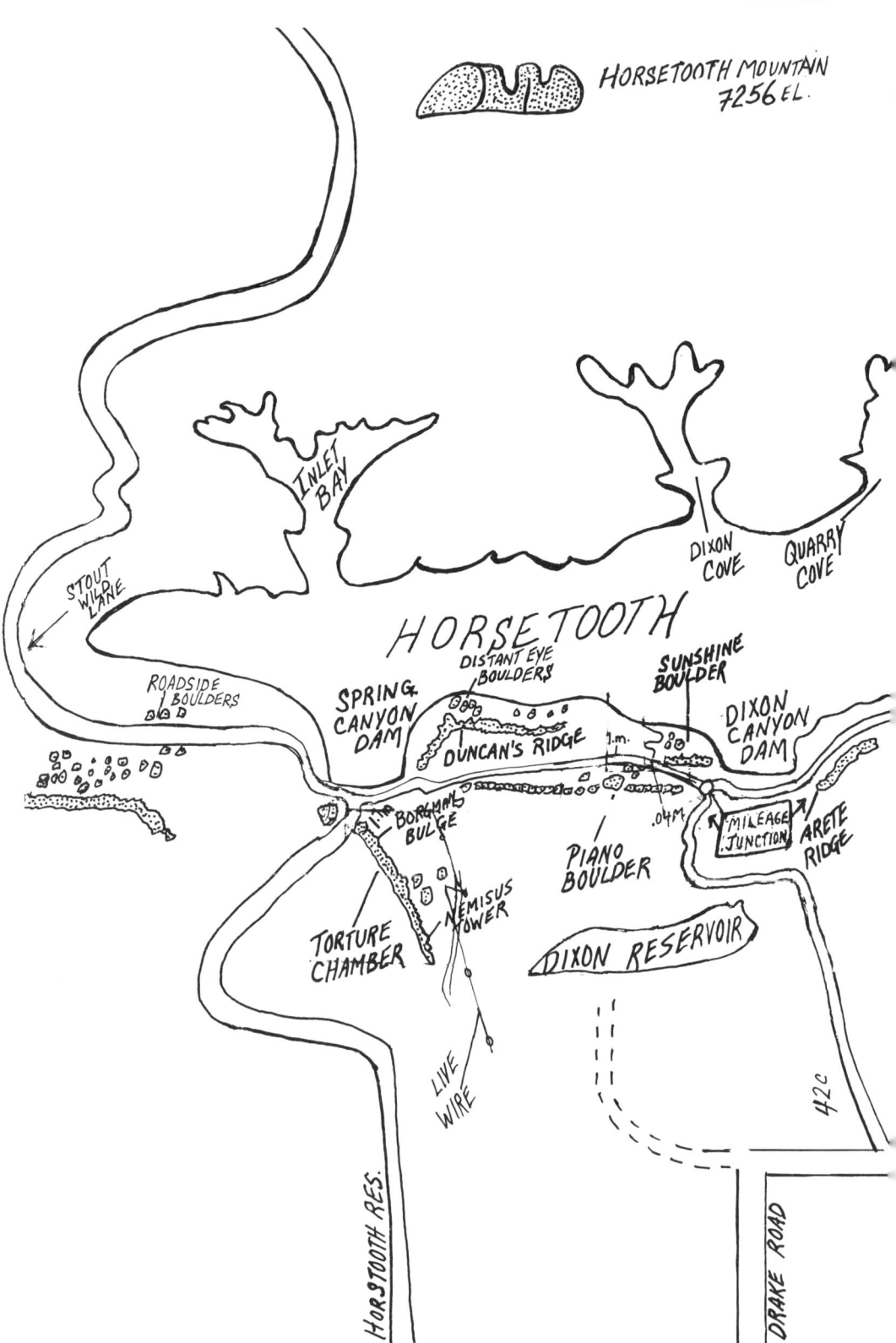

Horsetooth Reservoir — 11

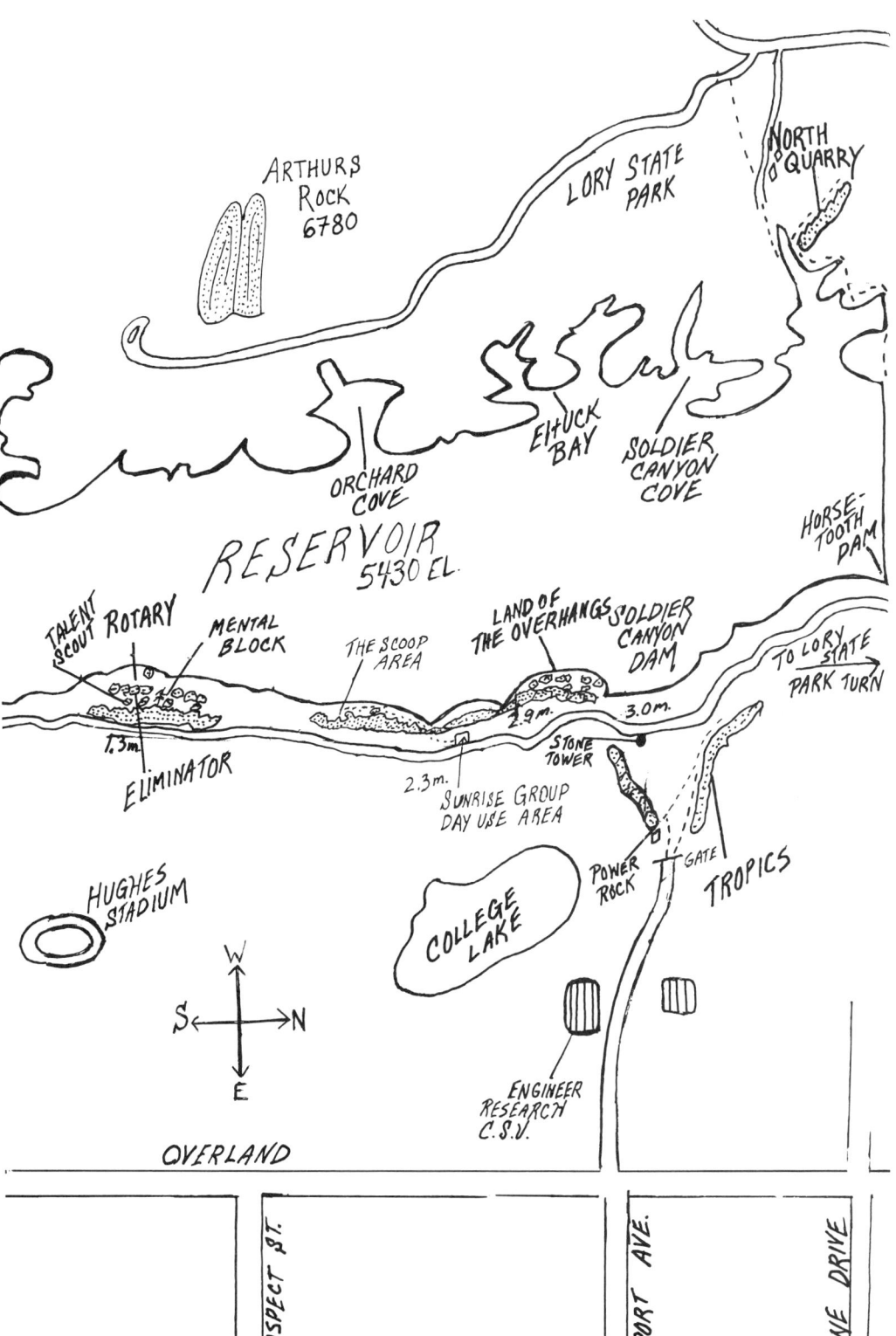

ROTARY PARK

From the mileage junction head up the dirt road to the north for 1.3 miles until a group of small rocks will be seen planted along the road. Park anywhere along the rocks and walk out west towards the reservoir. A faint trail leads to the edge of the ridge and down through a low angle break. Below are an amazing array of classic boulders filled with some of the problems that made John Gill a legend.

SHIP'S PROW

By walking south along the ridge from the break you will see this pointy arete with a prominent southwest-facing jagged crack.

Curving Crack B5.8
This problem takes the obvious crack on the southwest face of the Ship's Prow and offers some serious exposure.

Southwest Face B.1
To the left of the crack there is an arete with a thin face on its right side. Climb the delicate face, avoiding the arete.

West Arete B5.10
This problem takes the prow of the Ship's Prow.

ELIMINATOR BOULDER

Just below the Ship's Prow there is a large rectangular-shaped boulder with some classic Gill problems on its west side.

Mammen's Traverse B.2
On the south face of the Eliminator there is a cove formed by a connecting boulder. The traverse starts inside the cove and works its way to the right, ending at a crack and mantle. This is said to be the area's most difficult traverse. FA: S. Mammen 1980s.

The Prow B.1−
Down from the traverse to the south there is a overhanging arete on the southwest corner. Pinch your way to the pointy top.

Right Eliminator B.1
This classic Gill problem can be found on the far right hand side of the boulder's west face; look for the painted arrow. A small brown crystal is used with one hand and a small edge is used with the other. Crank up on these small holds and reach for a good jug. Moving left from here adds another challenge. FA: J. Gill 1960s.

Left Eliminator B.1+
This incredible problem on the left side of the west face can be done statically, one arm lunged or double lunged. From a small edge with your right hand make a long reach up and out left to a good ledge. Look for the painted arrow. FA: J. Gill 1960s.

Arete Crack B5.9+
Just to the left of the Left Eliminator there is a right-angling wide crack that can be laybacked. The far right side of the crack is where you reach on the Left Eliminator Problem. This is a good fun pump.

MEDITATION BOULDER

Just below the Eliminator Boulder and to the northwest is found this somewhat round, flat-top boulder. Many good face problems can be done, including a traverse around the whole boulder. A flat summit makes for a peaceful place to relax while gazing into the still waters below.

MENTAL BLOCK
Slightly up and to the north several hundred feet from the Meditation Boulder is this overhanging test block. Many very tenuous problems exist on its west face, including a wild pinch overhang and a strenuous traverse. Look for the painted arrows and head up the overhang.

Layback Overhang B.1 −
On the far right side of the west overhang of the block there is an obvious foot-long corner with a barndoor layback move to gain the top mantle shelf. FA: J. Gill 1960s.

Pinch Overhang B.1 +
This intense pinch problem requires a leap for the sloping shelf above from a 4 by 4 pinch with the right hand. A good grip is crucial on this powerful move. FA: J. Gill 1960s.

Standard Route B.1 −
This overhanging face climbs up the edges on the northwest corner of the block. The mantle on the top has been known to spit people off, leaving them in the bush below. FA: J. Gill 1960s.

Corner Crack B.1
Immediately left of the Standard route is an overhanging problem that reaches up to a small finger lock in a little corner. FA: J. Gill 1960s.

Willie's Lunge B.1
From a good hold at the start of the North Roof and another good hold at the start of the Corner Lock, lunge up to the top of the block and mantle. FA: unknown

North Roof B.1
Left of the Corner Lock there is another thin problem that starts out the right side of the small roof and moves up the thin edges towards the arete on the left edge of the boulder's north face. FA: J. Gill 1960s.

North Arete B5.8
On the left side of the north face there is a prominent arete with a short fun problem.

Block Face B5.9
Just to the south of the Mental Block and connected to its southwest side there is another small block with a classic face up its south face.

PITCH PENNY BOULDER
Downhill to the northwest of the Mental Block there is a fun moderate boulder with some very good faces and traverse on it. Several pennys where found on the top of this boulder that had probably been pitched from the top of the ridge.

THE CAVE
East of Mental Block and slightly north along the top ridge there is a cave-like formation with some difficult problems out a protruding roof. A short face problem can be found on a south-facing wall just to the north in the cave area. If you continue along this ridge to the north you will run across other types of problem with good challenges.

Rotary Park

A SHIP'S PROW
1. Curving Crack B5.8
2. Southwest Face B.1
3. West Arete B5.10

B ELIMINATOR BOULDER
1. Mammen's Traverse B.2
2. The Prow B.1−
3. Right Eliminator B.1
4. Left Eliminator B.1+
5. Arete Crack B5.9+

C MEDITATION BOULDER

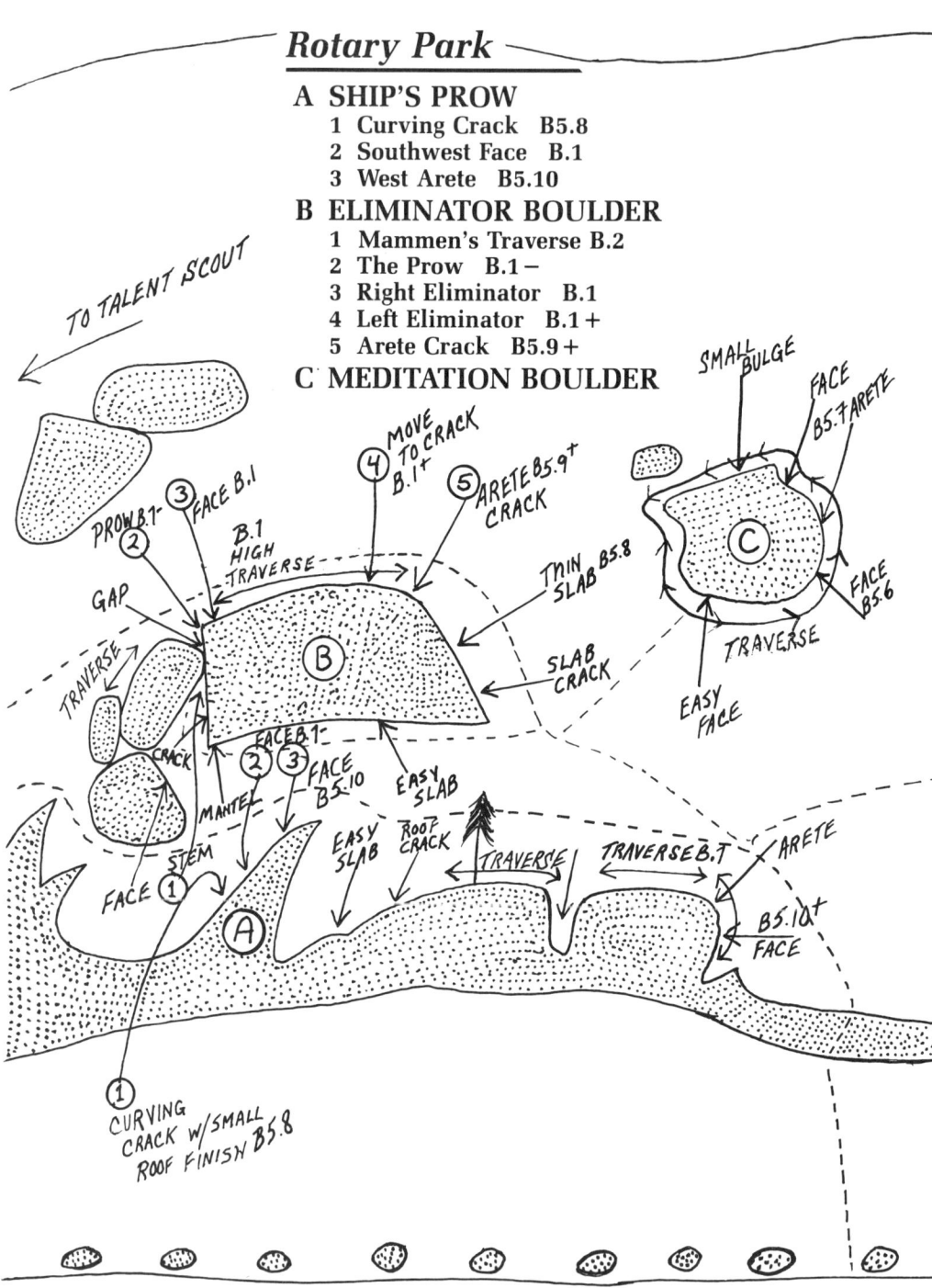

Horsetooth Reservoir — 15

D MENTAL BLOCK
1. Block Face   B5.9
2. Layback Overhang   B.1−
3. Pinch Overhang   B.1+
4. Standard Route   B.1−
5. Corner Crack   B.1
6. Willie's Lunge   B.1
7. North Roof   B.1
8. North Arete   B5.8

E PITCH PENNY BOULDER

F THE CAVE

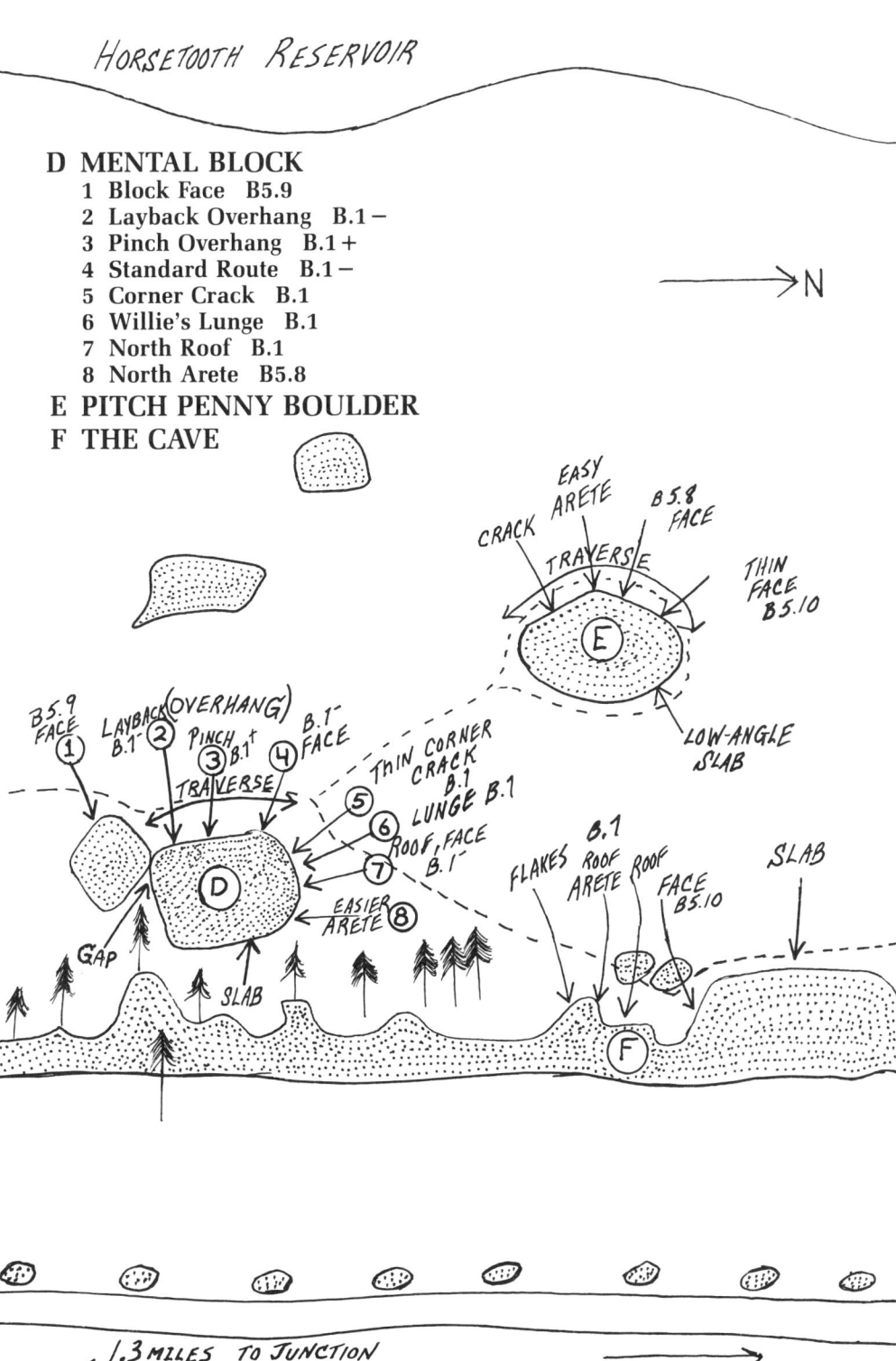

ROTARY PARK
BOLT WALL
From the Ship's Prow head along the ridge to the south until you come across a steep face with a right-facing dihedral crack on its right end. Two bolt holes can be seen just above the ground on the bulging face to the left of the dihedral. Many excellent problems exsist all along this wall. The wall continues around the corner to the south where an obvious crack under a large roof or ceiling can be found.

Classic Flake B5.7
On the west face of the far right wall, just to the right of the undercling roof crack, a large flake leads up off the ground to the roof.

Corner Cling B5.9
Left of the layback flake a prominent corner system rises to the ceiling. Follow this to the crack and undercling out to the left under the roof.

Cat's Eye B.1−
On the south face of the wall just below the ceiling undercling there is a thin-edged face leading straight up to the undercling. This is a problem with delicate moves high off the ground.

West Bulge B5.10
Left of the Cat's Eye and around the corner is a bulge just off the ground that can be ascended to the arete. A traverse problem starts on the left side of the bulge just right of the Classic Dihedral and works its way around to the right across the Cat's Eye face, offering a strenuous start to a delicate face.

Classic Dihedral B5.10+
Just to the left of the bulge is an obvious right-facing dihedral with a thin finger crack up its corner.

The Faces
Just left of the Classic Dihedral there is a steep west-facing wall with many variation up it. The routes range from B5.8 to B.1+.

Another Mammen Traverse B.1+
From the Classic Dihedral, traverse to the left just above the ground all the way across the face to easier ground. FA: S. Mammen 1980s.

Classic Crack B5.9
To the north from the Bolt Wall is this prominent line with small corners.

Bulging Traverse B.1
Farther to the north but still south of the Ship's Prow is a bulging north-heading traverse just above the ground that leads around a corner and up a steep face.

TALENT SCOUT
This is the small block located just to the west about fifteen feet from the Bolt Wall. Its northwest face has some thin problems.

Standard Route B5.10+
On the right side of the northwest face there are some good holds to use to make a long reach to a bucket. The polished foot holds make this a real challenge. FA: J. Gill 1960s.

Roof Direct B.1+
This tight move on the left side of the northwest face is ascended by avoiding the left arete. Pull up on the thin edges, undercling the small roof and reach over to thin edges. Pull to the top. FA: J. Gill 1960s.

Left Arete B5.9
This takes the arete on the far left side of the northwest face.

Many other variations can be done on this northwest face, including some lunge problems.

GILL PINNACLE
Straight north from the Talent Scout you will see a small blocky pinnacle with easy access to its short summit. Some fun moderate problems can be done on all sides.

PUNK ROCK
This long rounded boulder sits hidden down slope from the Gill Pinnacle. Its short bulging west face has a long strenuous B.1 traverse that was dug out by the locals.

WATERWAY BOULDER
Down from Punk Rock, near the waterline, this boulder has good problems on its west side. This boulder is sometimes under water.

Mike McCarron (right) ascends the Cat's Eye (B.1−) while Mark Wilford climbs the Bolt Wall's Bulge Route (B.1).

18 — Horsetooth Reservoir

HORSETOOTH RESERVOIR

Rotary Park

A BOLT WALL
1. Classic Flake B5.7
2. Corner Cling B5.9
3. Cat's Eye B.1−
4. West Bulge B5.10
5. Classic Dihedral B5.10+
6. Classic Crack B5.9

B TALENT SCOUT BLOCK
1. Standard B5.10+
2. Roof Direct B.1+
3. Left Arete B5.9

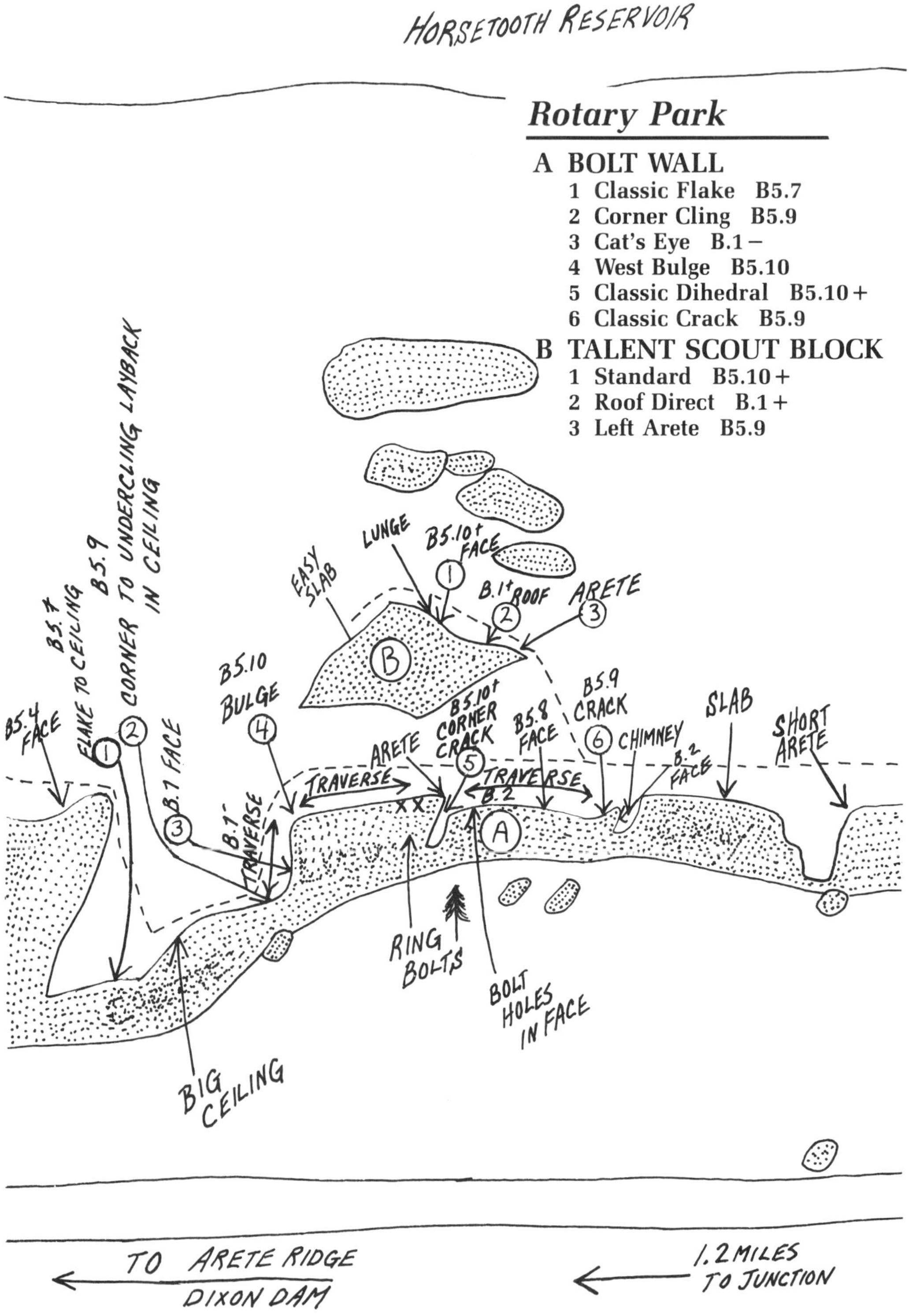

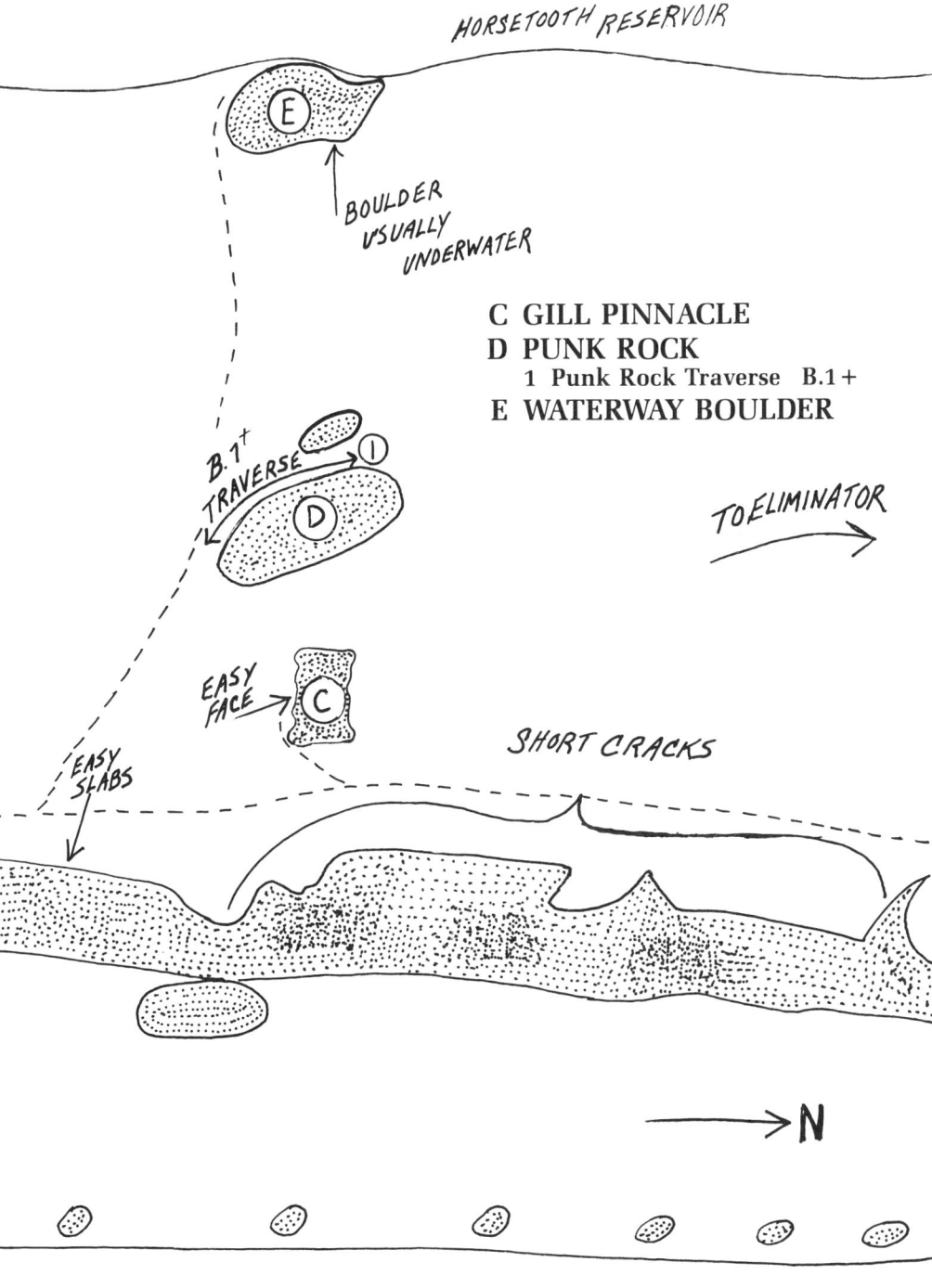

THE SCOOP AREA

Continue to the north along the dirt road from Rotary Park for about a mile. On the left side of the road you will see the Sunrise Group Parking Area. From the parking lot, hike due south down a faint trail to a gully that runs down towards the reservoir. From a quarried break in the ridge head up to the south along the ridge. Soon you will run across a good number of quality problems, including a classic overhanging crack.

Classic Crack B5.10 (TR)
If you hike uphill to the south along the base of the ridge you will soon come across this prominent west-facing, overhanging finger/hand crack.

Bulging Face B.1+ (TR)
Immediately left of Classic Crack is a bulging wall with a short corner start.

WEST PROW
Uphill to the south even farther is a prominent rounded white prow leaning out from the ridge. Several routes can be done on and around this, including a classic dihedral.

THE SCOOP WALL
Uphill to the south of the West Prow is this beautifully smooth section of the ridge. A prominent white scooping west face just left of a corner system has some delicate face problems.

Standard Scoop B5.10
On the left side of the white scooping face is a set of good edges leading up and to the left. FA: M. Wilford 1980s.

The Scoop B.1
This high quality face problem ascends the middle of the smooth face to the roof and then exits to the right via sloping holds. FA: M. Wilford 1980s.

Arete Hook B.1−
The right side of The Scoop forms an arete. Layaway with your left hand on the arete and reach out and up to the far right for a good edge. From this position you must hook your foot on the arete and match hands. FA: M. Wilford 1980s.

The Corner B5.8
To the right of the Arete Hook is a short corner with a thin layback crack.

Slab Ridge B5.7
To the right of the corner is a laid-back arete which can be ascended with the slab on its left side.

Master of Disaster B.1+
To the right of the Slab Ridge is an obvious undercling in the bulging wall with a short right-leaning corner. Undercling the bulge and reach up for a sloping pocket. The next delicate move is very intimidating. FA: M. Wilford 1980s.

Horsetooth Reservoir — 21

Powering over the bulge of Master of Disaster (B.1+), The Scoop Area. The Scoop Face can be seen just to the left. photo: Tom Henry

22 — Horsetooth Reservoir

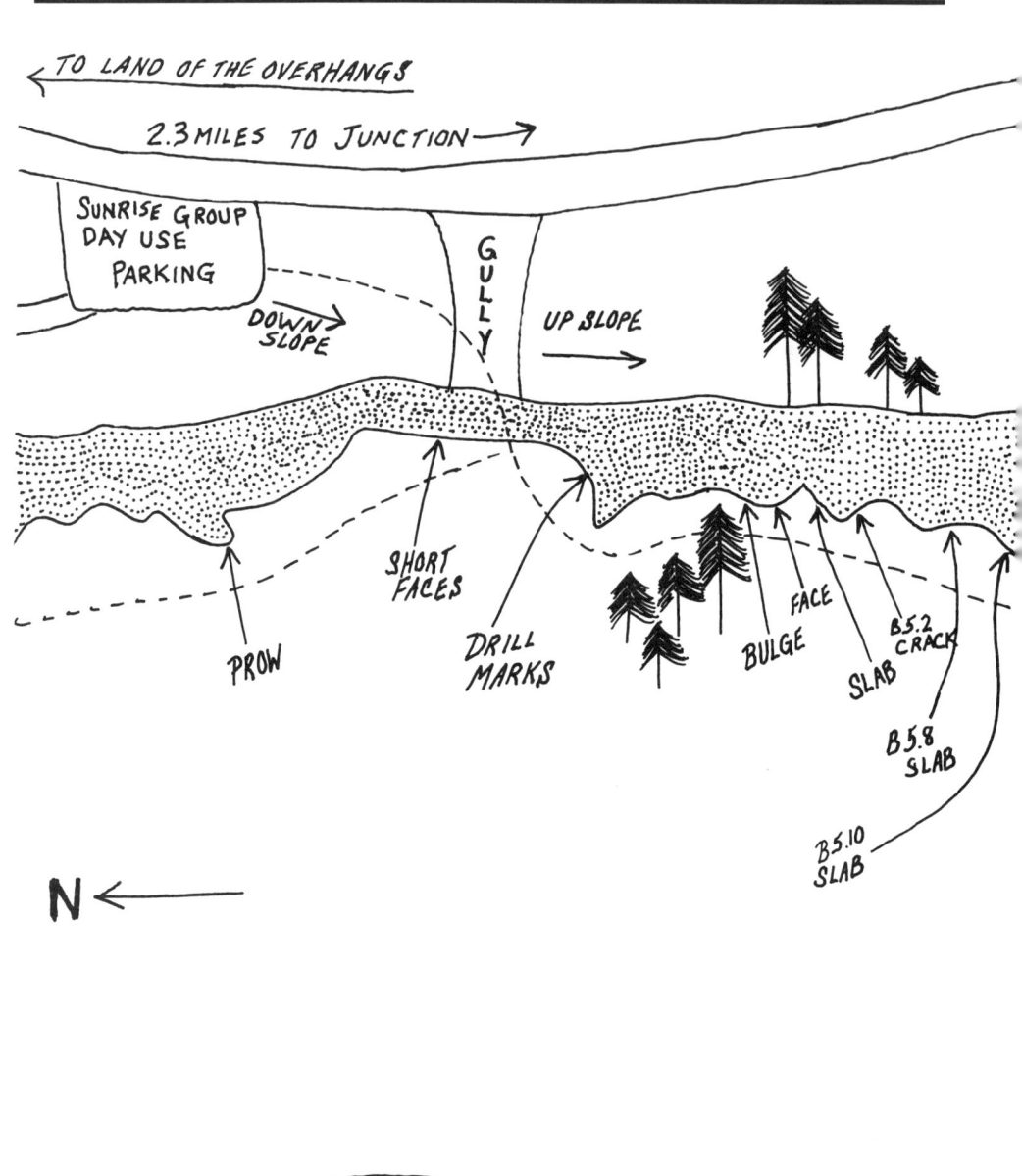

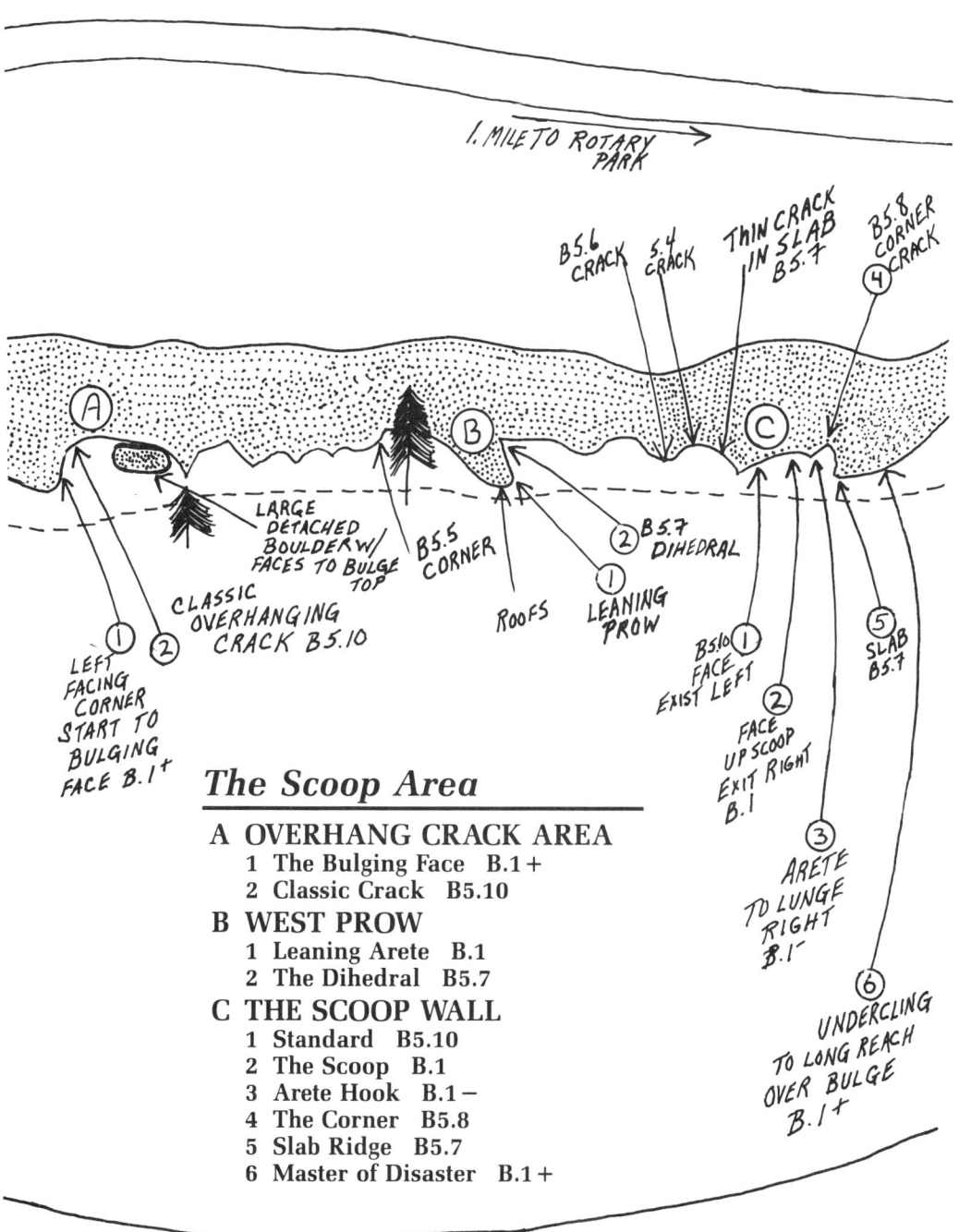

The Scoop Area

A OVERHANG CRACK AREA
  1 The Bulging Face   B.1+
  2 Classic Crack   B5.10

B WEST PROW
  1 Leaning Arete   B.1
  2 The Dihedral   B5.7

C THE SCOOP WALL
  1 Standard   B5.10
  2 The Scoop   B.1
  3 Arete Hook   B.1−
  4 The Corner   B5.8
  5 Slab Ridge   B5.7
  6 Master of Disaster   B.1+

LAND OF THE OVERHANGS

From the Scoop Wall continue on the dirt road to the north for six tenths of a mile. Just before a curve that heads down to Spring Canyon Dam pull off to the shoulder and park. From here reach the Land of the Overhangs by walking southwest to a break in the ridge or walk down hill to the northeast to the bottom of its ridge. Many overhanging outcrops fill this ridge with challenging problems.

BEACH ROCK
On the lower north end of the ridge there are some slabs and blocks off the beach. Beach Rock is the prominent black block with a steep north face, a left-leaning arete and a low angle west-facing slab.

North Face B5.10
On the north face of the Beach Rock there is a fun face with some good holds.

Direct B.1
To the right of the North Face is a contrived problem that avoids using the holds on the left side of the face. Reach straight up to the pocket from the smaller edges.

Black Arete B5.10+
On the right, northwest corner of the rock is a left-leaning arete with delicate moves to gain the top.

West Slab B5.7
On the west face of the rock is a smooth slab with some fun moves. Many variations can be done on this slab to gain the top.

CORNER BEACH
Just up the ridge to the south are some prominent corners and cracks with good challenging problems.

BEACH BLOCK
Across from Corner Beach, through the rocks to the southeast is a prominent blocky rock with a short problem up its north face.

THE OVERHANG
Head farther uphill from the beach area past a clump of trees for several hundred feet to reach a prominent overhang sticking out from the ridge. On its west side, close to the ground is a small chalked-up flake.

Easy O B5.8
On the left side of The Overhang is a crack leading up from the ground.

Roof's Way B5.9
To the immediate right of the crack is a set of good holds that lead out the roof to the right.

Flake Lunge B.1
From a sitting position under the overhang a small finger flake can be used for a long lunge up to the lip. FA: J. Bachar 1970s.

Lip Traverse B.1−
From left to right across the lip and back again is a sure way to get a good pump.

SHIP'S CORNERS
To the right of The Overhang about thirty feet is found a prominent set of corners with an overhanging underside. Various routes can be done all over these blocky outcroppings.

Roof Arete B.1
On the left side of the block a difficult move leads out the roof and up the arete.

Hank's Hang B5.10
To the right of the Roof Arete is another roof problem that surmounts the west side to a thin crack in the slab.

Continue up and along this ridge to the south for more desperate overhanging outcroppings. Eventually this will take you clear over to the Scoop Ridge.

RESERVOIR ROCK
Just below the Ship's Corners and towards the reservoir is a severely overhanging outcrop with a prominent overhanging slot on its left side. Excellent problems exist all over this west-facing wall.

Squeeze Slot B.1 –
This grunting, overhanging slot is found on the left side of the wall. Hand stacks are useful at one point.

Right Bulge B5.10+
Immediately to the right of the slot is a bulging overhang with some good holds. FA: B. Horan 1980s.

Flakey Overhang B5.10
This long roof problem can be found about fifteen feet to the right of the slot. Long reaches from good holds lead to the lip.

H's Lunge B.1 –
To the right of the Flakey Overhang about six feet or so there is another shorter roof. From a small edge, lunge up and over the lip to a good hold. Pull over the lip to a stance. FA: B. Horan 1980s.

From the road that leads across the Spring Canyon Dam the Tropics Ridge can be seen down the slope to the northeast. See Tropics.

26 — Horsetooth Reservoir

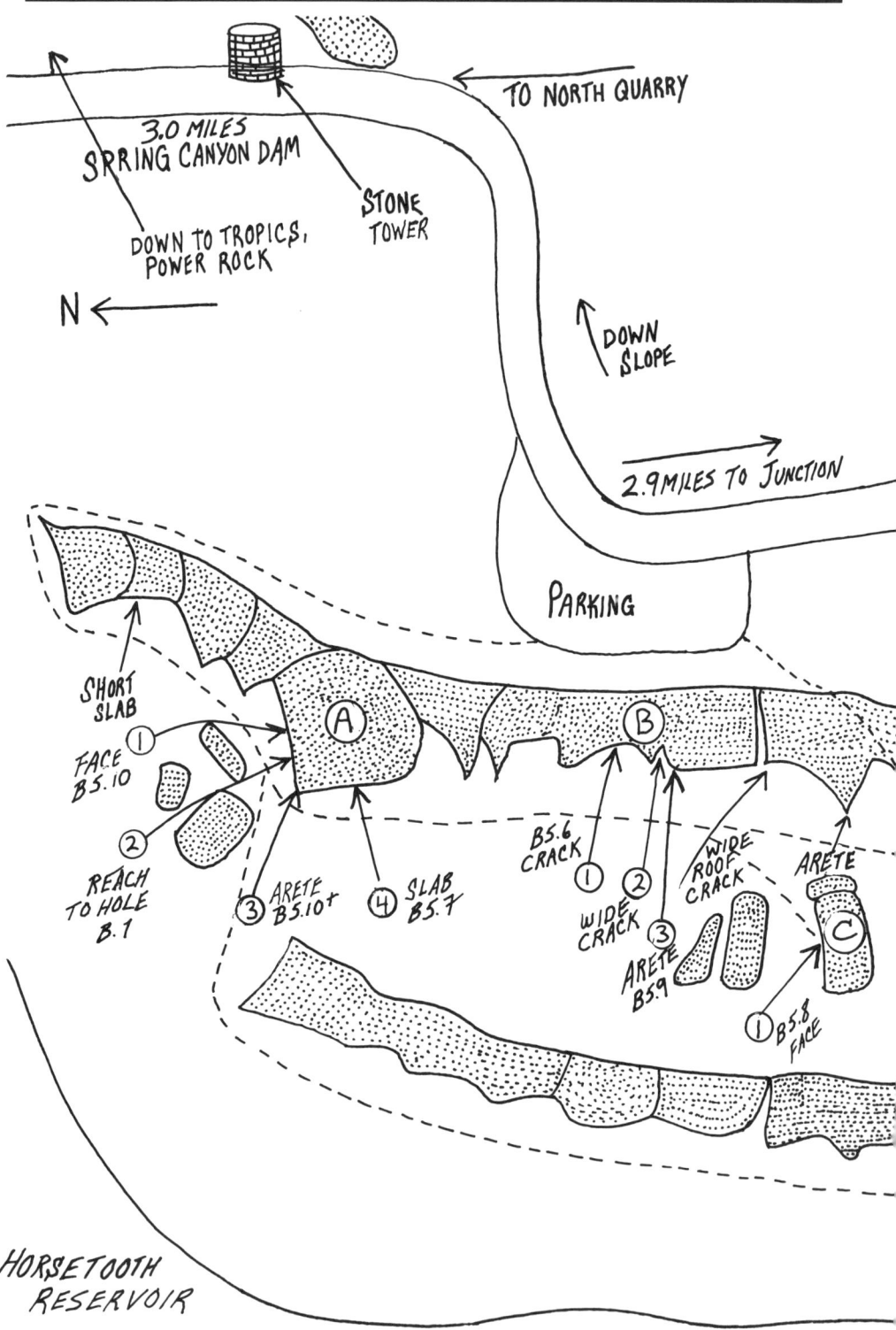

Land of the Overhangs

A BEACH ROCK
1. North Face B5.10
2. Direct B.1
3. Black Arete B5.10+
4. West Slab B5.7

B CORNER BEACH
1. Crack B5.6
2. Wide One B5.7
3. Aerial Ballet B5.9

C BEACH BLOCK
1. North Face

D THE OVERHANG
1. Easy O B5.8
2. Roof's Way B5.9
3. Flake Lunge B.1
4. Lip Traverse B.1−

E SHIP CORNERS
1. Roof Arete B.1
2. Hank's Hang B5.10

F RESERVOIR ROCK
1. Squeeze Slot B.1−
2. Right Bulge B5.10+
3. Flakey Overhang B5.10
4. H's Lunge B.1−

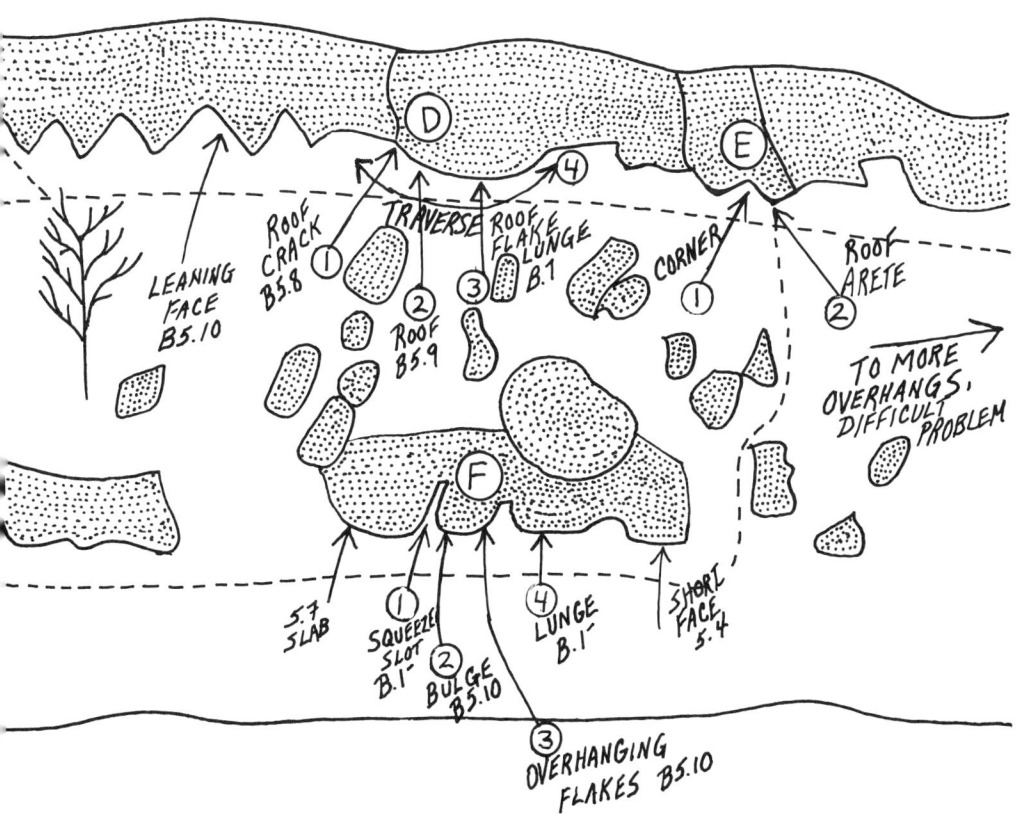

NORTH QUARRY

The square cut red sandstone walls of the North Quarry offer some of the best face climbing at the reservoir. There are actually two different ways to approach the sheer outcropping. One way is to park on the west side of the Horsetooth Dam and walk west along the shore line until you reach the quarry. Another way is to head farther north past the Horsetooth Dam until you see the sign pointing to Lory State Park. Head west on the paved road until you reach the entrance station to the park. Park just outside the entrance station at a designated parking area along the main road. From here walk down to the east on a faint trail leading to an obvious gully. A house with a small horse stable can be seen on the left side. Continue past this through the gully and soon the quarried walls on the north side can be seen. The unique sheared-off blocks of sandstone fill the walls with classic aretes, corners and slabs.

Cinch B.2
At the lower far east end of the wall a cable hangs down the wall. From a mantle position, lunge to a sloping hold out right. Continue up the dihedral to another mantle up high. FA: M. Wilford 1980s.

Physical Graffiti B.1 (TR)
Up the wall to the left of the Mantle Lunge and just right of an arete about ten feet is a small corner system that leads up the face to some good ledges. The number 5430 is painted on the left side of the face. FA: B. Horan 1980s.

Little Arete B.1 −
Just to the left of Physical Graffiti is a short arete problem that uses the right face to gain a good ledge.

Magazine Face B.1
Around the corner to the left of the Little Arete and uphill a bit, another arete has some fun moves. Just to the right of this arete is a steep face with a set of finger edges leading to the ledge above. This problem was pictured on the cover of *Climbing* magazine in the summer of 1981. FA: M. Wilford 1980s.

Leaning Dihedral B.1 −
Just around the corner and up-slope from Magazine Face there is a prominent left-facing flakey dihedral with some balancey moves up its corner.

Desert Crack B.1
Up the wall from the Leaning Corner is a thin finger crack with strenuous moves leading off the ground. Continuing to the top is a scary feat. The number 5400 is painted just around the corner to the left.

Motion Picture Slab B.1
From the painted number 5400, walk up-slope to the second corner. The thin west-facing micro-thin slab has the words "Motion Picture" carved into it. A prominent drill groove can be seen on the left side of the slab. Just to the left of the right-hand arete is a thin slab with two small edges. Get hold of these edges and lunge up to the good ledge. FA: M. Wilford 1980s.

Arete Motion B5.7
This ascends the short arete on the right side of the west face.

Layback Drill Mark B5.9
Left of the Motion Picture Slab a drill groove can be face climbed.

Sunshine Face B5.10 +
About 20 feet up and left along a smooth south-facing wall from the Motion Picture Slab a classic face leads up some good edges.

Many other problems can be discovered on this long wall of high-quality sandstone. Let your imagination wander.

Horsetooth Reservoir — 29

Joy climbing on the Classic Arete of the Motion Picture Slab, North Quarry.

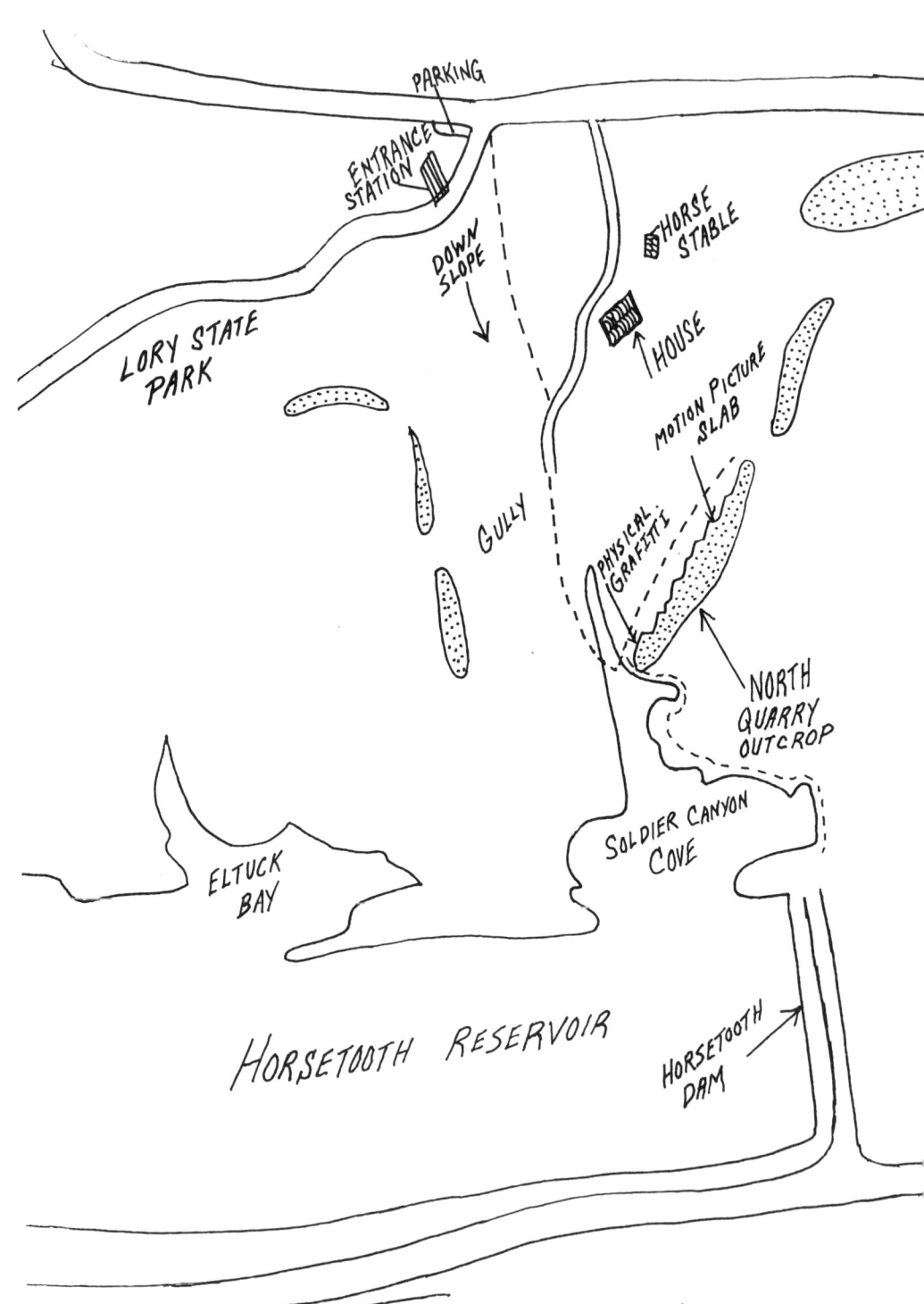

Horsetooth Reservoir — 31

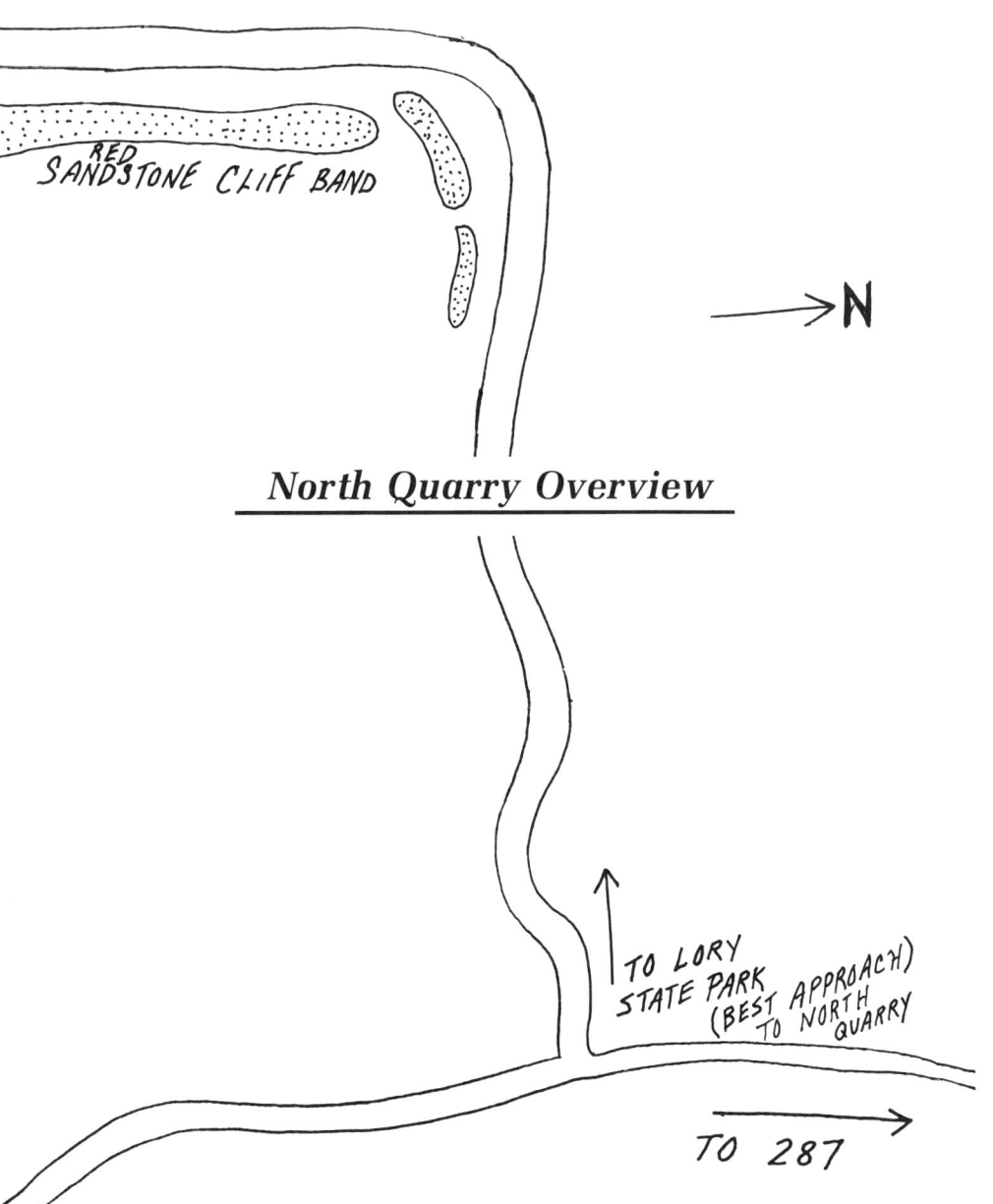

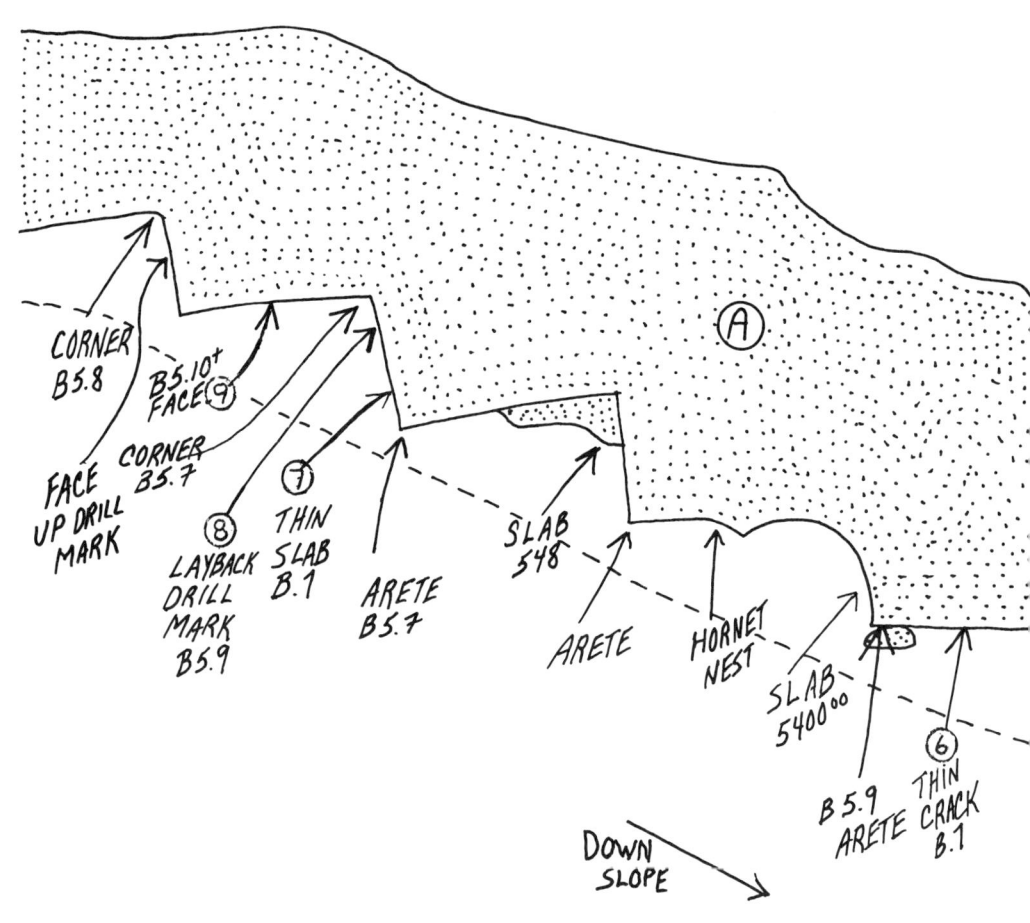

North Quarry

A NORTH QUARRY WALL
1. Cinch B.2
2. Physical Graffiti B.1
3. Little Arete B.1−
4. Magazine Face B.1
5. Leaning Dihedral B.1−
6. Desert Crack B.1
7. Motion Picture Slab B.1
8. Layback Drill Mark B5.9
9. Sunshine Face B5.10+

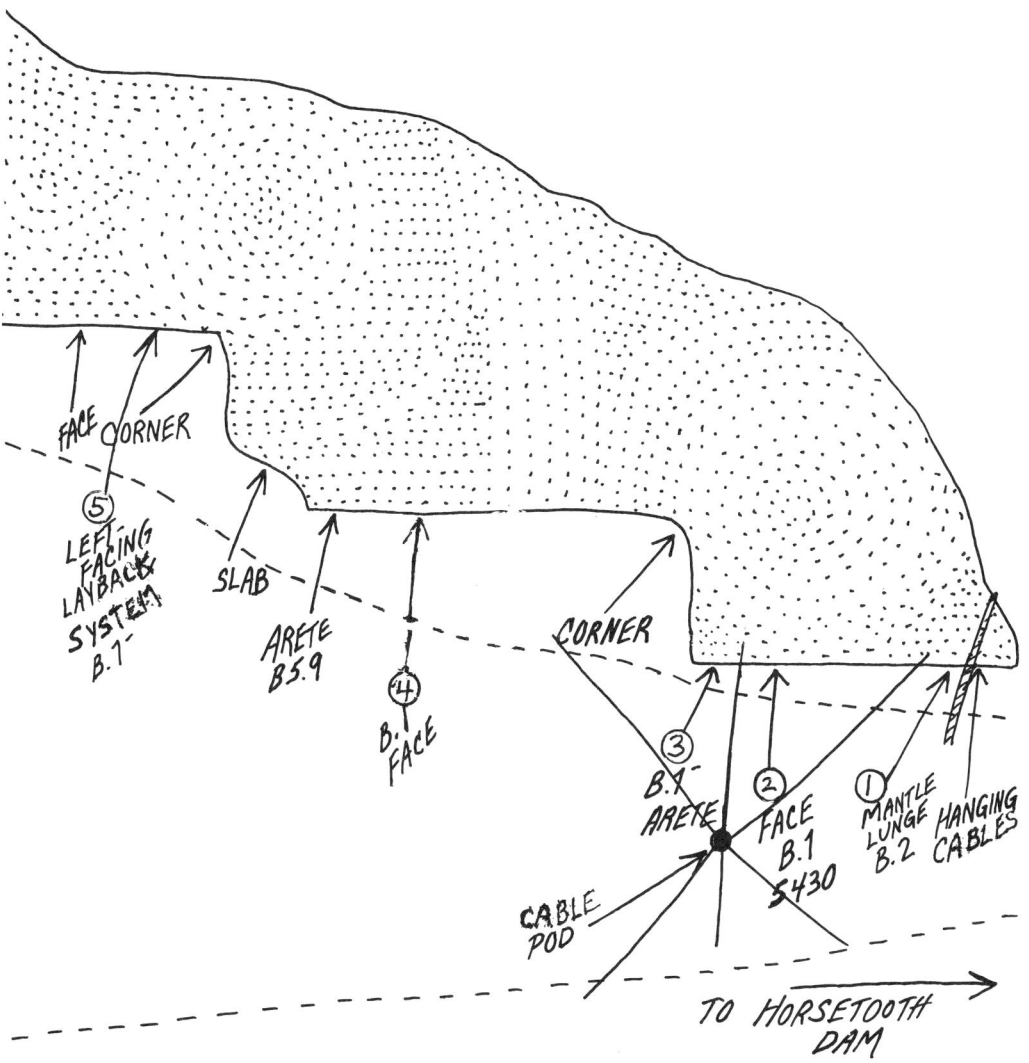

MARINA RIDGE AREA

From the mileage junction just left of the Dixon Canyon Dam, continue around the curve on the paved road to the south for 0.4 miles, where a gate will be seen on the right side of the road. Behind the gate there is a sailboat-shaped sign that reads "Sail and Saddle." Park along the road and head down hill on a faint trail to the northwest. The rocky ridge extends to the north and is loaded with many good problems. Below the ridge is a boulder-filled slope. Gill problems can be found on the Sunshine Boulder.

SUNSHINE BOULDER

This is a large single boulder below the main ridge. From the parking area head down towards the reservoir, angling to the northwest. Soon after is this classic hunk of sandstone with its slightly overhanging west face.

The Horn B5.8
On the southwest corner of the boulder is a short problem that requires a reach up to a prominent horn.

Muscle Cling B.1+
Just left of the horn a thin overhanging face starts from an undercling and reaches up to a small edge. FA: J. Gill 1960s.

Standard Route B.1
On the left side of the west face a ledge system angles up from right to left. This overhanging face ascends from the middle of the leaning ledge system to a mantle on the sloping top. FA: J. Gill 1960s.

Sunshine Traverse B.1
From the far left side of the boulder traverse around to the right, ending on the south side with a short face climb to the top.

PIANO BOULDER

From the Marina parking continue along the paved road to the south for 0.6 miles. Pull over to the side of the road and look up to the east. Sitting among the many rocks along this spiney ridge can be seen a prominent round boulder with a crack going around it. The traverse along the crack is one of the area's best problems.

Piano Traverse B.1
This is the circular traverse around the Piano Boulder. Heel hooks, hand jams and small finger edges are used to complete this strenuous problem.

Many short problems go up all around the Piano Boulder. Pick a set of holds and go for it.

Bootie B5.10
About 40 feet to the right of the Piano Boulder is a steep west-facing slab just left of a crack. Good edges lead the way.

Continue farther down the spiney ridge to the south to discover many good problems, including a Gill arrow route.

Horsetooth Reservoir — 35

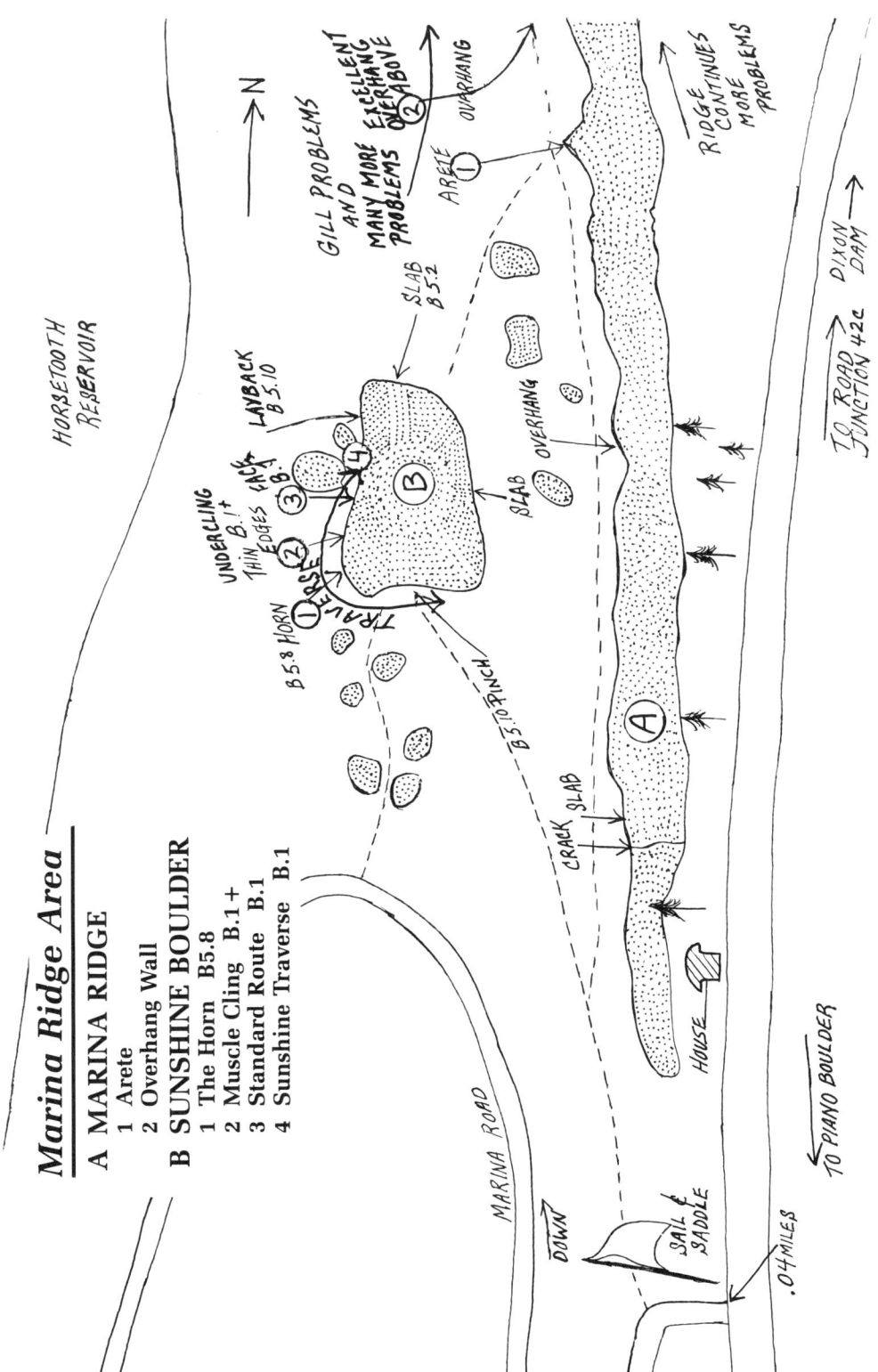

Marina Ridge Area

A MARINA RIDGE
1 Arete
2 Overhang Wall

B SUNSHINE BOULDER
1 The Horn B5.8
2 Muscle Cling B.1+
3 Standard Route B.1
4 Sunshine Traverse B.1

Reaching out of the Muscle Cling (B.1+), on the Sunshine Boulder, Marina Area.   photo: Mike McCarron

Horsetooth Reservoir — 37

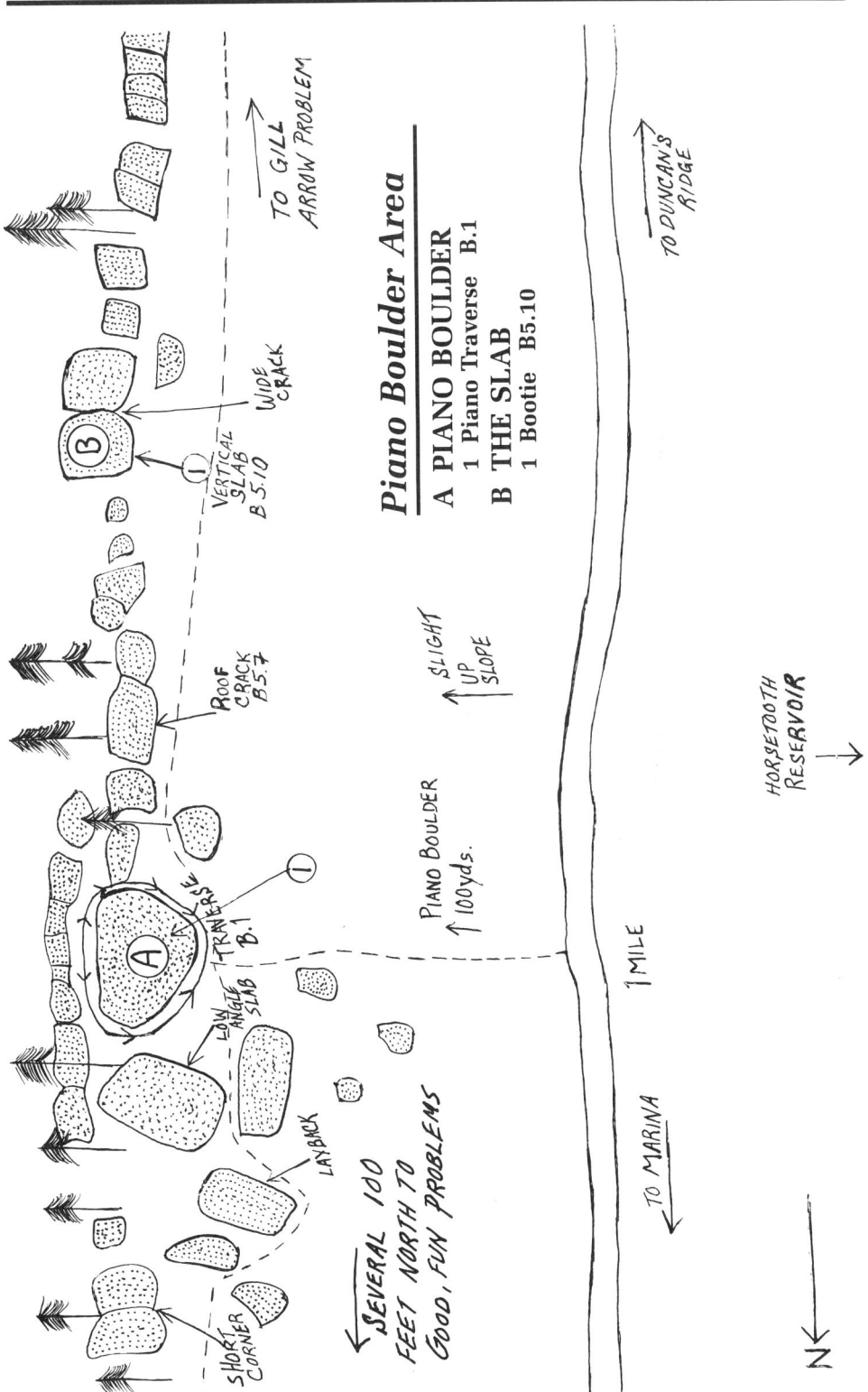

DUNCAN'S RIDGE

From the mileage junction head south past the Marina Area and the Piano Boulder for 1.3 miles or until you come to the north end of the Spring Canyon Dam. Park along the road here and walk down towards the reservoir. Duncan's Ridge starts along the shore line and then rises up to the northwest for some distance. Great Gill problems can be found along the shore and as you walk up the ridge to the north an incredible number of higher top-ropes will be discovered.

Thin Crack B.1 (TR)
This thin line is found at the start of Duncan's Ridge, off a large shelf, just above the ground.

Leaning Cling B.1 −
Farther to the west of the Thin Crack, this vertical face lies just off the beach. Ascend the small right-leaning corner system to the obvious undercling and reach for the top. FA: J. Gill 1960s.

The Layaway B.1
Just to the left of the Leaning Cling is another prominent block with a steep face. Different variations to this south face can be done. The Layaway uses a small layback hold on the right side and reaches up to the good edges. FA: J. Gill 1960s.

Regular Line B5.10+
Lying on the southwest corner of where the ridge begins to head up hill to the north, this problem follows a crack to a small roof.

Direct Bulge B.1
This is a direct start to the Regular Line. Little edges in the bulge can be used to gain the crack. The landing is not very good.

DISTANT EYE BOULDERS

From the beach area of Duncan's Ridge, walk along the shore and follow it around to the north. These boulders can be seen a little ways up hill in the brush. Good problems exist in the clump.

Up the Layaway (B.1) at Duncan's Ridge. The Leaning Cling face can be seen just to the right.

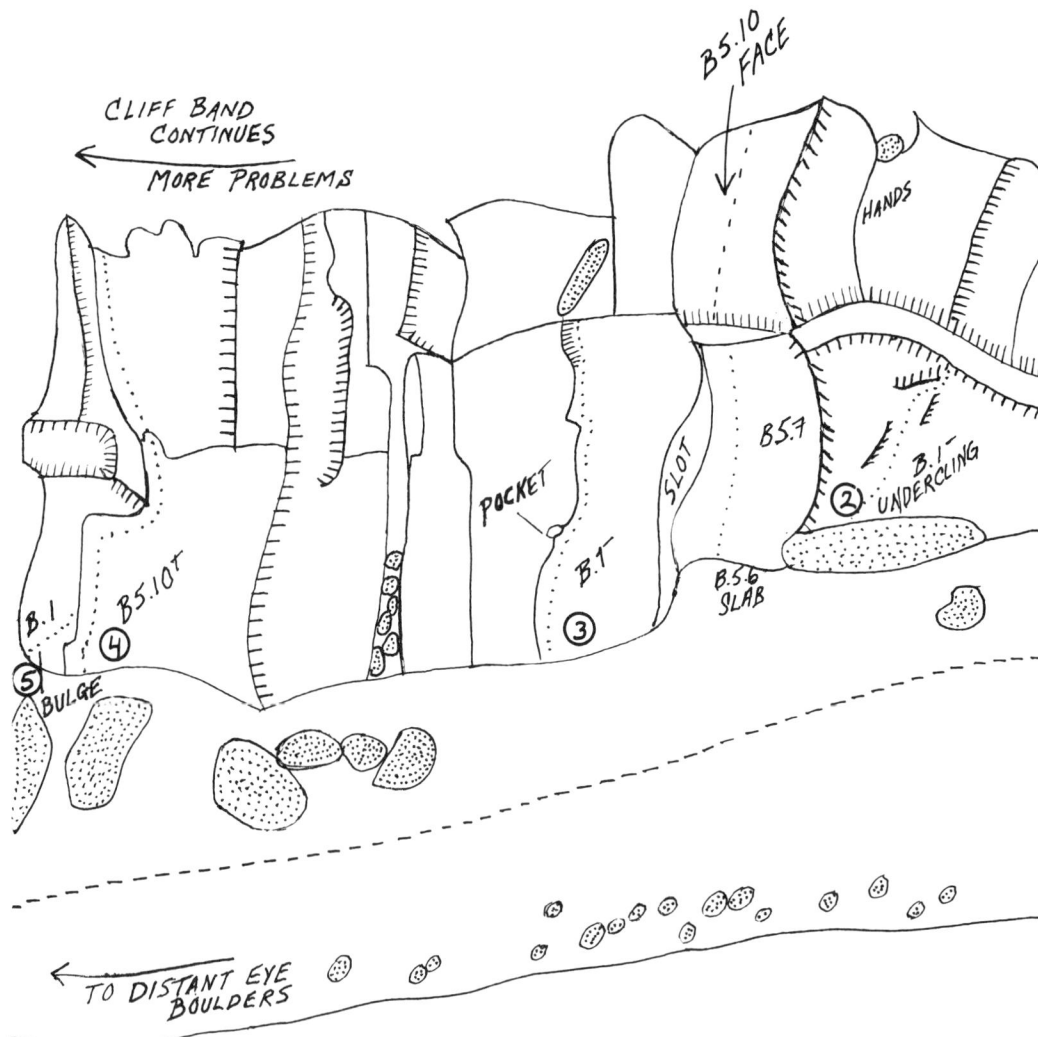

Horsetooth Reservoir — 41

Duncan's Ridge Beach Area

1 Thin Crack   B.1
2 Leaning Cling   B.1 –
3 The Layaway   B.1
4 Regular Line   B5.10
5 Direct Bulge   B.1

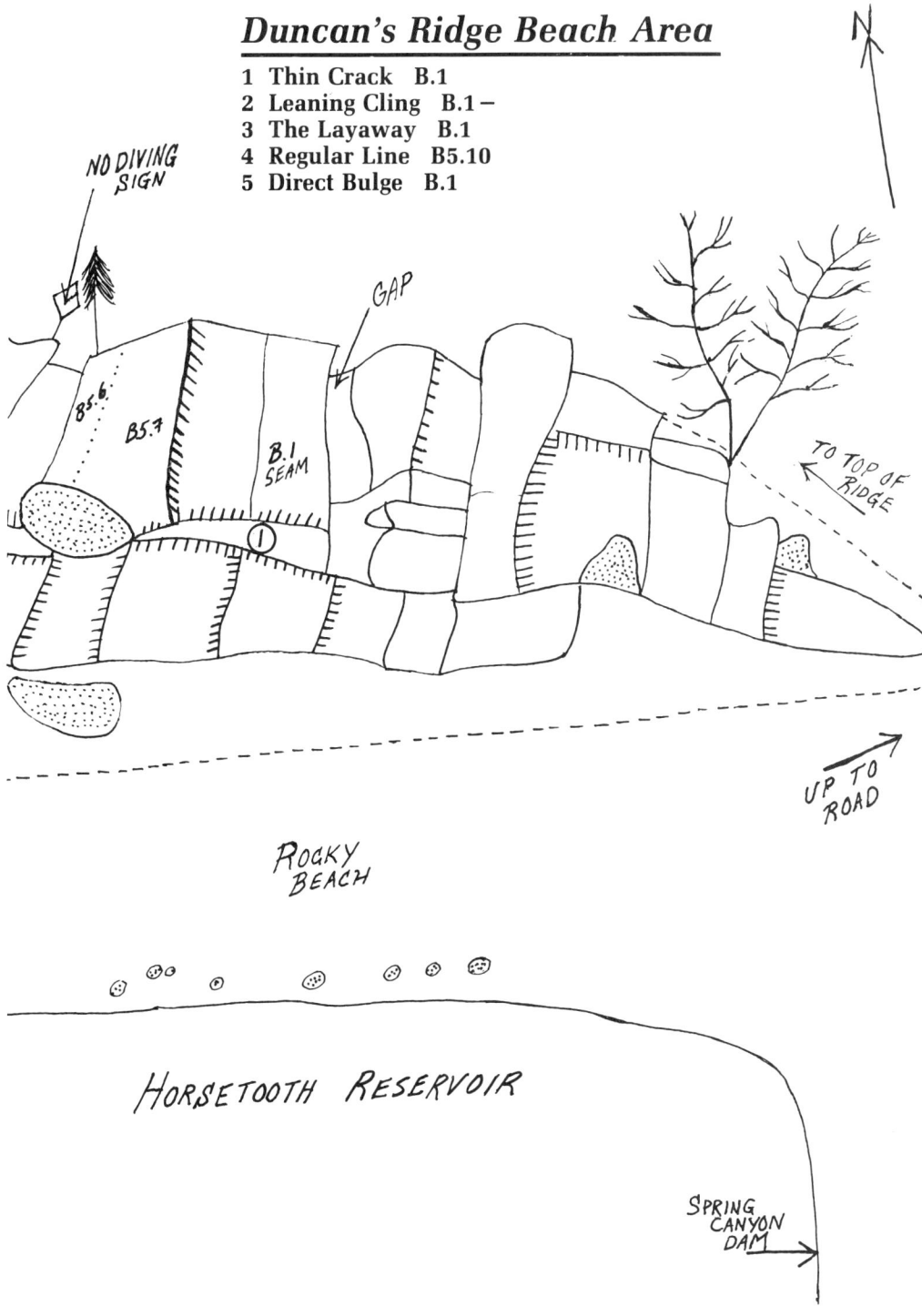

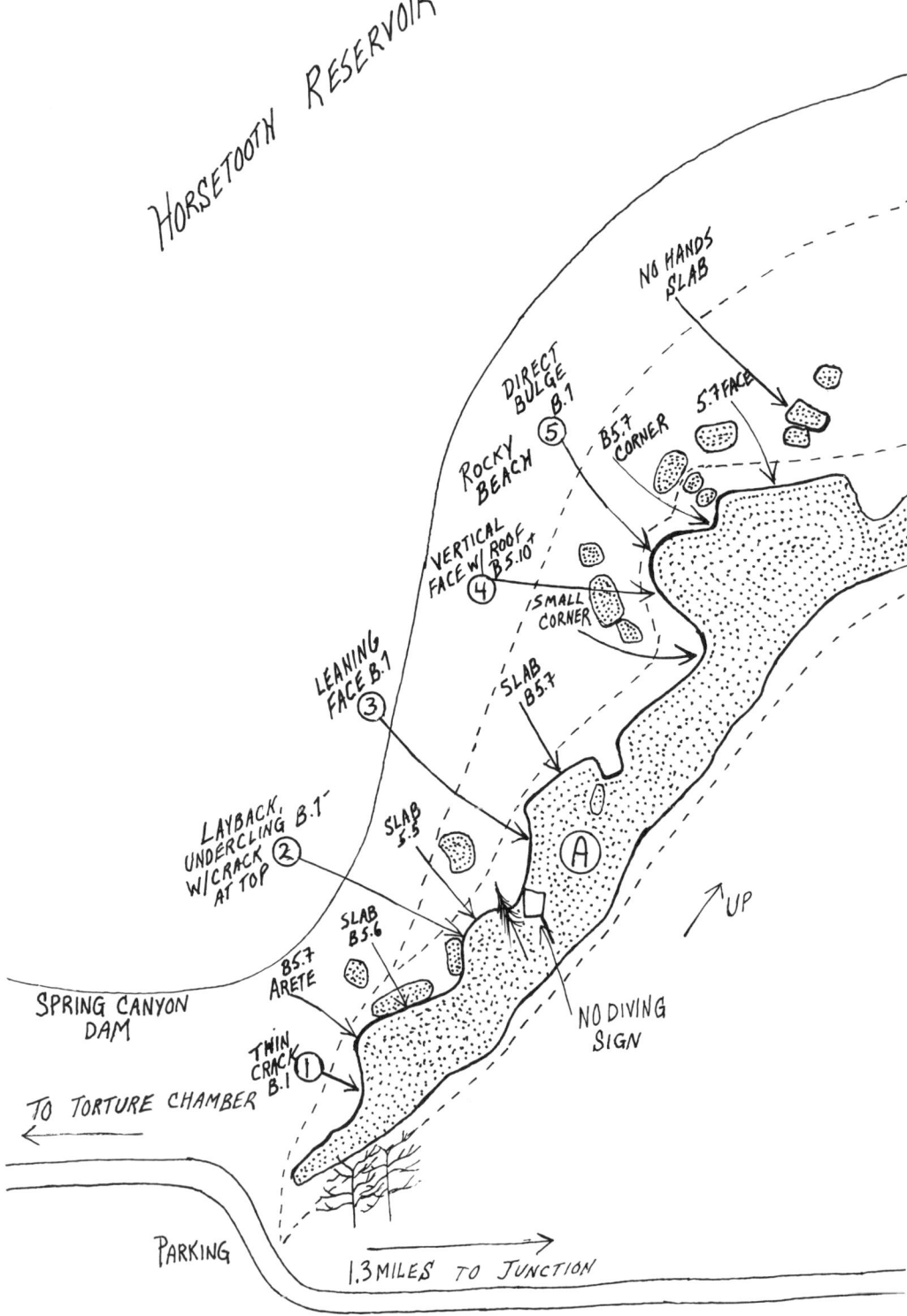

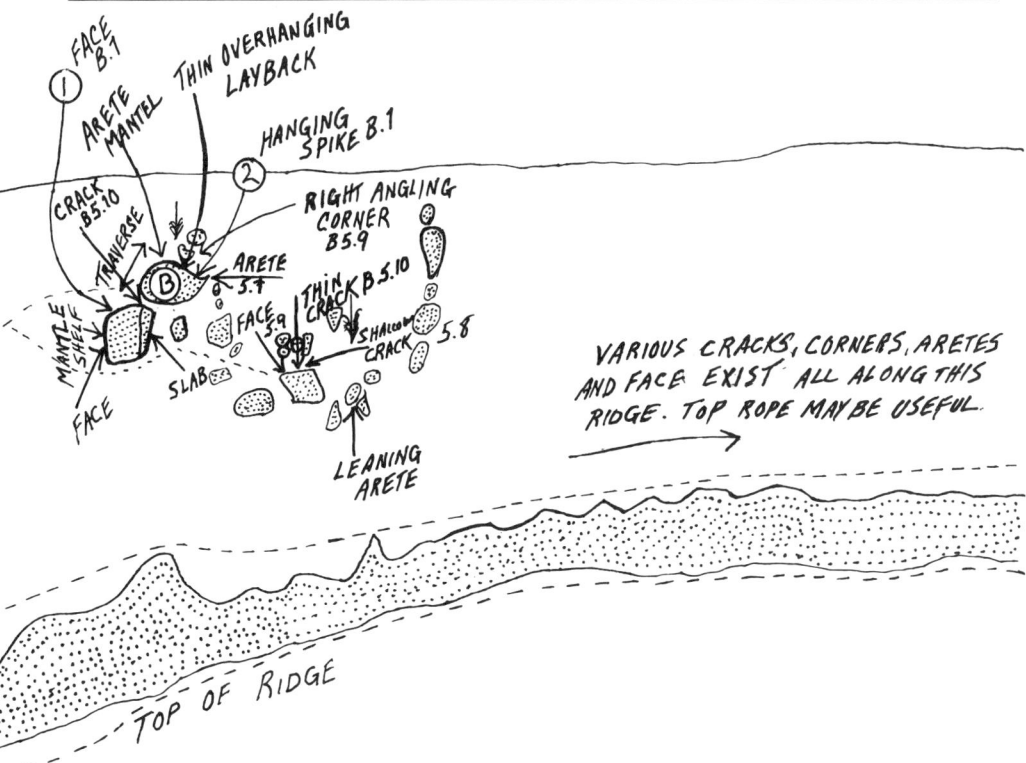

Duncan's Ridge Beach Area

A DUNCAN'S RIDGE
   1 Thin Crack   B.1
   2 Leaning Cling   B.1 –
   3 The Layaway   B.1
   4 Regular Line   B5.10
   5 Direct Bulge   B.1

B DISTANT EYE BOULDERS
   1 Face Up   B5.7
   2 Hanging Spike   B.1

TORTURE CHAMBER

From the north side of Spring Canyon Dam, the Torture Chamber's downsloping ridge can be seen across the dam to the southeast. From the roadside parking of Duncan's Ridge, continue on the road south over the dam to a stop sign. Hang a left and drive about a block to the east. Just before a curve in the roadcut, pull off the road to a parking area on the left. The top of the ridge will be seen from here. If you continue around the curve through the roadcut this road would take you out east to Fort Collins.

The Torture Chamber is most famous for its Gill traverse of the upper west end of the ridge and the B.2 top-rope problem on the Nemesis Tower. Many other classic top-ropes exist, including some of Horsetooth's best crack routes, which can be found on the far east end of the ridge.

Torture Chamber B.1
This is perhaps a name given to describe the feeling you get after traversing back and forth along this good-edged lip. The traverse moves along the lip of an undercut roof system close to the ground for many feet. FA: J. Gill 1960s.

Borgman's Bulge B.1+
Just left of the Torture Chamber a prominent bulge problem has cracks around its left side. This is one of the reservoir's most difficult bulges. FA: J. Borgman 1960s.

Big Roof B5.10+
Continue down the ridge for some distance to this prominent roof block that sticks out into the trees. There are many variations to this roof section, including a classic B5.10+ regular route.

NEMESIS TOWER

This is a separate pinnacle/block downhill several hundred feet from the main ridge, just past some prominent boulders lying in the slope. Many excellent top-rope problems have been done on its steep sides.

West Crack B5.8
On the west side of the tower an obvious crack runs up to the top of the block.

West Flake B5.9
Immediately left of the crack a fun flake system leads to the top.

Nemesis Standard B.2 (TR)
To the left of the flake there is a scoop-like face with some very small edges. Crank on these edges, eventually reaching the arete on the left. This problem was done on-sight by Dave Breashears in the 1970s. Some of the holds have broken down since the first ascent, leaving an even harder start.

North Arete (TR)
On the north corner of the tower there is an obvious arete shooting up to the top.

Northeast Face B.1− (TR)
This thin top-rope problem ascends the northeast face just to the left of the North Arete. After making your way up the smooth short corner move right, connecting with the North Arete. A difficult direct line that moves straight up the face from the smooth corner has also been done.

Dihedral Line B.1− (TR)
Just to the left of the previous routes is a classic corner with a thin finger crack. They don't get much better than this.

CRACKS WALL
Just to the left of Nemesis Tower is a good condensed section of wall with many classic cracks. These are some of Horsetooth's best crack lines.
The Thin One B.1 (TR)
Downhill from Nemesis Tower several feet and just to the left of a prominent tree is this thin crack.
S Crack B.5.10+ (TR)
This is a crack that is hard to miss. Its curvy shape gives it its name. The steep line has a tricky move at the top.
Cracky Face B5.10+ (TR)
Just to the left of the S Crack is yet another classic thin line that can be face climbed.
Final Finger B.1- (TR)
To the left of Cracky Face is another crack with great moves.

Along the Torture Chamber Ridge there are an endless number of excellent boulder problems. Some may require a top-rope while others are short enough to boulder out. Climbers of all abilities will be right at home along this pleasant ridge.

Torture Chamber

1. Torture Chamber Traverse B.1
2. Borgman's Bulge B.1+
3. The Big Roof B5.10+
4. Nemesis B.1+
5. S Crack B5.10+

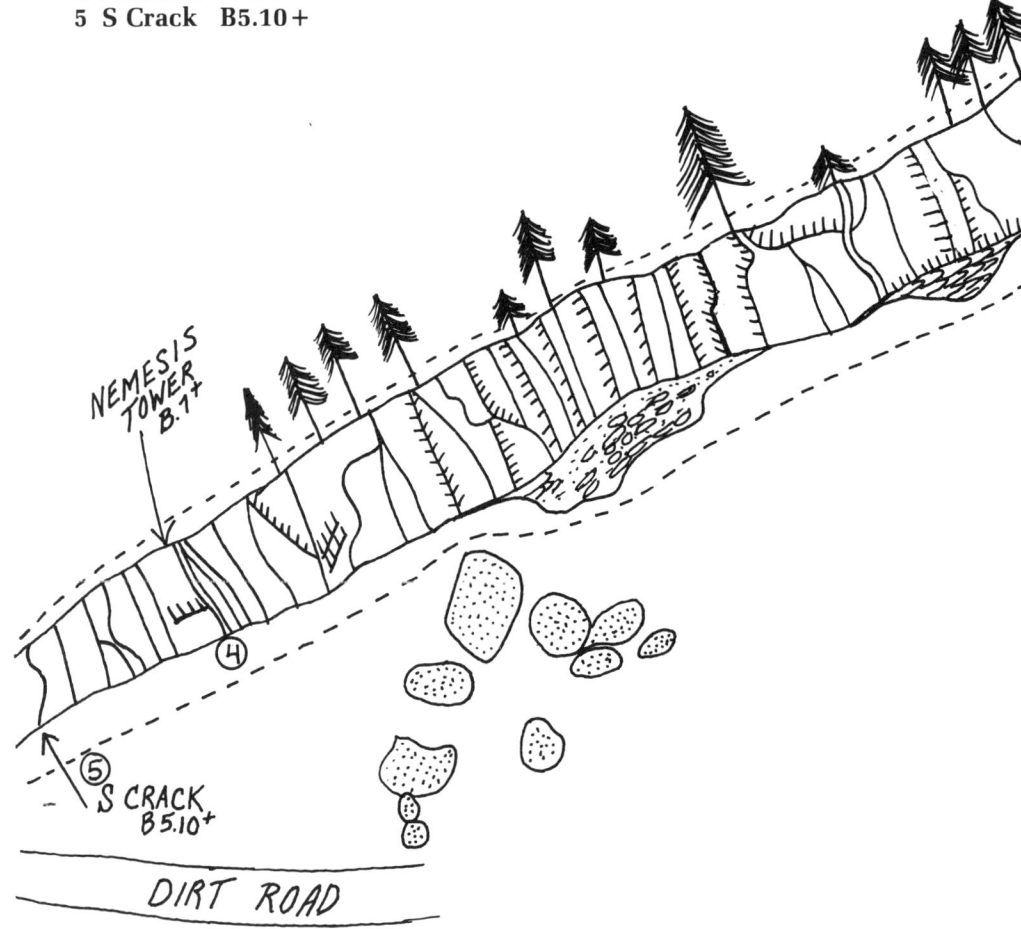

HORSETOOTH ROAD
B.7
TORTURE CHAMBER
1.7 MILES
TO 42C JUNCTION
1
2
BORGMAN'S BULGE B.1+
3
BIG ROOF B5.10+
N
SPRING CANYON DAM
TO DUNCAN'S RIDGE

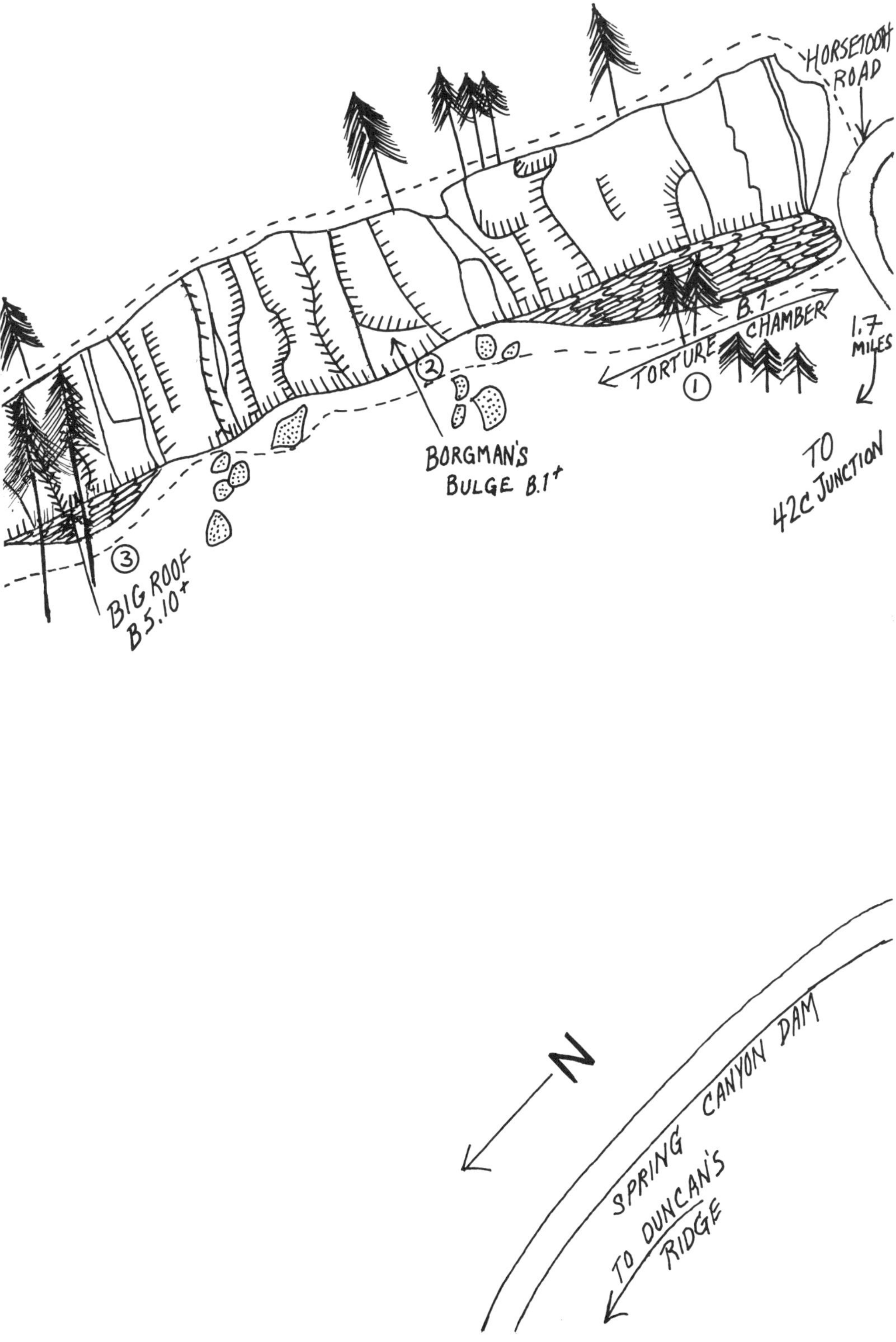

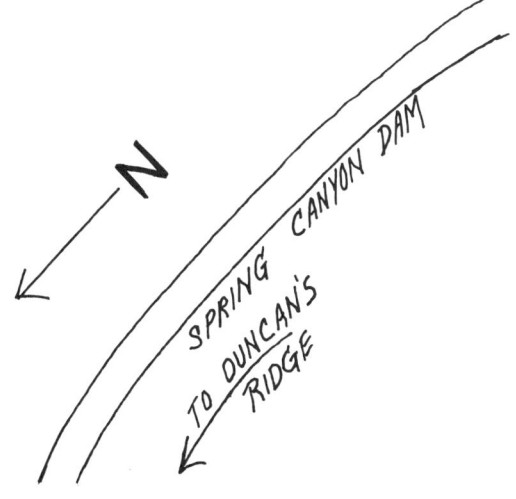

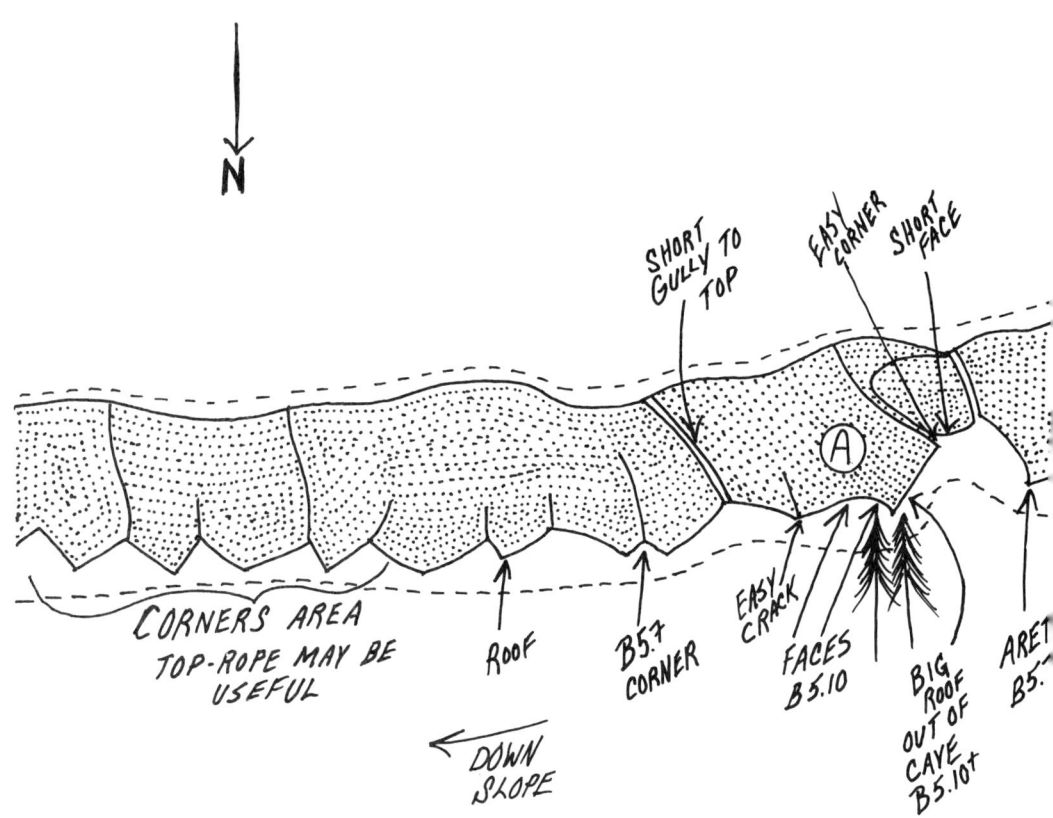

Torture Chamber Outcrop

A BIG ROOF
B BORGMAN'S BULGE
C TORTURE CHAMBER TRAVERSE

Horsetooth Reservoir — 49

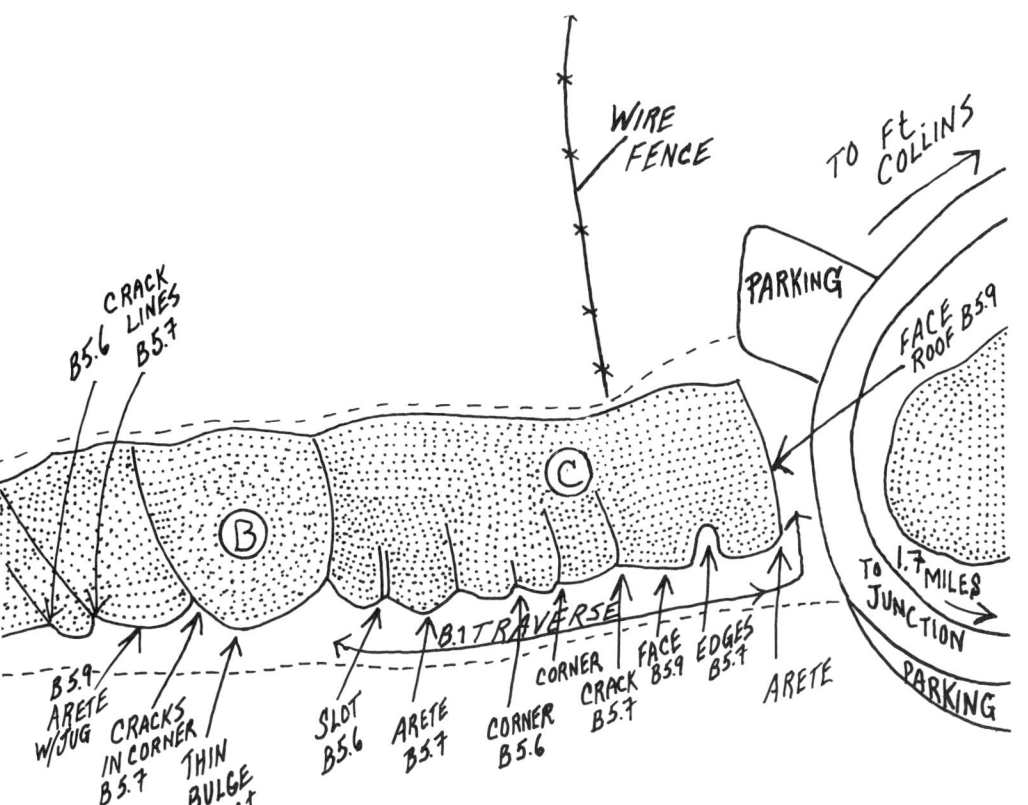

Torture Chamber Outcrop

A CRACKS WALL
1. Final Finger B.1−
2. Cracky Face B5.10+
3. S Crack B5.10+
4. Thin One B.1−

B NEMESIS TOWER
1. Dihedral Line B.1−
2. Northeast Face B.1−
3. North Arete
4. Nemesis Standard B.2
5. West Flake B5.9
6. West Crack B5.8

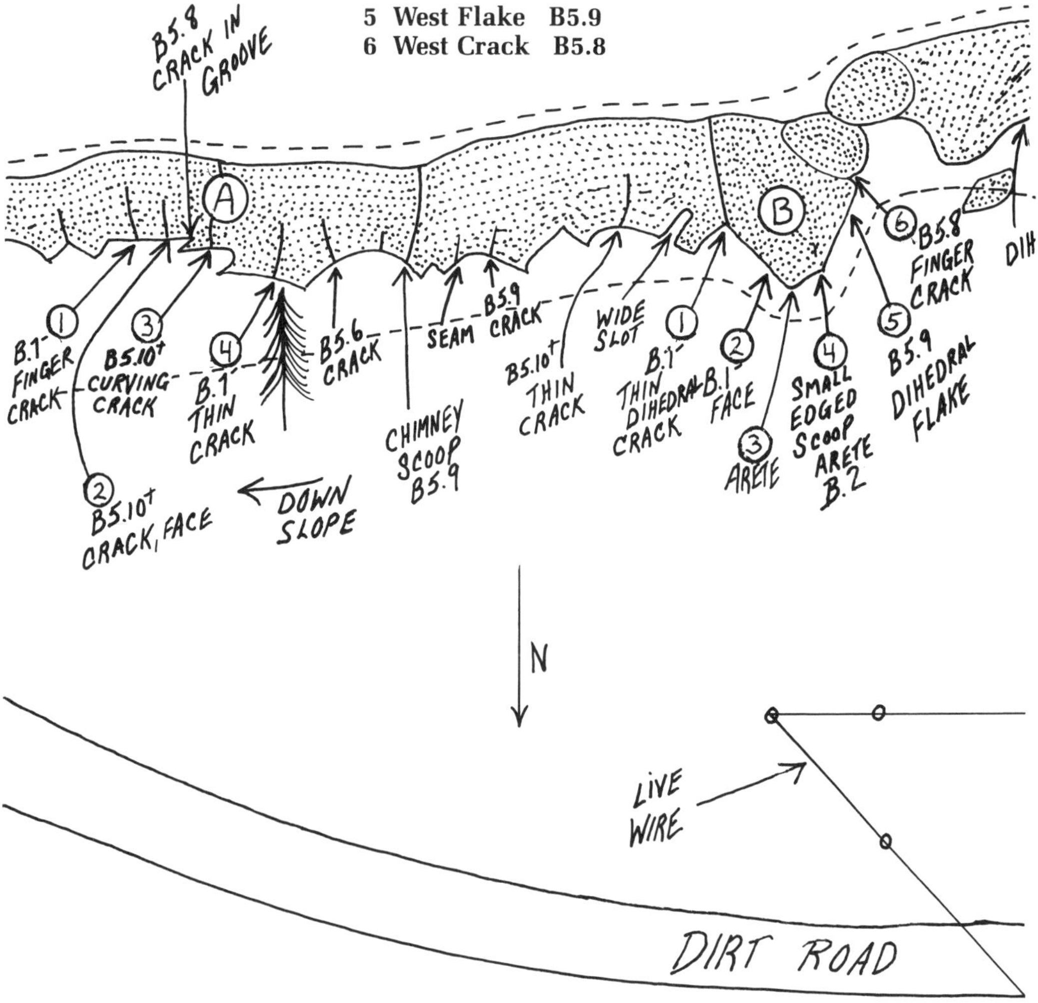

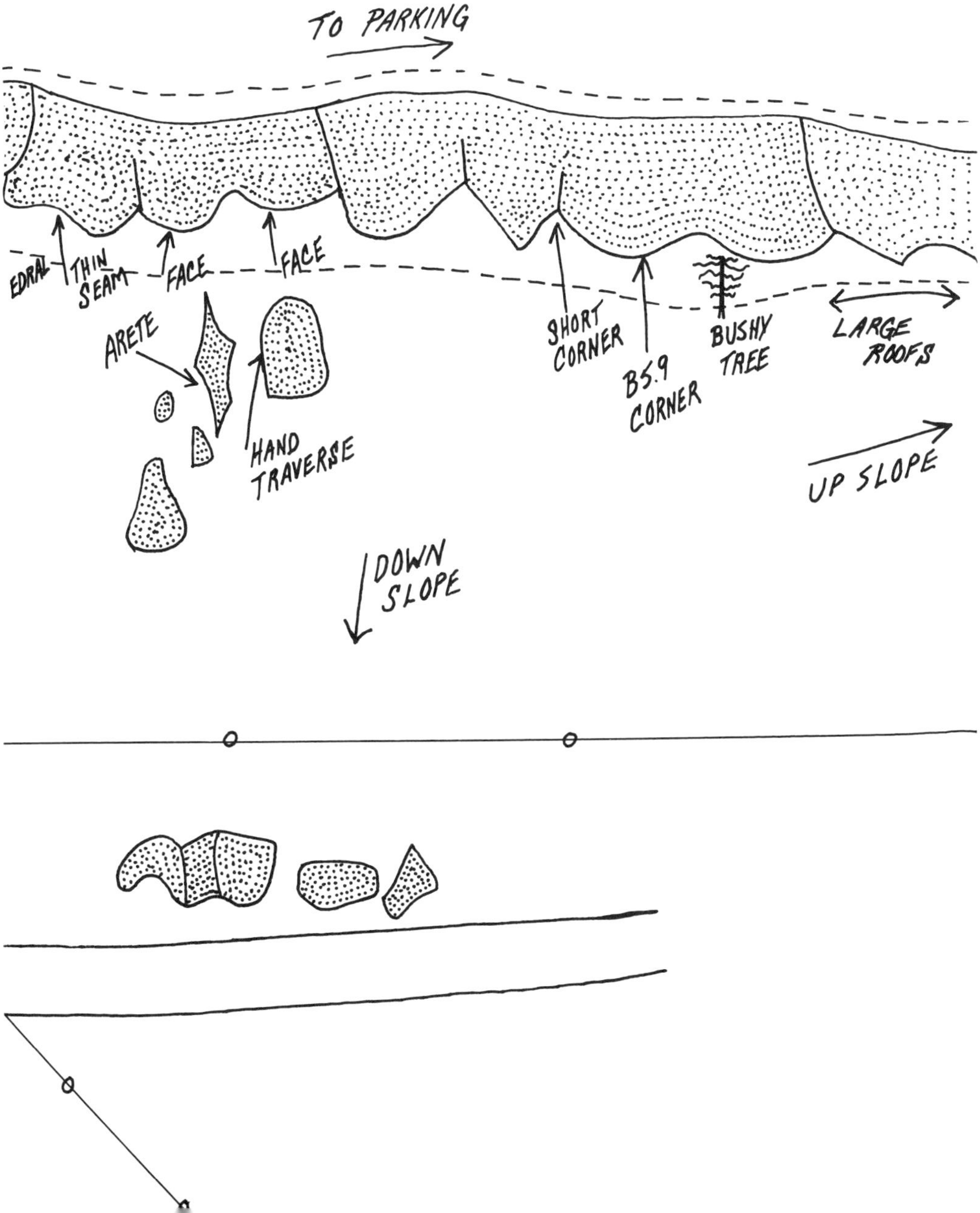

Horsetooth Reservoir — 51

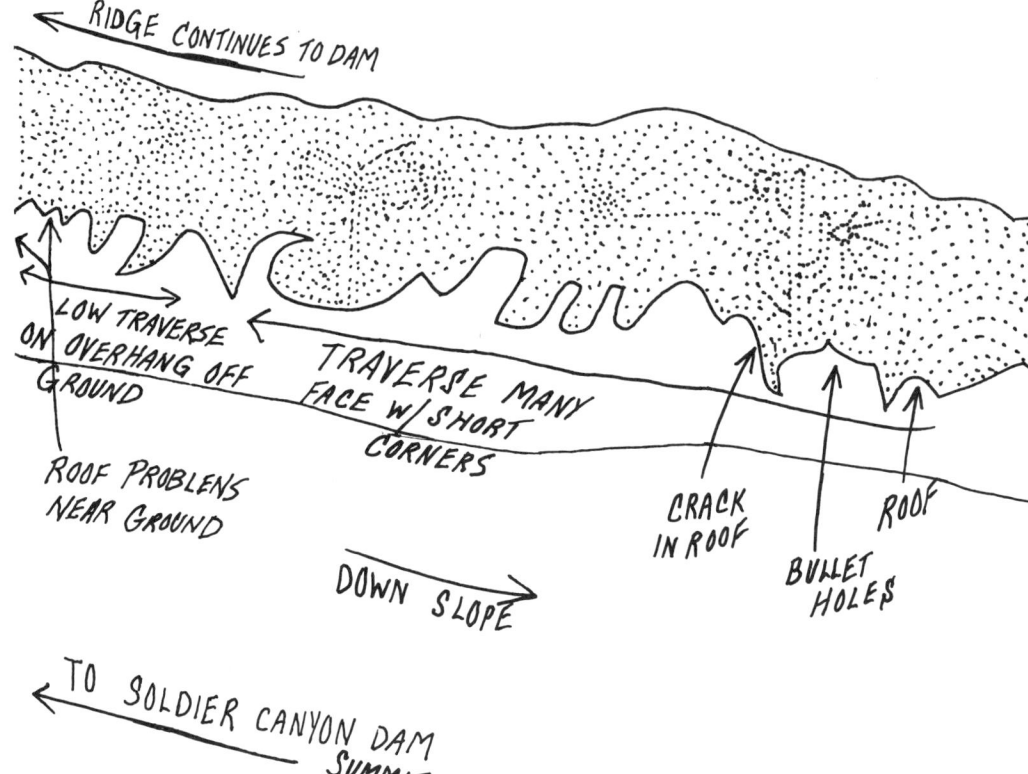

LAPORT STREET
From Overland Road, which runs north-south past the east side of the Colorado State University football stadium, locate Laport Street, north of the stadium. Take Laport Street straight west, past the CSU engineering research buildings until the road comes to a dead end. Two ridges run down hill from Soldier Canyon Dam. The south-facing northern ridge offers good bouldering during the colder months of the year. A large variety of problems, from moderate to extremely difficult, exist here.

TROPICS
This is the lengthy northern ridge of the Soldier Canyon. Traverses, aretes, good faces and roof problems exist up and down this solar collector.

POWER ROCK
On the far east end of the southern ridge there is a big blocky-looking section of rock hidden in the bushes. This is a great place to get a pump going from large holds. The area was cleaned out by some of the more active locals.

Circular Traverse B.1
This is a traverse that moves in a circular manner on the top and bottom of the north-facing overhang. FA: M. Wilford 1980s.

Many different roof problems can be worked out on the north face of this unique block.

Horsetooth Reservoir — 53

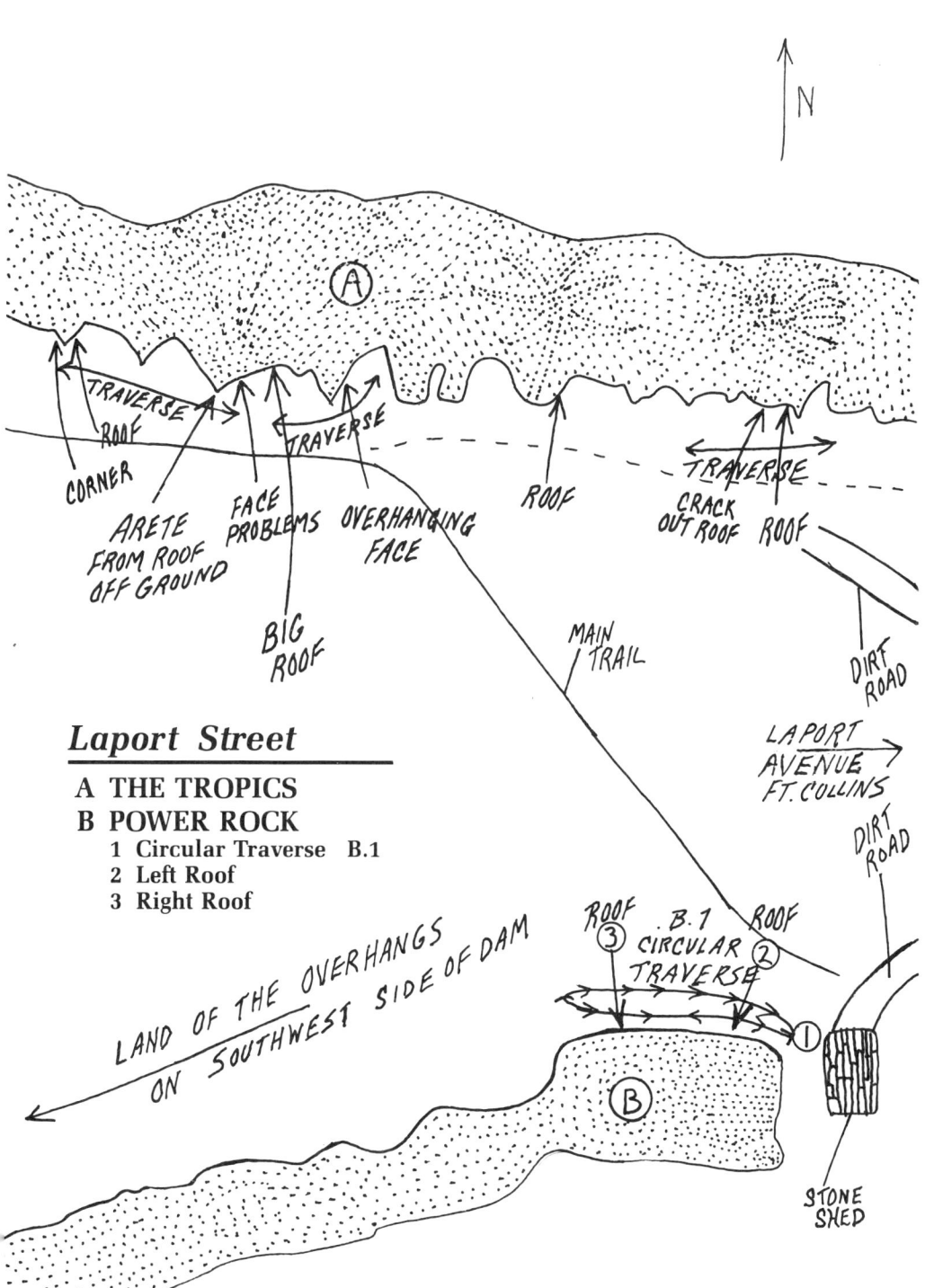

Laport Street

A THE TROPICS
B POWER ROCK
   1 Circular Traverse B.1
   2 Left Roof
   3 Right Roof

Carter Lake Reservoir

This recently discovered area, with its mile-long stretch of high quality sandstone boulders and outcroppings, has an atmosphere unmatched by any other area along the Front Range. Below the the boulder-filled slopes is a refreshing lake. To the west you can clearly see the gleaming Rocky Mountain high country, dominated by the Diamond on Long's Peak.

Carter Lake Reservoir is located just west of the town of Berthoud. West of town on Highway 287 the road curves to the south towards Longmont. At this prominent curve is a gas station. The road behind (west of) the gas station will take you almost straight to the reservoir, and is well-marked with signs. When you enter the reservoir area you will come to a split in the road. One way goes north towards the dam and the other leads south around some curves to a parking lot on the right side of the road. From this parking area the beginning of the boulder field lies just to the north.

Many of the boulder problems that you will come across in this long stretch were pioneered by Steve Mammen, the most active climber to develop this lakeside area.

Reaching up the West Face (B.1−) of Chain Rock on the slopes of Carter Lake. photo: Shane Rymer

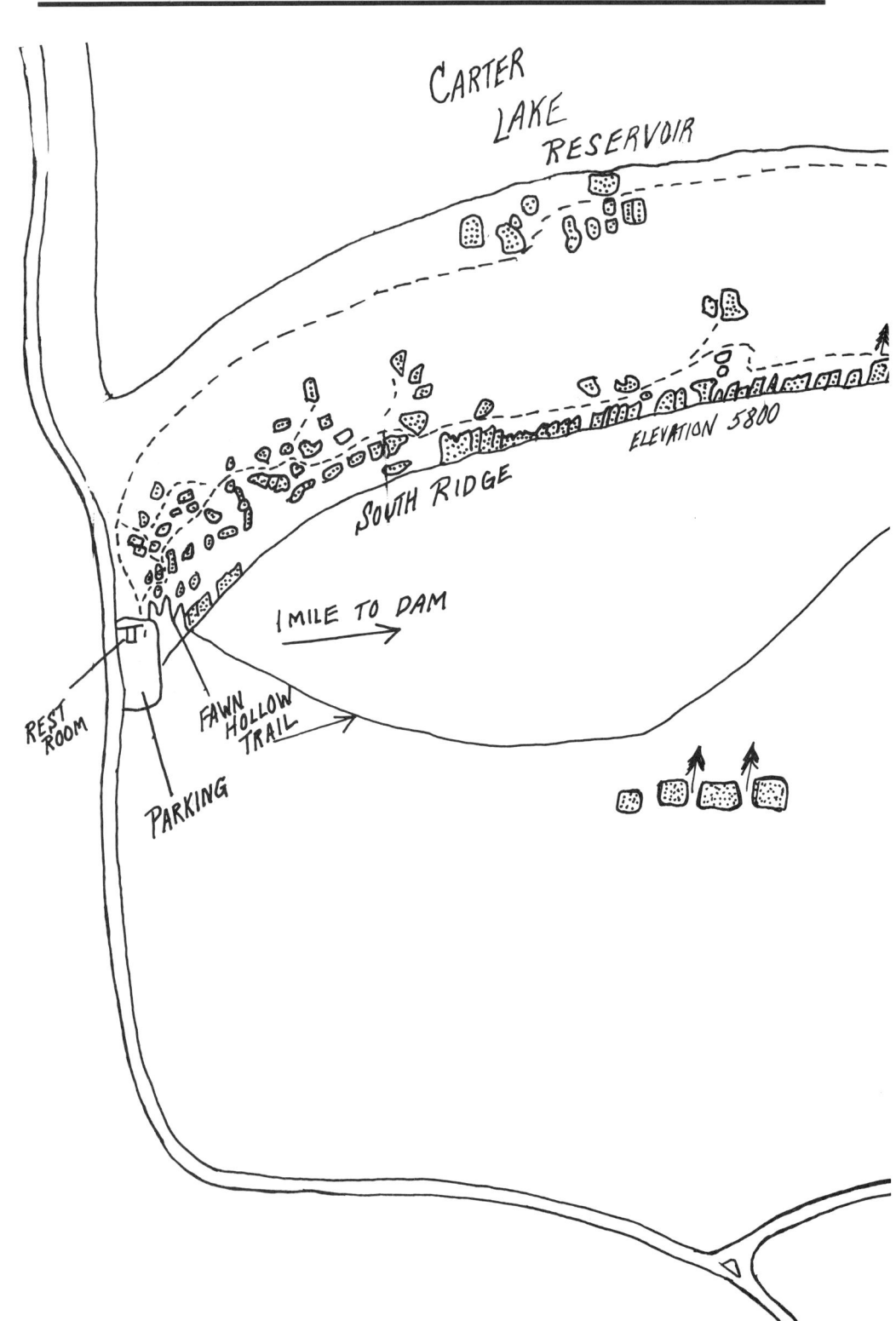

Carter Lake Reservoir — 57

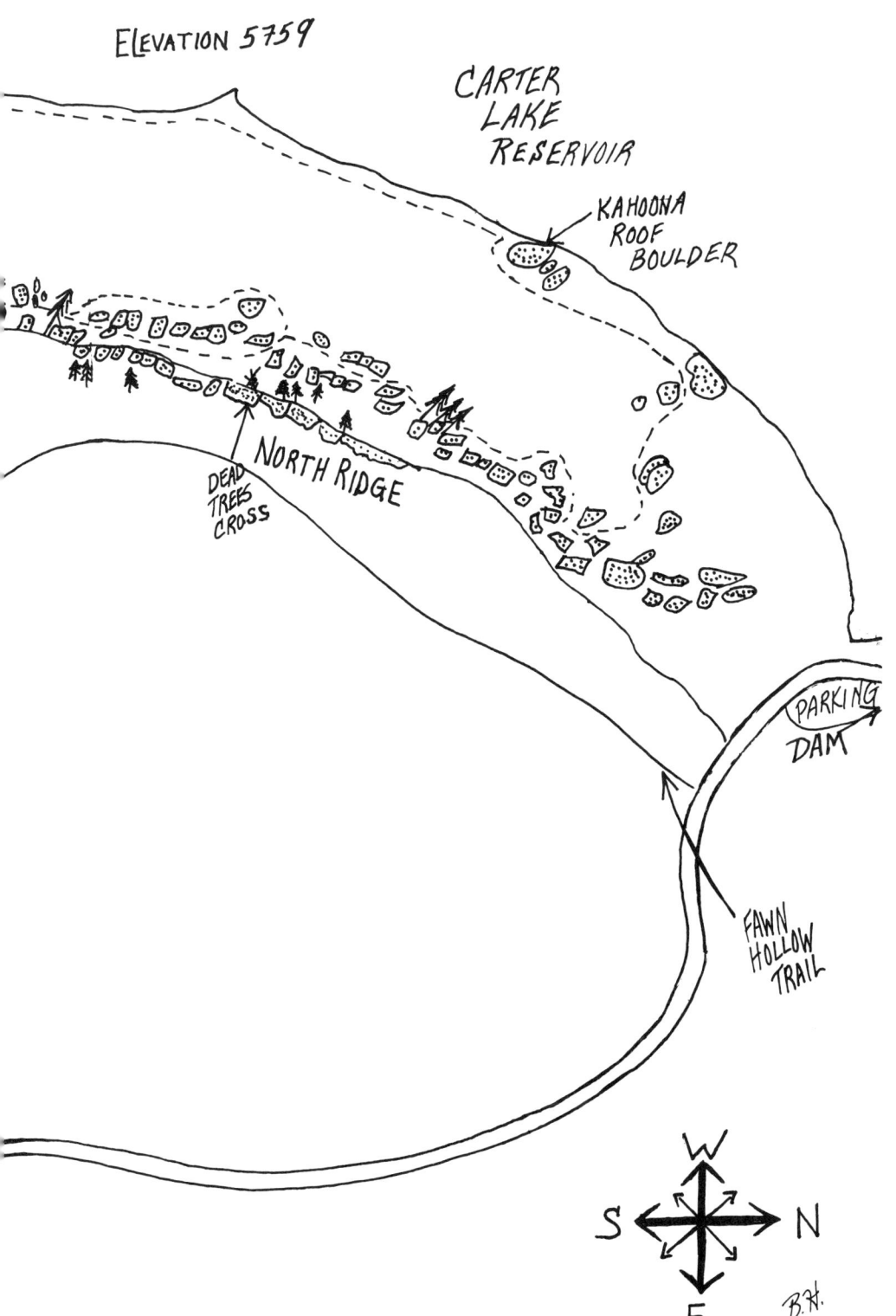

Shane Rymer leaps his way up the South Line (B.1).

SCENIC BOULDER
This is the first prominent boulder from the south parking lot that you will see. It has an overhanging south face with a crack on its left side and a obvious pocket on its right side. Look for the chalk.
Pocket Lunge B.1 –
From the pocket on the right side of the face lunge up to the top of the boulder. FA: B. Horan 1988.
Standard B.1 –
This line takes the pocket on the right with a heel hook and a reach to a small finger lock. Reach from this to the top and mantle. FA: S. Mammen.
South Line B.1
This is the problem up the line on the left side of the boulder. Reach to the sloping holds and go for the top. FA: S. Mammen.
West Bulge B.1 –
On the far left side of the boulder is a bulging problem that reaches out to the right from the corner. FA: B. Horan 1988.

BOOK ROCK
Directly behind Scenic Boulder is an obvious corner in the middle of a rock.
West Corner B5.8
Stem up the prominent corner to the top.

CLASSIC ROCK
Behind Book Rock and slightly west is a rock with a classic crack on its north side. This is a fun B5.8 problem.

CAVE BOULDER
Just behind Classic Rock is a short boulder with a roof problem that starts off the ground. Rocks were cleared away to create a longer problem called Flake Hang. FA: B. Horan 1988.

BIG BLOCK
Continue to the north through the boulder field until you come across a prominent block sticking out from the top of the ridge. Its west face has a big roof just off the ground with a small layback corner over the lip.
Big Block Roof B.1
This is the west-facing roof problem on the Big Block. It can be ascended by grabbing hold of the corner from the lip and making a high step move into a layback positon, or you can start from a sitting positon under the roof and grab hold of a small flake and make a long reach for the lip. It was done from a sitting position by B. Horan in 1988.

THE SPACESHIP
Down below Big Block there is a spire that looks like a spaceship when looking at its west face.
Southern Arete B5.10
On the south corner of the west side of the spire is an arete with some good holds.
Leaning Face B5.10
On the west face of the Spaceship is a set of good holds that leads up from the lower left to the upper right.

SLABBY
This describes the low-angle slab a few rocks north of the Spaceship. Some short but fun problems can be found on the slab.

PROW ROCK
Heading up to the outcrops on the top of the ridge, one sees a prominent outcrop with a west-facing prow and a steep north face. This same rock connects with another prominent wall to form a left-facing inside corner.
North Pockets B5.10+
Around the corner to the left of the prow is a steep face with pockets in it. FA: S. Mammen.

CHAIN ROCK
This is the classic west-facing wall which connects with Prow Rock. It has a prominent cave with a crack leading out of it. Many good face routes as well as a leaning arete have been done.
West Face B.1−
On the right side of the face is a small seam with finger pockets around it. FA: S. Mammen.
Chain Reactor B.1
Just to the left of the West Face is this obvious, left-leaning arete. FA: B. Horan 1988.
North Face B5.10+
Left of the prominent cave and around the corner to the north is a steep face with some good edges.

Carter Lake Reservoir

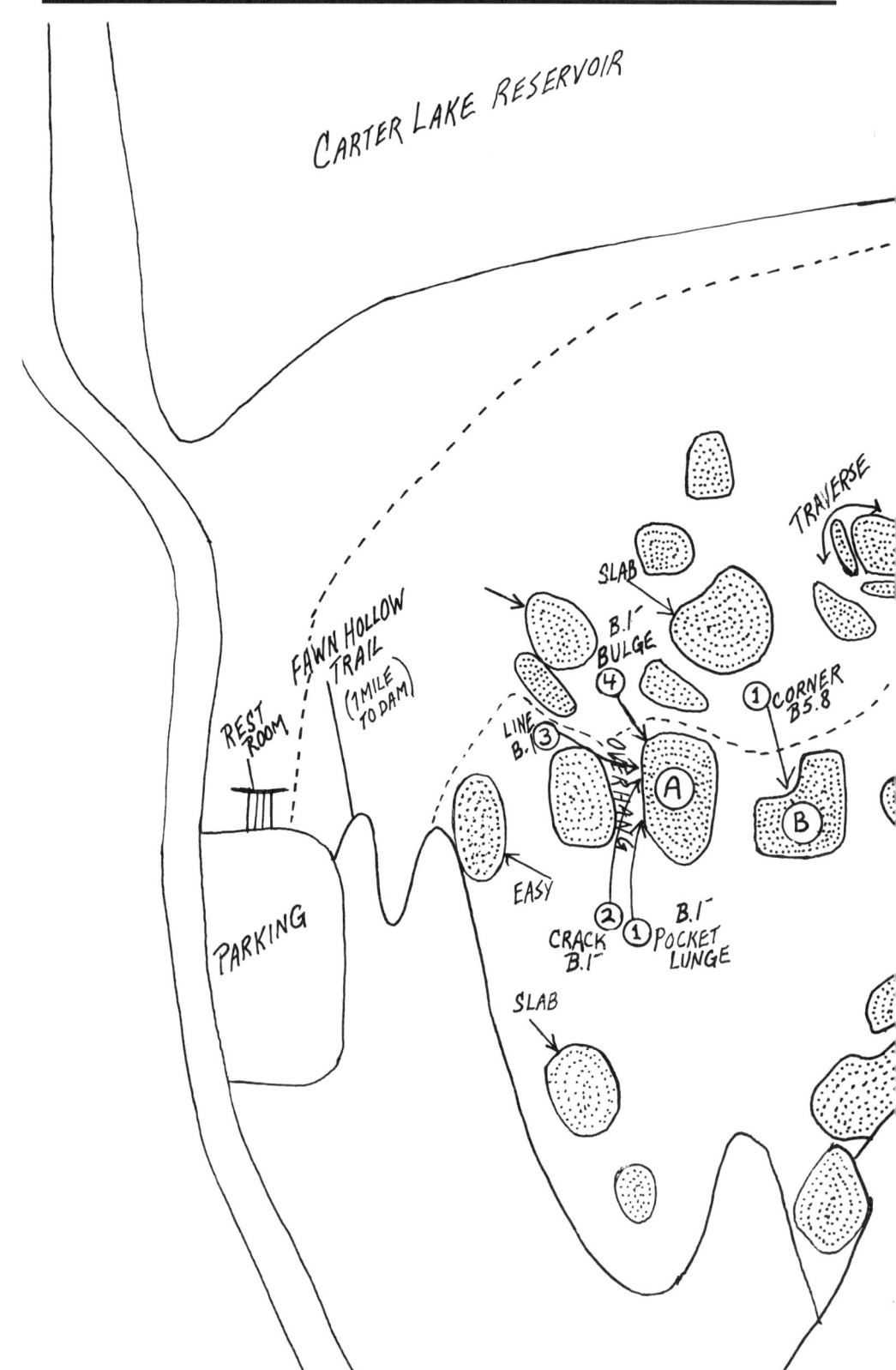

Carter Lake Reservoir — 61

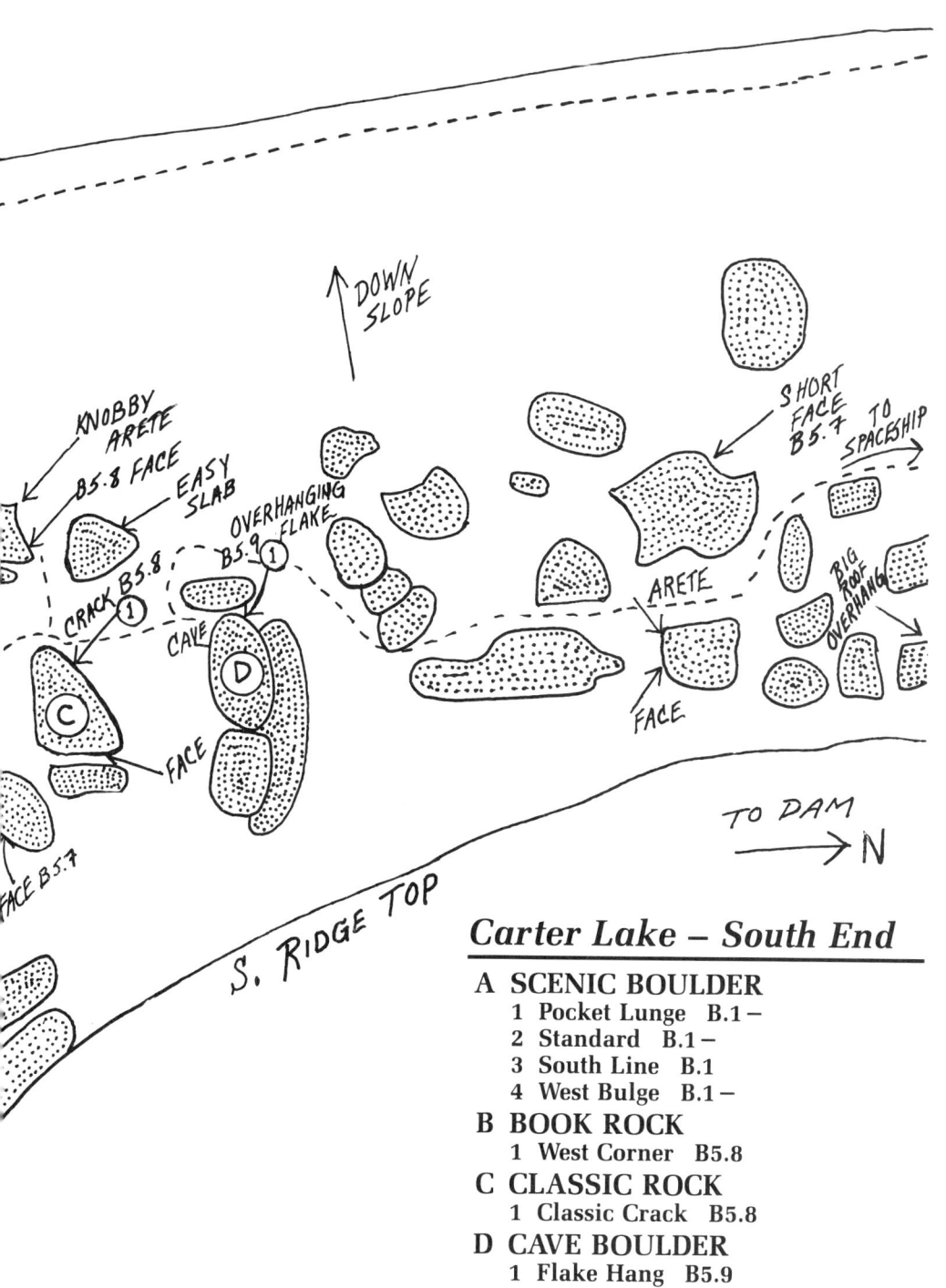

Carter Lake – South End

A SCENIC BOULDER
1. Pocket Lunge B.1–
2. Standard B.1–
3. South Line B.1
4. West Bulge B.1–

B BOOK ROCK
1. West Corner B5.8

C CLASSIC ROCK
1. Classic Crack B5.8

D CAVE BOULDER
1. Flake Hang B5.9

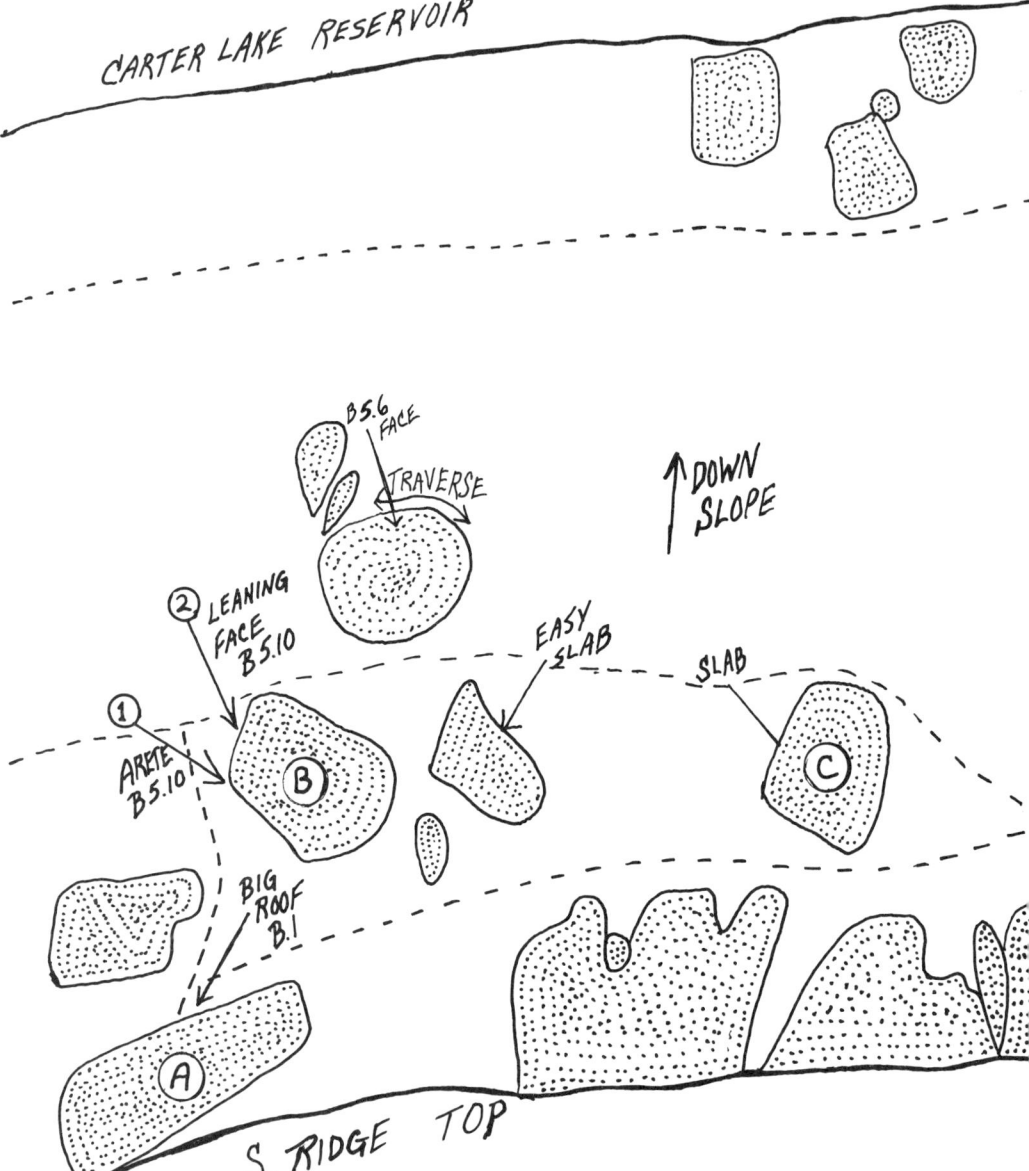

Carter Lake Outcrops

A BIG BLOCK
    1 Big Roof B.1
B THE SPACESHIP
    1 Southern Arete B5.10
    2 Leaning Face B5.10
C SLABBY
D PROW ROCK
    1 North Pockets B5.10+
E CHAIN ROCK
    1 West Face B.1−
    2 Chain Reactor B.1
    3 North Face B5.10+

GRAFITTI ROCK
This is a landmark rock just uphill from Chain Rock. It has been painted on its west side.

LITTLE BOULDER
Just northwest of Grafitti Rock is a little boulder with two good moderate problems on its northwest face.

Little Face B5.9
This is a short face on the rock's right side.

Little Crack B5.8
This takes the thin crack on the left side.

CRAYOLA ROCK
Just west of Little Boulder is a rectangular rock with a overhanging northwest face. The colors on this rock appear to be melting.

Melting Traverse B5.10+
This is the traverse of the entire northwest face of Crayola Rock. Many other problems exist all over this northwest face.

LAKE BOULDER
If you look down the slope towards the lake you will see a fairly large boulder with a split in it. Some fun little problems can be found on this, including a wide west-facing crack.

MIGHTY WALL
Looking up north to the top of the ridge from Crayola Rock you will see a classic, slightly overhanging wall with an overhanging corner up its middle.

Regular Route B.1−
On the right side of the wall is a steep face that comes in from the right side. FA: S. Mammen.

West Corner B.1
This ascends the overhanging corner in the middle of the face. FA: S. Mammen.

Dicey Prow B.1+
Left of the West Corner, on the far left side of the wall is an arete with good flakes leading up to the top. FA: S. Mammen.

SCOOP ROCK
Traveling up along the ridge to the north you will come across a face with a short scooping wall. These moderate problems offer some fun challenges.

HANDY ROCK
This is just to the north of Scoop Rock; a small cave can be seen on its left side. A strenuous traverse exists on its west side.

POCKET WALL
North a few more outcrops from Handy Rock is a block with a pocketed prow leading to a short corner.

Northwest Pockets B.1−
This ascends the pockets on the northwest corner of the wall to a short right-facing corner with hidden single-finger pockets in and around it. FA: B. Horan 1988.

North Seam B.1
On the north face of Pocket Wall is this thin crack that can be laybacked. FA: B. Horan 1988.

LONG WALL
Just to the north of Pocket Wall is a long wall with some short problems on it. This wall extends north to a split in the ridge.

BARREL ROCK
Where the ridge splits at the north end of Long Wall, there is a smooth barrel-shaped rock sitting up and above. This rock starts off the rocks of the upper split in the ridge.

Mighty Wall's Regular Route (B.1 −).

Carter Lake Outcrops

- **A GRAFFITI ROCK**
- **B LITTLE BOULDER**
  1. Little Face   B5.9
  2. Little Crack B5.8
- **C CRAYOLA ROCK**
  1. Melting Traverse B5.10+
- **D LAKE BOULDER**
- **E MIGHTY WALL**
  1. Regular Route B.1−
  2. West Corner   B.1
  3. Dicey Prow   B.1+

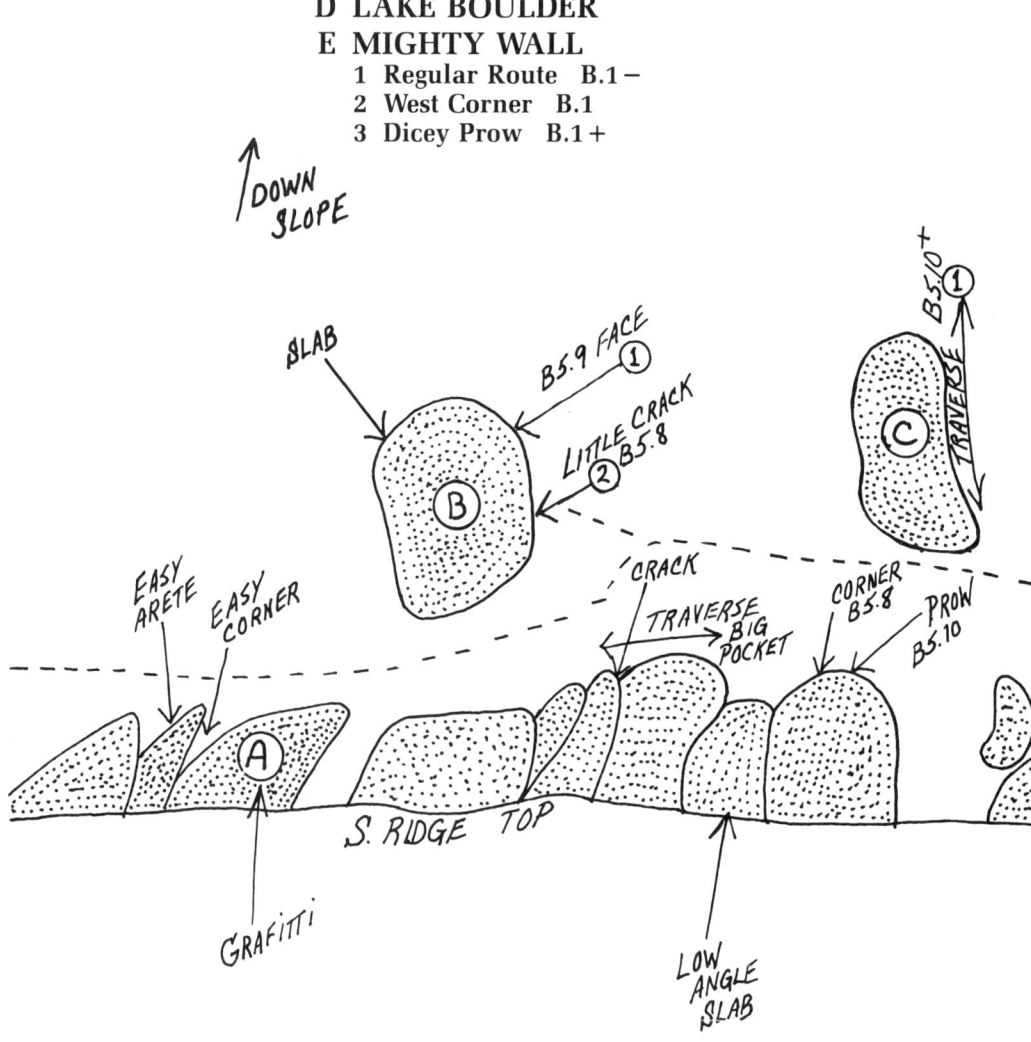

WIDE CRACK
CORNER
FACE
D

DOWN SLOPE
POCKETED FACE
B5.9 LEANING CORNER
1
B.1 FACE
OVERHANGING CORNER
B.1
2
B.1+ PROW
3
TRAVERSE
E
SLAB
B5.10 FACE
N

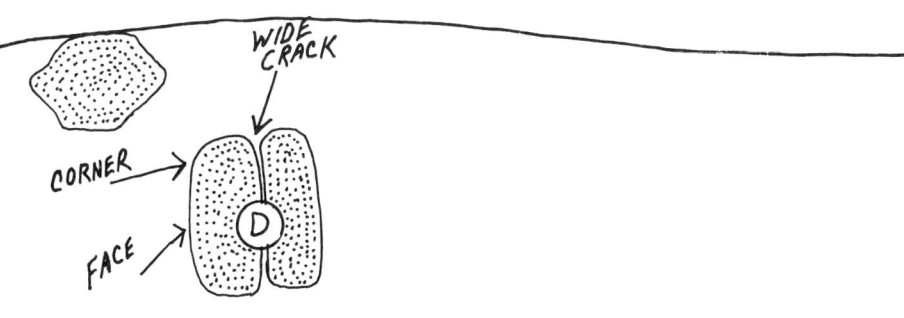

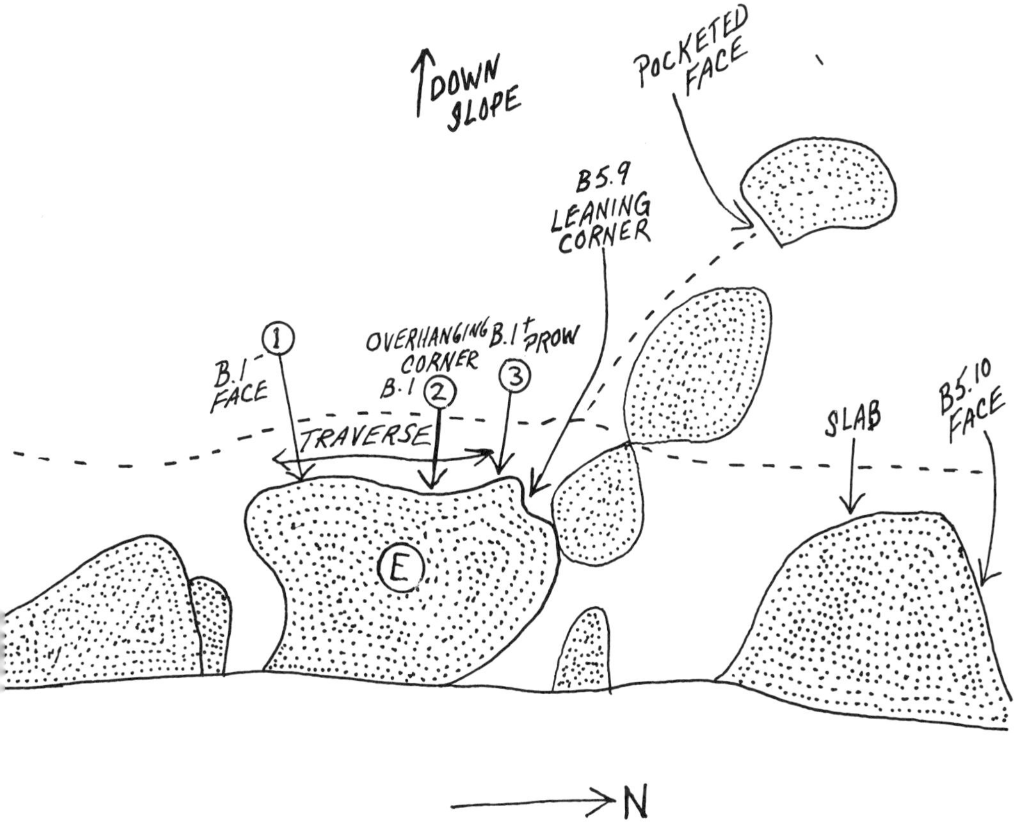

Carter Lake Reservoir

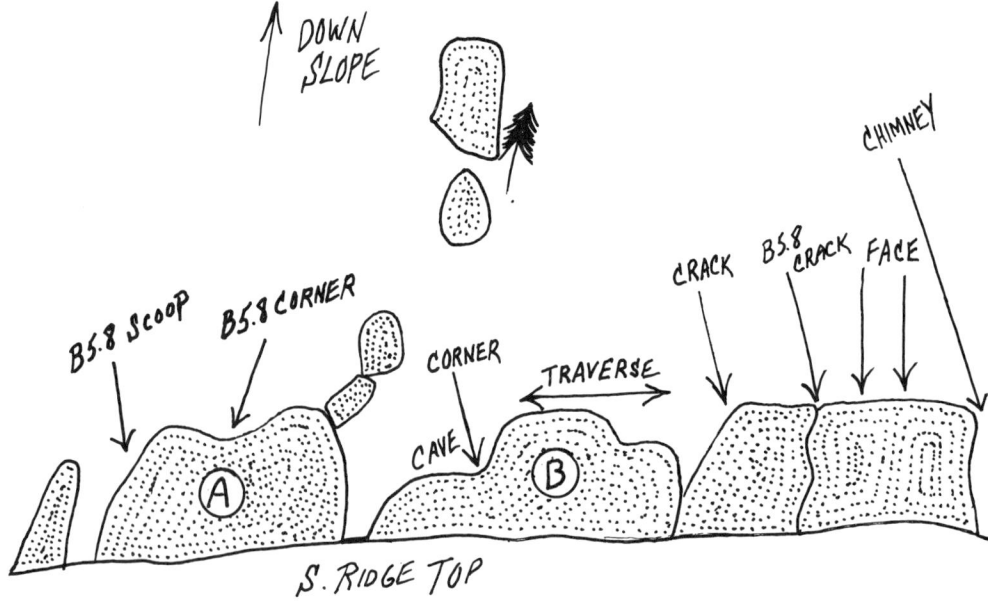

Carter Lake Reservoir — 69

Carter Lake Ridge Split

A SCOOP ROCK
B HANDY ROCK
C POCKET WALL
    1 North Seam B.1
    2 Northwest Corner B.1–
D LONG WALL
E BARREL ROCK

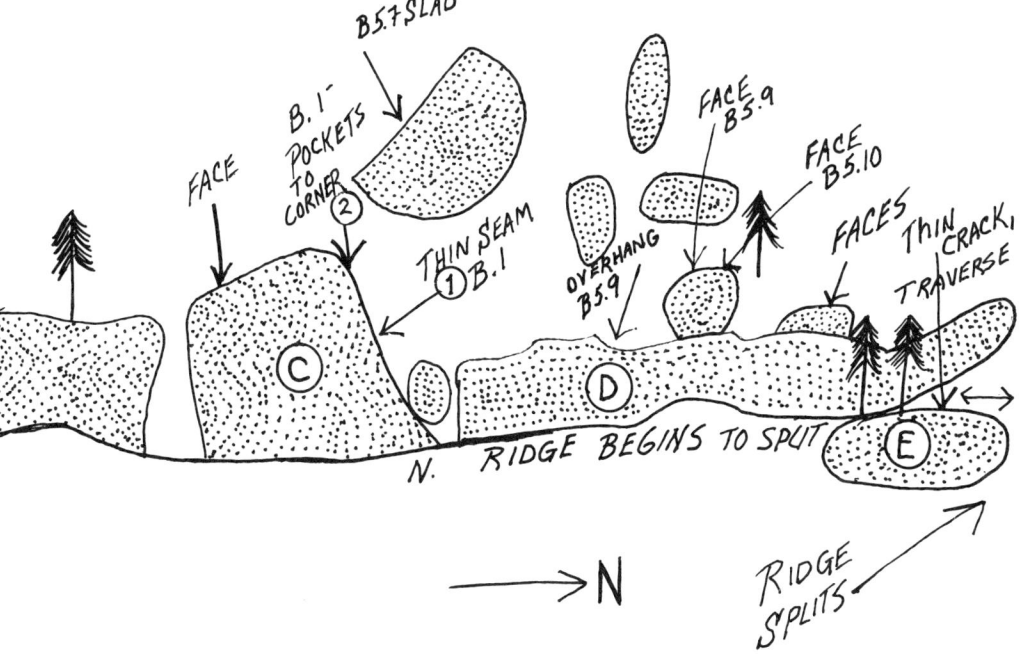

LONE STAR BOULDER
Continue north along the upper ridge split until you run across a prominent boulder with a thin crack splitting its southwest face.
Southwest Crack B5.10
This climbs the classic thin crack.
Areteach B5.9
Left of Southwest Crack is an arete with some good holds.

DEAD TREES ROCK
Just north of Lone Star Boulder is a rock with dead trees lying against it. Another useful landmark to guide yourself by.
Roof Cave Crack B5.10+
Moving even farther north on the upper ridge of rock, just left of the Dead Trees Rock, is a overhanging roof crack that comes out of a short cave. Hand jam out to the lip. FA: M. Pennings 1988.
Flakey Pull Roof B.1+
Just left of the roof crack is another roof. Some layaway pockets are used to gain the lip; a tricky maneuver from here is the crux. FA: B. Horan 1988.

LOWER ROCK
Just below the roof cave on the lower ridge split, walk north for a few boulders until you see this bulging west face.
The Bulge B.1−
On the right side of Lower Rock is a nice bulge that starts from under a roof.
The Crack B5.9
To the left of The Bulge is an obvious crack leading over a small bulge.

MANTLE BOULDER
Where the ridge north of Lower Rock begins to break up into a field of massive boulders, you will note an oval-looking boulder sitting alone to the west. A good short B5.8 face can be done on its west side and a mantle shelf can be found on its south side.

EXTENSION ROCK
A few rocks to the north you will see this exposed high face with a problem up the middle of its west side.
West Face B.1 (TR)
On the west face of the rock is a high face with some long reaches between the holds. FA: S. Mammen.
Rocky Top B.1−
To the left of West Face is an enjoyable layback problem. FA: B. Horan 1988.

MONSTER BOULDER
Heading north from Extension Rock and slightly down slope you will see this large boulder with an exposed northwest face. An interesting problem goes up the far left side of the northwest wall just above a manmade rock platform. FA: S. Mammen.

GIANT PEBBLE
From Monster Boulder head down the slope to the northwest, past a couple of boulders lying on the slope, and you will come across this rounded boulder. Three routes on its south and west faces were done by B. Horan 1988.

Carter Lake Reservoir — 71

KAHOONA BLOCK
This is the awesome boulder that sits beside the water, just to the left and downhill from Giant Pebble. Its west face has an incredible thin overhang.

Kahoona Roof B.2
On the west face of Kahoona Block, facing the water, is a set of edges that are used to leap up to a sloping shelf. From here you must reach up to the short overhanging corner and mantle to the top. FA: S. Mammen 1988.

BIG BUD BOULDER
To the right of Giant Pebble is another large, rounded boulder. Many problems exist on all sides.

A refreshing Carter Lake ripples as the Southwest Crack (B5.10), on Lone Star, is ascended.   photo: Shane Rymer

Carter Lake Ridge Split

A LONE STAR BOULDER
  1 Southwest Crack   B5.10
  2 Areteach   B5.9
B DEAD TREES ROCK
C ROOF CAVE
  1 Roof Cave Crack   B5.10+
  2 Flakey Pull Roof   B.1+
D LOWER ROCK
  1 The Bulge   B.1−
  2 The Crack   B5.9

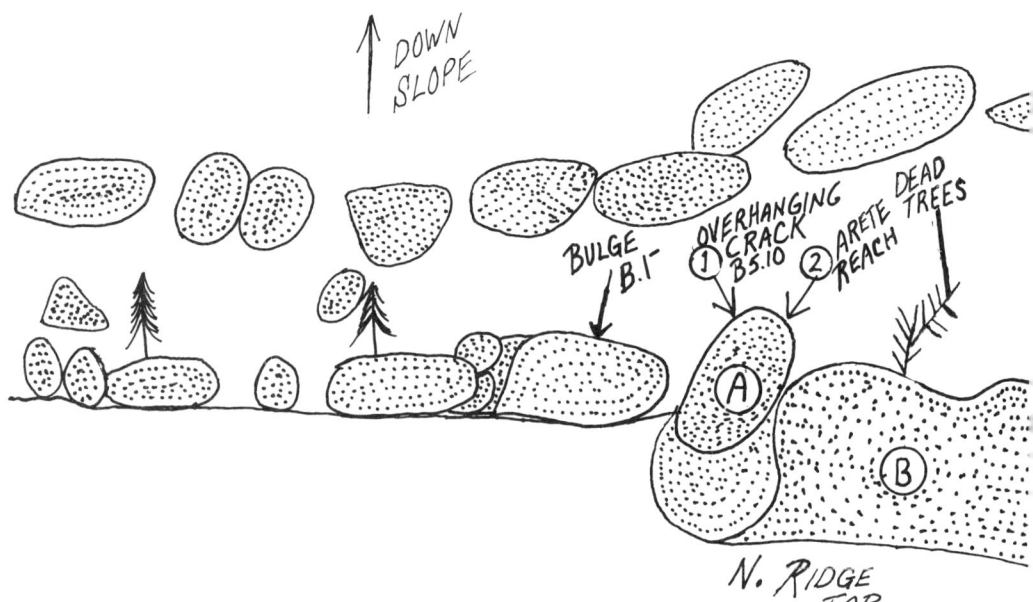

Carter Lake Reservoir

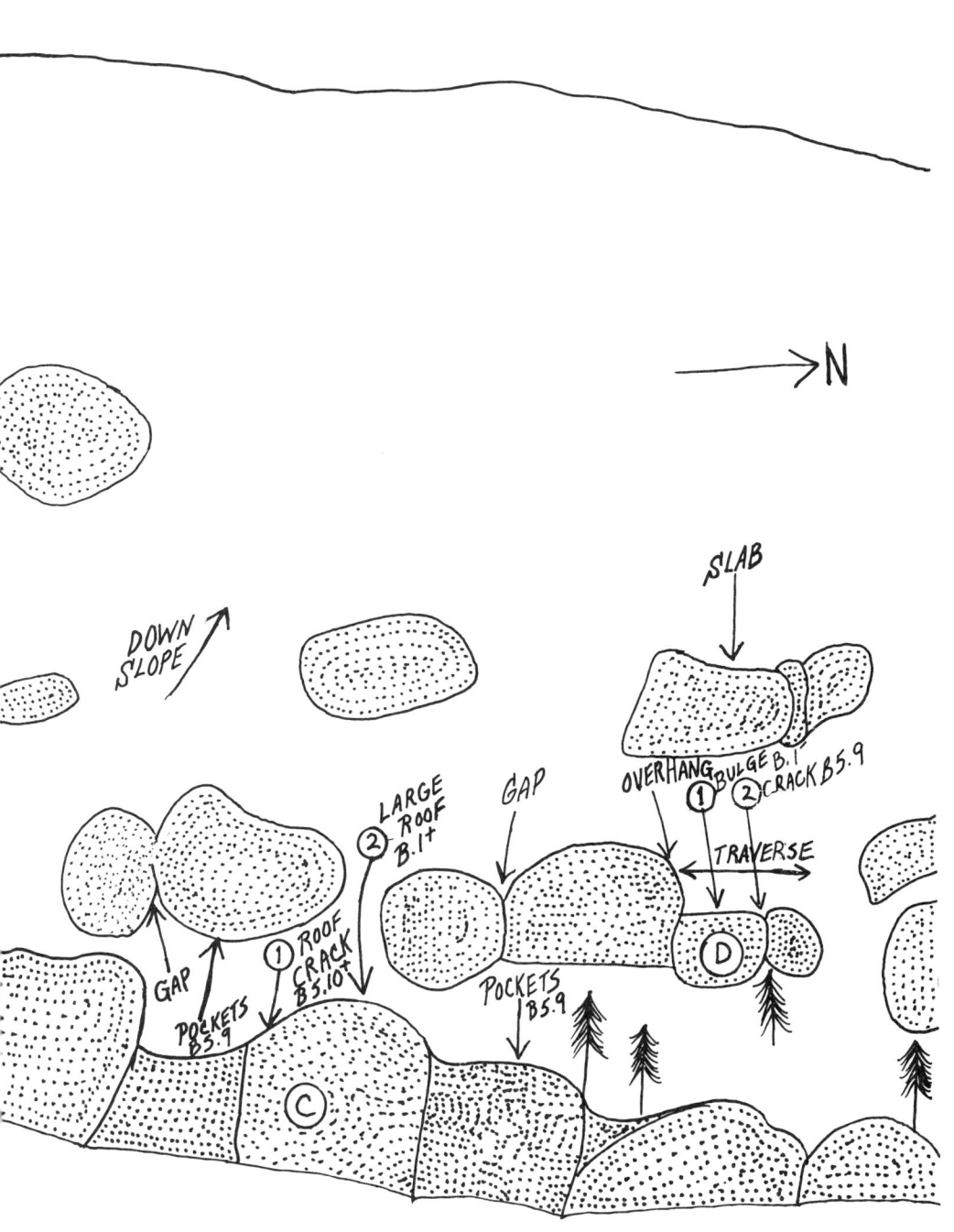

Carter Lake – North End

A MANTLE BOULDER
B EXTENSION ROCK
  1 West Face   B.1 (TR)
  2 Rocky Top   B.1−
C MONSTER BOULDER

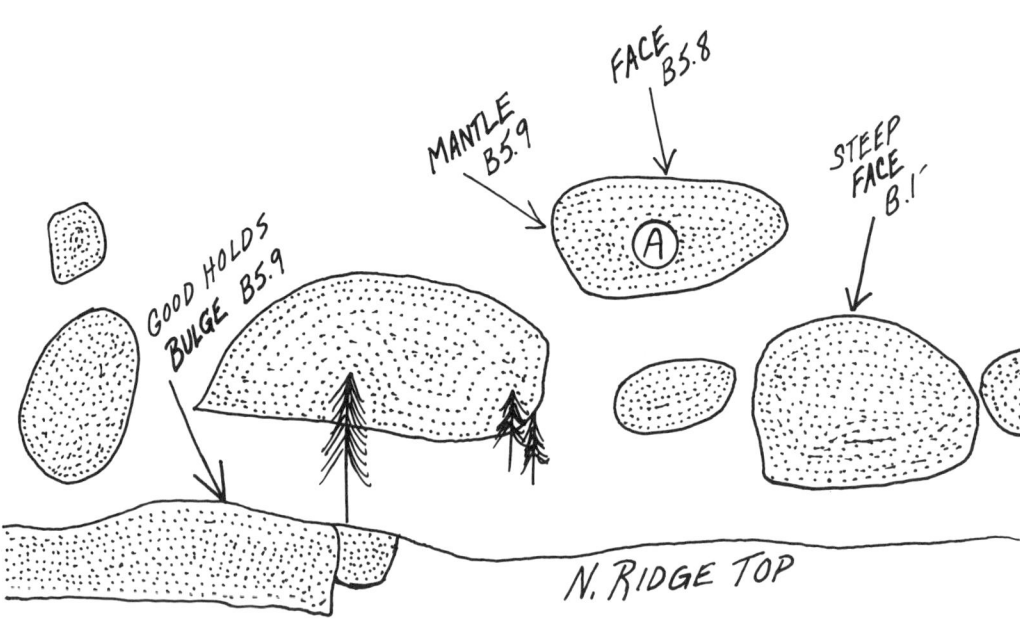

Carter Lake Reservoir

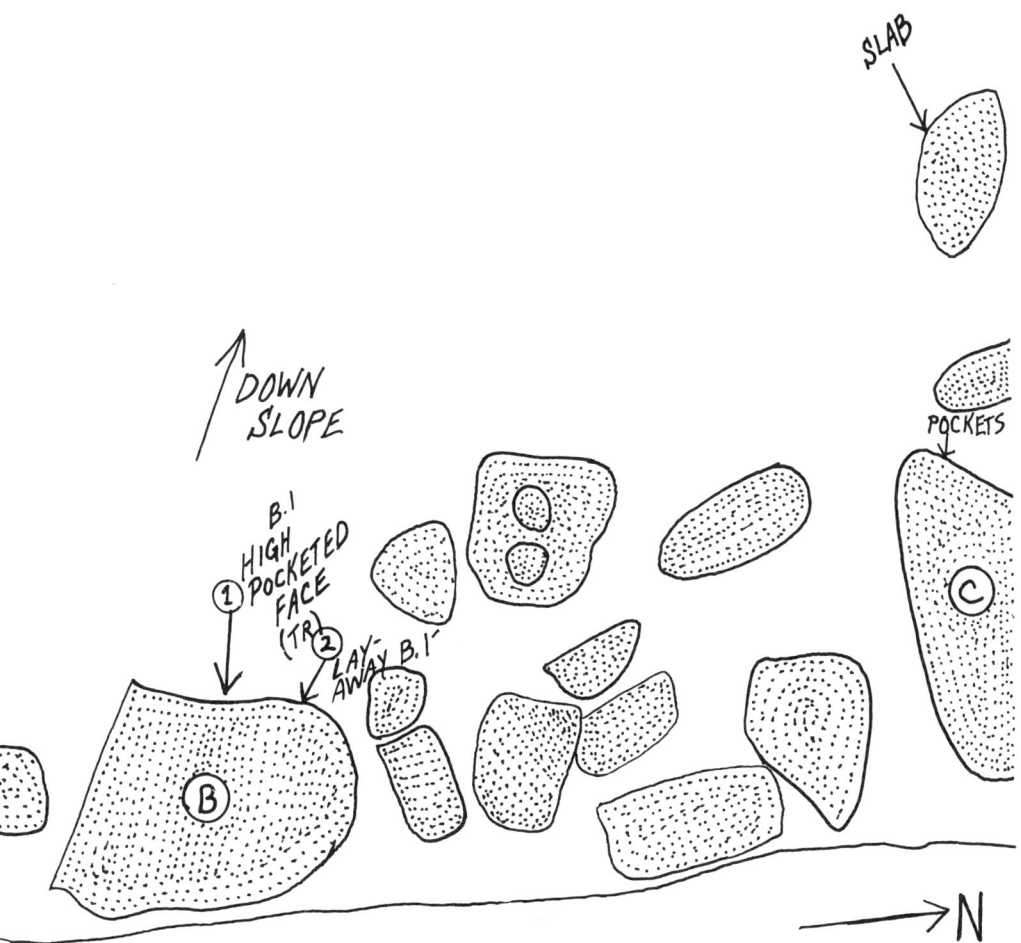

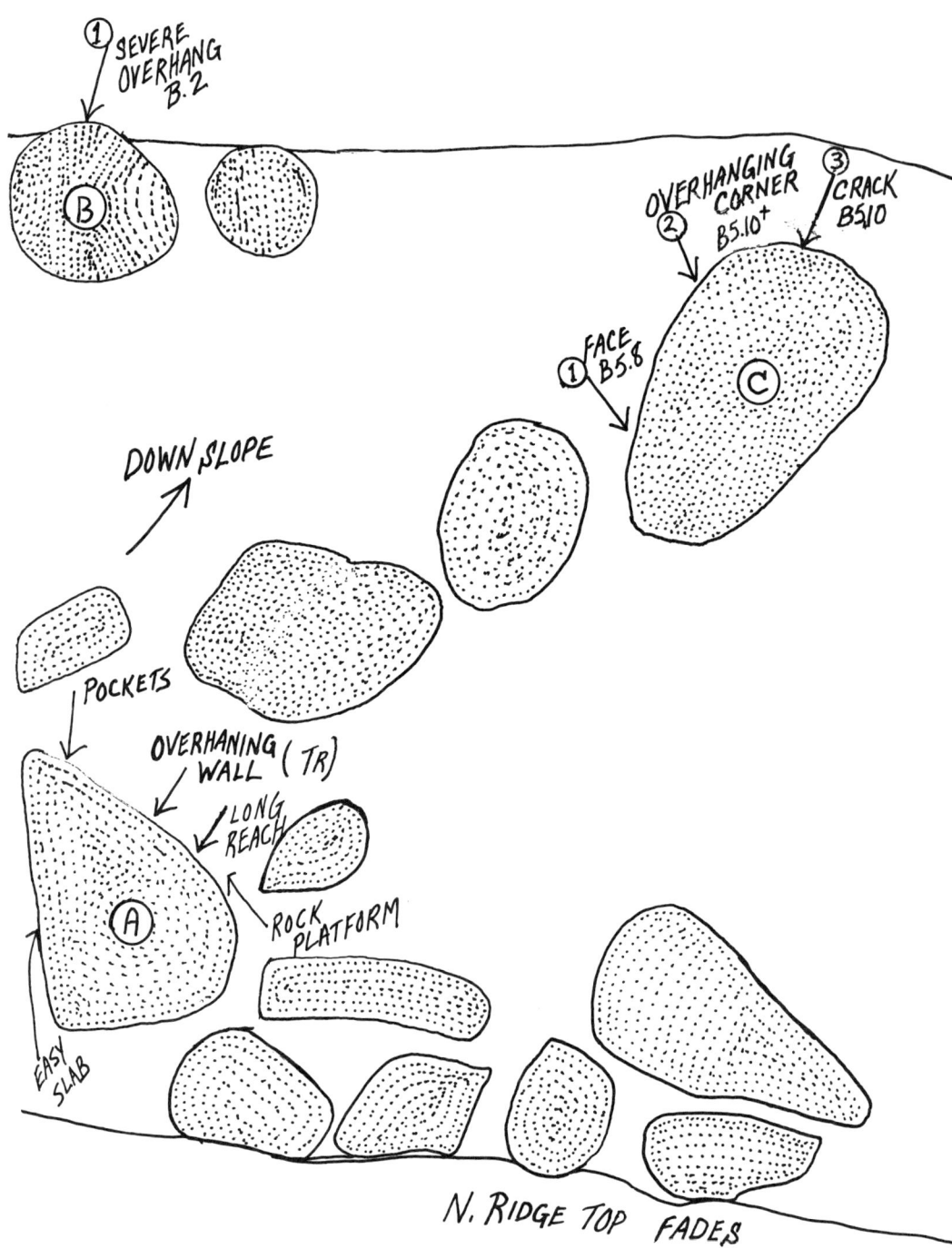

Carter Lake Reservoir — 77

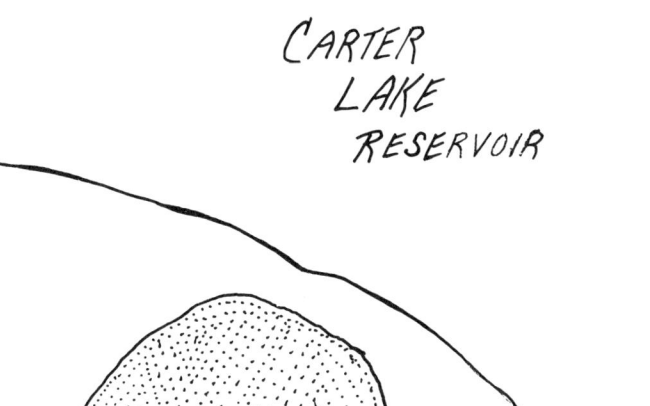

Carter Lake – North End

A MONSTER BOULDER
B KAHOONA BLOCK
    1 Kahoona Roof B.2
C GIANT PEBBLE
    1 South Face
    2 Southwest Corner B.1
    3 Crack Hang B.1 –
D BIG BUD BOULDER

Mount Sanitas

This spiny ridge of west-facing outcroppings is filled with moderate boulder problems that usually have good landings. A short hike uphill to the ridge will take you to a pine-scented conglomerate sandstone bouldering ground featuring enough rock to please all levels of ability.

To reach Mount Sanitas you must locate Broadway (Highway 93). This road runs north-south through the city of Boulder. Take Broadway to Mapleton Street (north Boulder) and head west towards the mountains. The small city park with its pavillion and fire pit is located about a half block west of the Memorial Hospital. Park near the shelter and walk up to the north over a foot bridge. Follow the trail around to the west and uphill until you come across the ridge.

The history of Mount Sanitas is not well documented. Many local and traveling climbers have come through this bouldering area. The north-stretching ridge filled with cracks, faces, and aretes is an enjoyable after-work, after-climb kind of place to go. Just look along the walls for the chalk marks and you will see the many well-tracked problems this fun little place has to offer.

Mount Sanitas — 79

Bouldering up the North Shelf Blocks of Mount Sanitas.
photo: Shane Rymer

Shane Rymer bouldering the B5.9 route on Classy Wall.

80 — Mount Sanitas

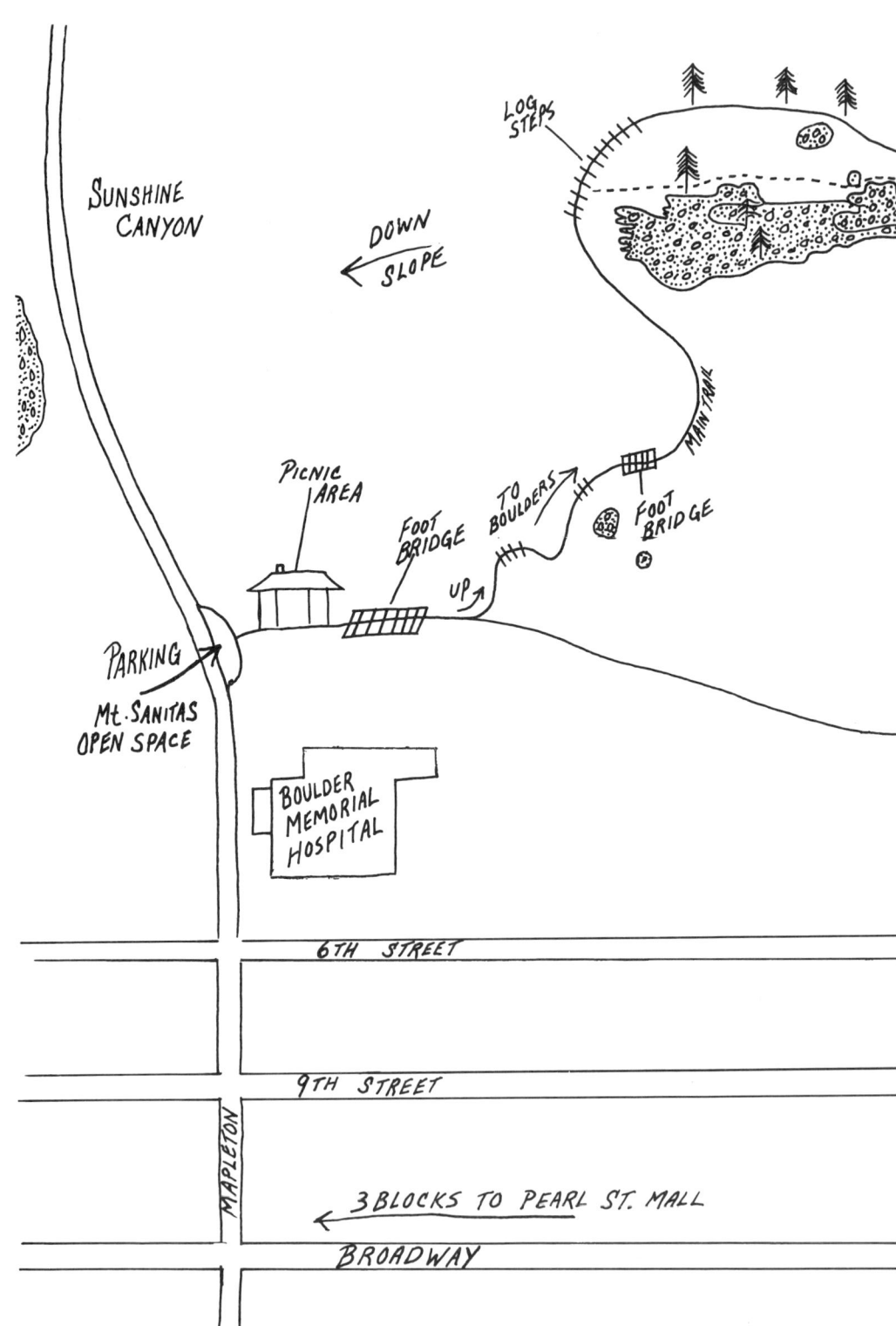

Mount Sanitas — 81

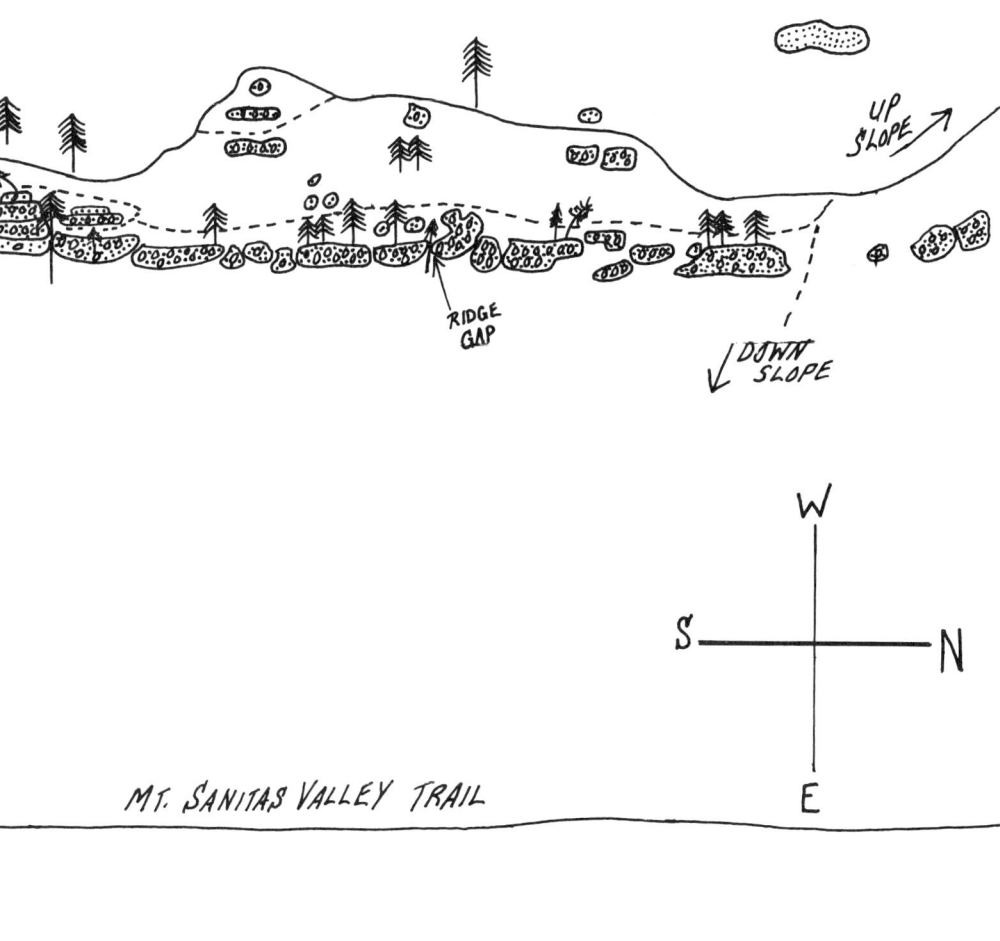

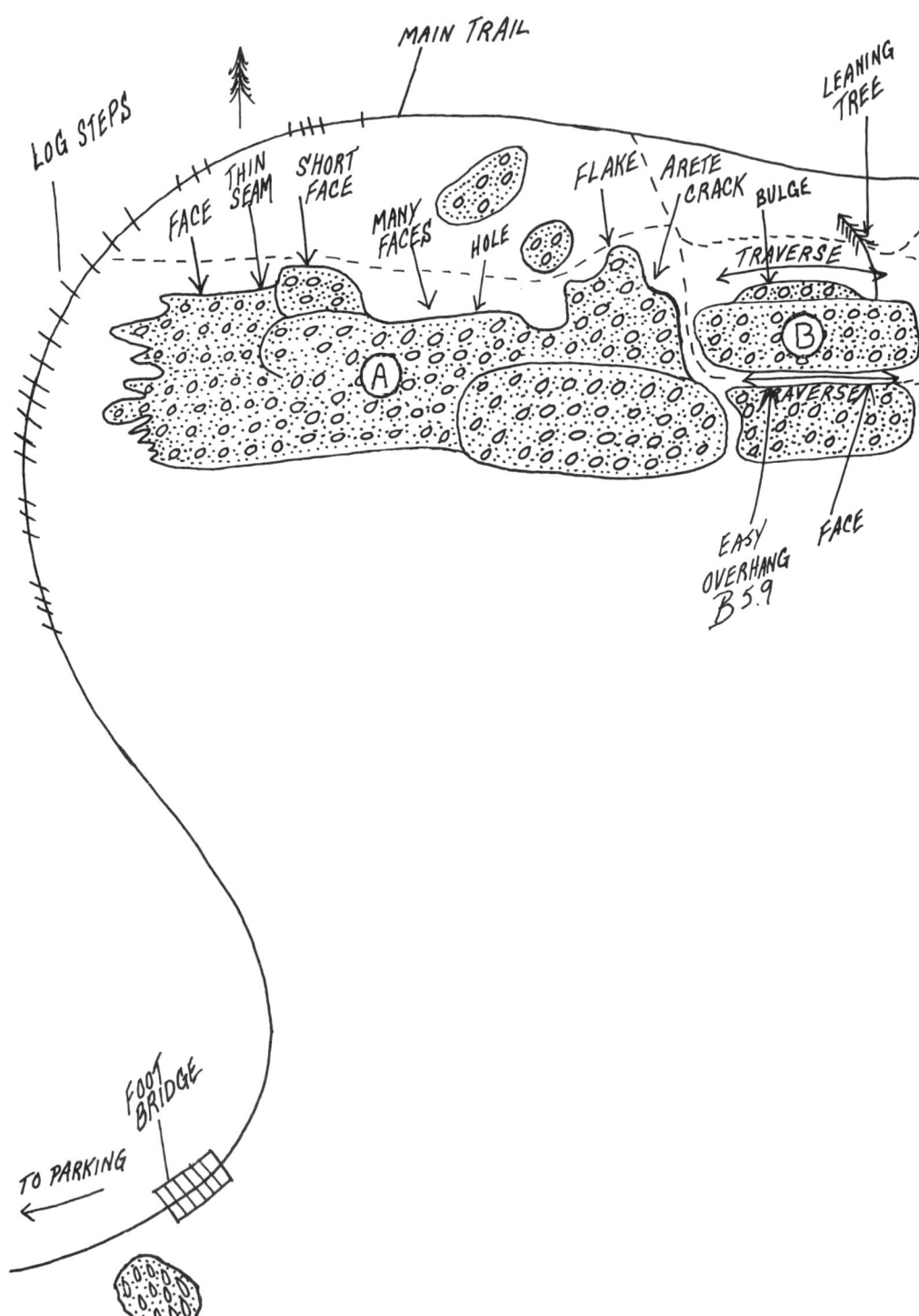

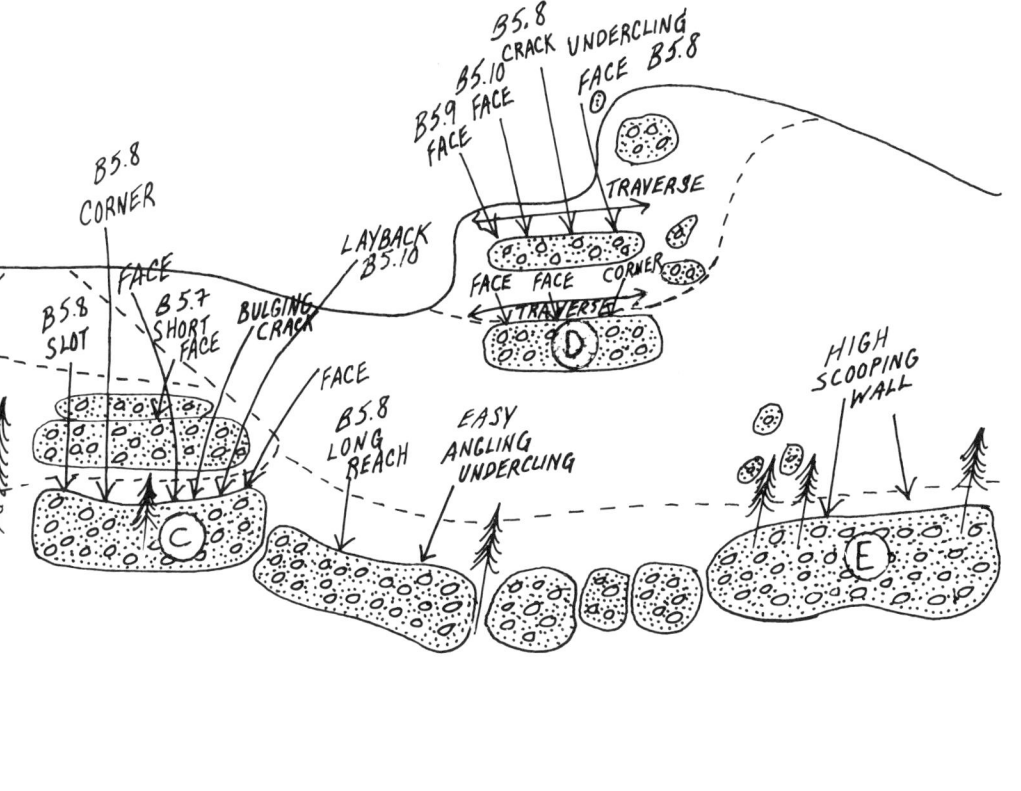

Mount Sanitas – South End

A SANITAS PROPER
B SOUTH SHELF BLOCKS
C NORTH SHELF BLOCKS
D TWIN FINS
E SCOOP WALL

84 — *Mount Sanitas*

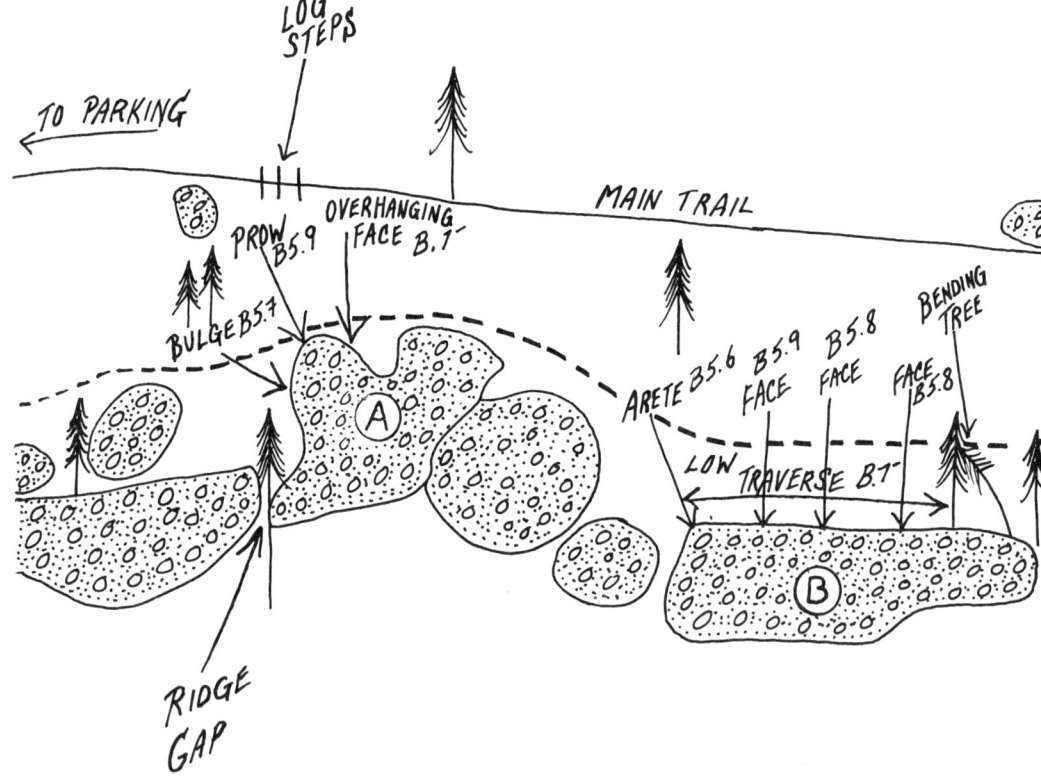

Mount Sanitas – North End

A CORNER ROCK
B CLASSY WALL
C RIDGE GAP WALL

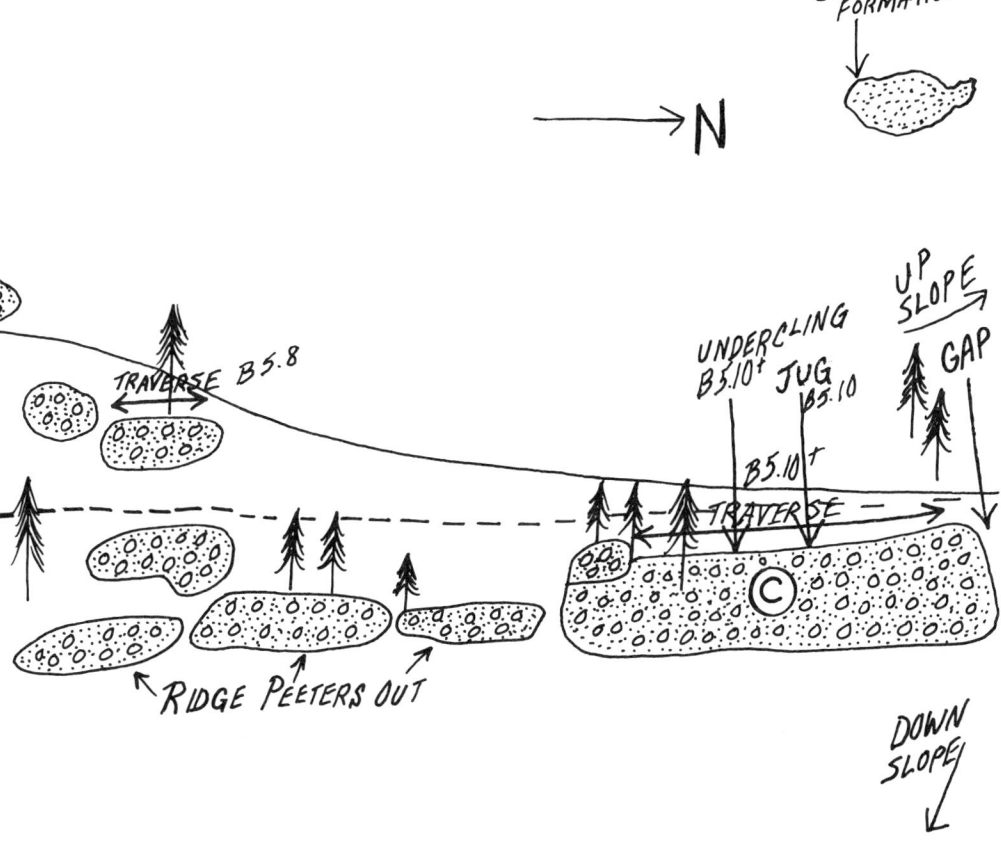

Flagstaff Mountain

When in the picturesque little city of Boulder, Colorado one should not miss the historic boulders of Flagstaff Mountain. Their easy access by car has made this natural playground an area favorite. Spread out magically amidst the pine-scented forested slopes are an awesome array of short, demanding problems for all levels of ability. The conglomerate sandstone boulders often resemble mini flatiron formations that are mostly quite solid. Flakes, pockets, edges, pebbles and crystals appear on the well-rounded rocks to create an unlimited variety of challenges.

   Many climbers have found this exciting area to be a little rough on the fingertips at first, but with a bit of conditioning the fingers will begin to adapt with nice calluses. Flagstaff has been the training ground for many of the area's top climbers and with the strength and endurance gained on these small outcroppings, the standards of fifth class roped climbs in the area have greatly advanced. The future of difficult rock climbing lies in the development in one's bouldering skills. Flagstaff has an abundance of these state-of-the-art problems.

Flagstaff Mountain — 87

Hanging high over Boulder on Sailor's Delight (B5.10), Cloudshadow Area.

photo: Jim Sanders

To find this fine bouldering area, locate Baseline Road, running east-west through the city of Boulder. Go west on Baseline until you reach the foot of Flagstaff Mountain. From here the road takes a sharp curve up and to the north, and Baseline turns into Flagstaff Road. The mileage markings used in this book begin at a small bridge located just as the road curves to the north at the base of the grade. A pleasant foot trail can also be taken up the mountain and is located just past this bridge on the west side of the road. While driving up the road you will most likely encounter bicyclists, some with rock shoes and chalk bags strapped to their backs. Be considerate of the wobbling cyclists, for the road becomes very narrow at times.

A new challenge of the eighties was not only climbing upward, but also traversing the faces until totally pumped. Many new desperate problems on Flagstaff and other areas are strenuous traverses of the outcroppings, both low and high. Flexiblity plays an important role in this type of problem.

88 — Flagstaff Mountain

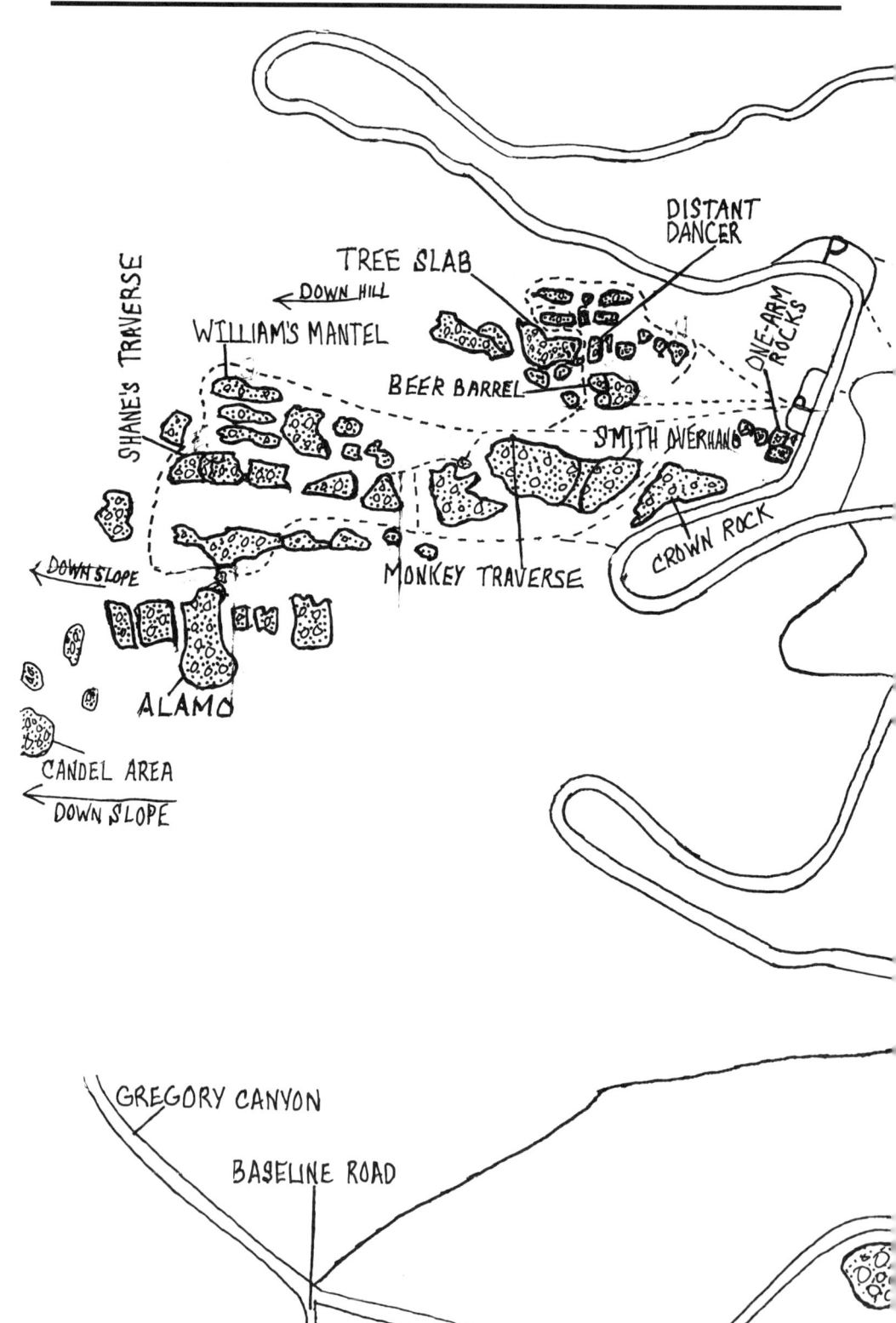

Flagstaff Mountain — 89

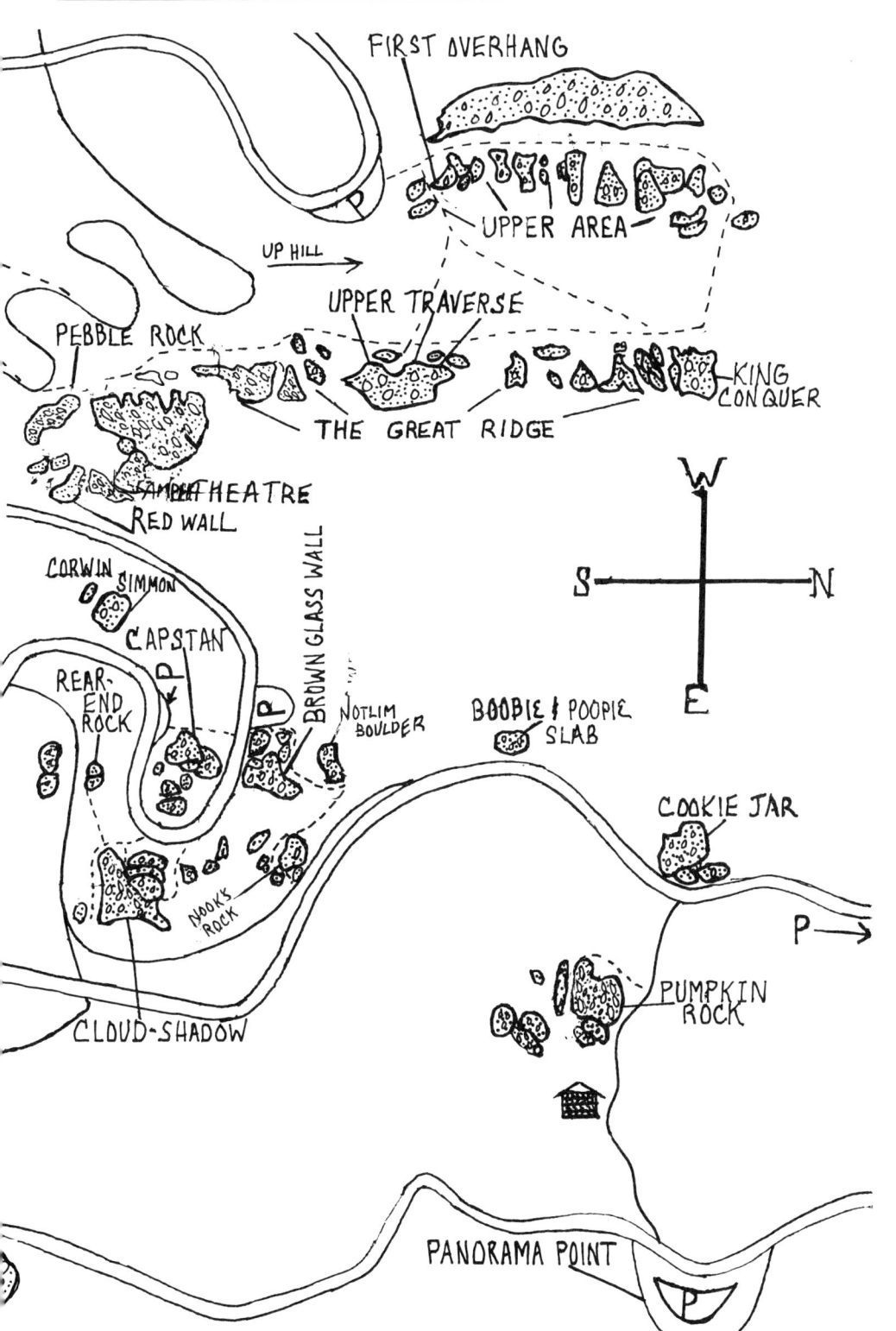

PUMPKIN ROCK
This large blob-like boulder sits on the west side of the road just southwest of the Panorama Point parking area. Many little problems can be found all around its base. Two steel eye bolts on top provide convenient top-roping, and a ramp on the south side gives easy access to its summit. Many excellent high problems are to be found on its northwest face.

Northwest Face B.1 –
This ascends the old aid line via pin scars to the summit. FA: unknown.

Northwest Right B.1
Climb the wall right of the pin scars. FA: unknown.

West Face Left B5.10
This climbs a scoop-like face to the right of the Northwest Face. FA: P. Ament 1968.

West Face Right B5.10+
This climbs an overhanging wall to the right of the West Face Left route. FA: Ament 1968.

COOKIE JAR ROCK
This is another prominent Flagstaff boulder which sits on the western side of the road 0.8 mile up the road, a short way past the Flagstaff House restaurant. Many classic problems are found on this formation. The south crack that splits this spire in half is probably one of the most climbed routes in the Boulder region. Steel eye bolts can be found on top.

The Shield B.1 –
This route climbs the bulging face just right of the Cookie Jar Crack.

Cookie Jar Crack B5.7
An excellent beginner's top-rope can be found on the south side of the Cookie Jar.

Russian's Nose B5.10
Climbs the overhang left of Cookie Jar Crack. There are several variations to this route.

Commitment B.1 –
On the west side of the north face, right of Jackson's Pitch is another bulge problem. FA: P. Ament 1968.

Jackson's Pitch B.1 –
Located on the north side of the rock, this ascends a bulge via an undercling to a fingertip hold.

Kor's Corner B5.9
Towards the road from Jackson's Pitch is a corner leading up to a bulge.

Northcutt's Roll B.1
Climbs the overhanging wall on the southeast face. This earned its name when Ray Northcutt came off the problem and ended up rolling down into the roadway.

Rough One B.1 –
Just below the Cookie Jar and to the right is a roadcut block with an overhang leading to a short dihedral. This is a fun and challenging problem. FA: P. Ament 1969.

SCALIWAG ROCK
This is a small boulder southwest of Pumpkin Rock.
Northeast Side
This climbs a face on the northeast side. FA: C. Griffith 1978.

BOOBIE AND POOPIE SLAB
This roadside slab is located on the west side just a short ways up from Cookie Jar Rock. The red slab's name was painted on it by two lovers. Many no hands problems and balance moves will be found on this little slab.

NOOK'S ROCK
This rock is located a short way south from Boobie and Poopie Slab, just after the curve in the road. The boulder sits on the south side of the road a little ways uphill and into the trees. The rock received its name from the nickname of Layton Kor. Many routes for all levels of ability can be found on this boulder.

Northeast Undercut B.10+
This problem ascends an overhang to a mantle on the northeast side of the boulder. FA: P. Ament 1960s.

Butt Slammer B.2?
Crank on the small frail edges on the east overhang of the rock. This problem has lost a few holds since its first ascent and has yet to be repeated. FA: R. Candelaria 1970s.

The Scoop B.1
This ascends the thin scoop/face just left of Butt Slammer. FA: B. Horan 1988.

That Flakes It B5.10
This is located on a small rock just south of Nook's Rock and climbs an obvious overhang. Look for the chalk. R. Candelaria 1975.

Wimpie's Revenge B5.9
Ascend a line near the tree on the west face of the boulder. FA: Rob Candelaria 1974.

Westside Traverse B.1
This is an impressive traverse that moves along the west face of the boulder.

92 — *Flagstaff Mountain*

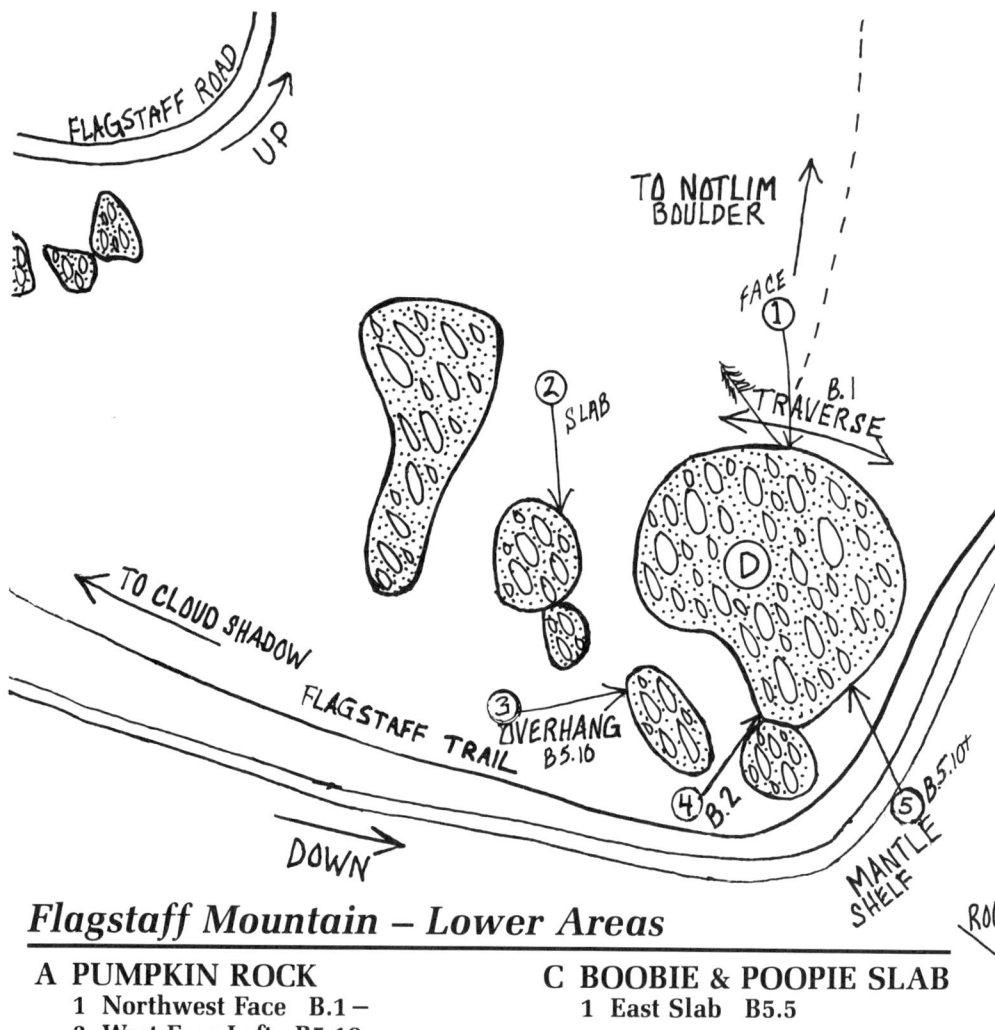

Flagstaff Mountain – Lower Areas

A PUMPKIN ROCK
1. Northwest Face B.1–
2. West Face Left B5.10
3. West Face Right B5.10+

B COOKIE JAR
1. The Shield B.1–
2. Cookie Jar Crack B5.7
3. Russian's Nose B5.10
4. Commitment B.1–
5. Jackson's Pitch B.1–
6. Rough One B.1–
7. Kor's Corner B5.9
8. Northcutt's Roll B.1

C BOOBIE & POOPIE SLAB
1. East Slab B5.5

D NOOK'S ROCK
1. Wimpie's Revenge B5.9
2. Easy Slab
3. That Flakes It B5.10
4. Butt Slammer B.2
5. Northeast Undercut B5.10+

Flagstaff Mountain — 93

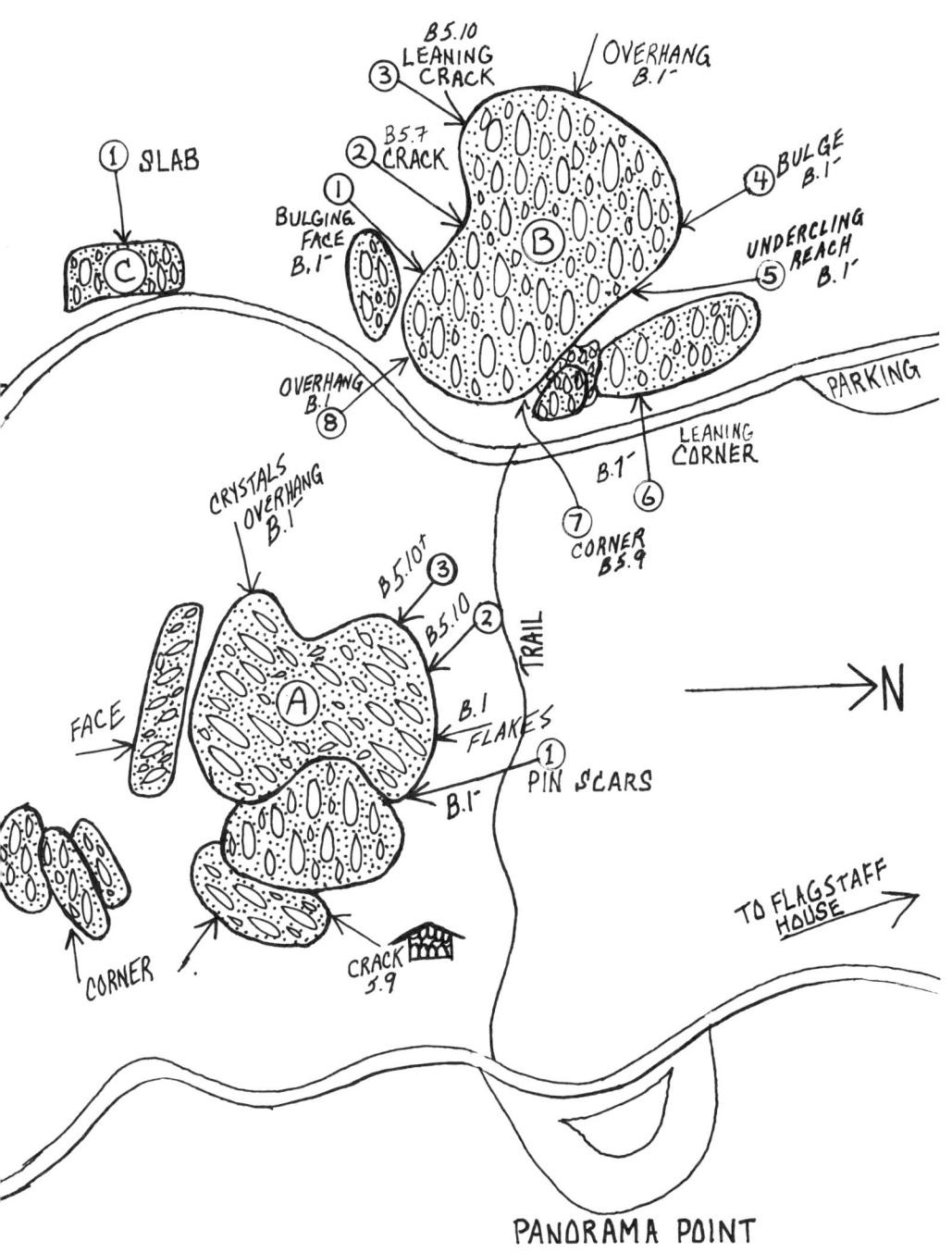

CORWIN SIMMONS' ROCK
About a mile and a half up Flagstaff Road, on the west side of the road at a curve, you will see this solitary boulder. It was given its name after a bouldering pioneer of the '50s.
North Face
Climb a thin face, probably done in the '50s, to the summit.
Northwest Corner
Climb small pebbles which become thinner at the top.

CAPSTAN ROCK
A short ways past Corwin Simmons' Rock, on the north side of the road about a mile and a half up Flagstaff Road, is this prominent spire with a pointy summit and an obvious curving crack on its south face. Numerous great problems of various length and difficulty make this rock one of the many sought-after boulders on the mountain. A top rope can be set up by slinging the big horn on its summit.
Easy Route
This is the easiest way to the summit of Capstan and climbs up from the road on the north side of the rock.
North Face Right B5.9
This is a challenging slab starting just off the road, right of the easy route.
Northeast Mantle B5.9
This is a self-descriptive route on the northeast corner, just above the road.
Northwest Edges B5.10
This overhanging problem climbs off the edge of the road and up the nothwest face via small edges. The rounded top offers a committing summit move.
West Face B5.10
This ascends the west face of Capstan with some interesting pockets and layaways. Soloers should beware of a few crumbly holds.
South Crack B.1 –
This ascends the obvious finger crack on the south face of the rock via pin scars from an early '50s aid ascent. FFA: P. Ament 1960s.
Sarabande B5.10+
This ascends the steep face just above the south crack. FA: R. Candelaria 1975.
South Overhang B.1
This climbs the bulge just to the right of South Crack. A few variations have been done on this bulge. One reaches left off a hole to a sloping edge, another reaches up statically to the right off a crystal and a hole and another problem lunges off the holds up to the left or right. FA: P. Ament 1968.
Just Right B.1+
This climbs the severe overhang to the right of the South Overhang. Pull onto the face with layaway moves, then reach with your right hand for a pocket. The top moves offer some delicate thin-edged balance moves. Spotters beware. FA: Jim Holloway 1973.
The Trough B5.9
This ascends the small bulge just right of Just Right. Once into the slanting trough the climb eases. FA: Dave Rearick 1961.
Diverse Traverse B.1 –
This fingery traverse moves along the bottom of the rock from an undercling at Just Right all the way past South Crack to the Northwest Edges route, then

back if your endurance allows. The small finger holes are reminiscent of climbing at Buoux in France. FA: Skip Guerin 1980s.

The boulders just east of Capstan Rock, offer some fun little problems. Go over and see what you can come up with.

ROAD SIGN ROCK
Just across the road, north of Capstan Rock, there is a somewhat rectangular rock with obvious drilled holes on its south face.

Road Side Traverse B.1+
A tight fit and stretchy moves pocket their way across this south-facing traverse, utilizing man-made drill holds that once held the road sign in place. FA: S. Guerin 1980s.

Several other face problems ascend via the drill holes on the south side of Road Sign Rock.

Northwestern Overhang B.1−
On the back (northwest) side of the Road Sign Rock an overhang close to the ground can be found. From a sitting start, ascend up to the minute smeary holds on the vertical face above. FA: P. Ament 1960s.

BROWN GLASS WALL
Just below Road Sign Rock and slightly to the east there is an amazing outcropping with a variety of high bouldering problems.

Bucket B.1−
This is behind Road Sign Rock, on an overhanging pillar. FA: R. Candelaria 1975.

Briggs' Bridges B.1
This climbs the arete on the west (right) side of Brown Glass Wall. The thin edges offer some delicate moves with an unpleasant landing; a top-rope may be advised. FA: R. Candelaria 1975.

V Crack B5.9
This is an obvious crack/flake system on the west side of the north-facing wall. A shakey flake above the airy bulge makes this a contemplative problem.

Crack Slot B5.10
This leaning off-size crack is jammed through the main overhang on the east side of the wall.

Back Extension B5.10+
This high problem surmounts the overhang just left of the slot on the east side of the north face. FA: R. Candelaria 1975.

Stem Rise
To the left (north) of Back Extension is this steep face by a tree. FA: R. Candelaria 1975.

NOTLIM BOULDER
Down the slope to the north of Brown Glass Wall there is an interesting boulder with a very bizarre route up its northern face. Spell this backwards and hike up Eldorado Canyon for a visit to another famous boulder.

Hollow's Way B.2
Fingertip your way up this desperate overhanging barndoor layback to the top. FA: R. Candelaria 1976.

Right Dihedral
This climbs the dihedral on the right side of the north face.

CLOUD SHADOW
At the first hairpin curve a few feet up the road from Capstan, and below the road to the south, you will find this incredible formation. A very unique traverse with solution pockets is located here as well as several difficult bulging face problems.

East Inside Corner B5.9
On the far east side of the traversing wall there is a small corner. This is a nice problem for all levels of ability. FA: P. Ament 1960s.

Sloping Mantle
Just right of East Inside Corner is a nice mantle problem. FA: P. Ament 1960s.

Bulge Traverse B5.10
From the inside corner traverse up and left on good holds. FA: Rob Williams 1969.

The Bulge B.1
Left of the inside corner is a prominent bulge above an undercling. Throw a heel over the bulge and proceed up the traversing shelf. FA: J. Holloway 1974.

A.H.R. B.2
This means Another Holloway Route, and is located just left of The Bulge. Grab for the illusionary edges and crank to the top. FA: J. Holloway 1975.

Consideration B.1 −
Left of the bulge routes, at another bulging section is a deep hole. From here, reach up to a good edge with your right hand, then up to a sharp smaller edge with your left, then reach to the top of the traverse shelf. FA: P. Ament 1969.

Reverse Consideration B.1
This is the same as Consideration, except that you switch hands in the hole and reach up with the other hand. A whole different balance point is created with this move.

Moderate Bulge B5.8
Slightly left of Consideration is a larger hole; get this as an undercling and make a long extended reach to the top.

Contemplation B5.10
This is a higher problem located to the left of the Moderate Bulge. Follow a seam curving to the left, then proceed with caution straight above. A bolt at the top of this makes for easy top-roping. R. Candelaria 1974.

Lower Bulge Traverse B.2
From Contemplation to East Inside Corner, this demanding traverse may be the hardest traverse Flagstaff has to offer. FA: J. Holloway 1970s.

Cloud Shadow Traverse
There are a few different ways to traverse this wall, one staying fairly high across the pockets, and one staying very low. From Consideration, traverse to the left until you cannot hold on any longer.

Williams' Pull B.1
Halfway across Cloud Shadow Traverse you will notice a nice circular pocket that you can cram both hands into. From here, place your left foot up onto a polished down-sloping ramp and crank in a dynamic motion up and slightly left for a large solution pocket. FA: R. Williams 1969.

Hand Traverse B.1 −
On the left side of Cloud Shadow Traverse, just before it gets thin and overhanging, is a left angling ramp leading upward. Hand traverse this to a difficult reach out left at the top.

Hagan's Wall B.1
Left of Hand Traverse is another bulging wall with a small flake for one hand and a solution pocket for two fingers with the other. Crank off the small boulder to a sloping hold above and work this to the top. FA: Paul Hagan 1969.

Dandy Line B.1
This strenuous problem climbs the steep face just left of Hagan's Wall via a small pebble. FA: Dan Stone 1980s.

Launching Pad B.1
Left of Dandy Line is a very difficult reach problem that launches off a small crystal up to a finger edge. The crystal since the first ascent has broken, creating a new challenge. FA: John Baldwin 1986.

REAR-END ROCK
From Capstan Rock walk south downhill and a little east along the main trail, and you will see this split boulder.

Crack Crack B.1 –
This jams the south crack of the formation. FA: P.Ament 1960s.

Left Bulge B.1 –
Climb the bulging face left of the crack via a tricky mantle. FA: P. Ament 1960s.

THE ALCOVE
Slightly uphill on Cloud Shadow Rock, and to the north behind its south face, is an alcove with some excellent problems.

East Overhang B5.10+
This is an obvious roof problem on the west side of the alcove. Follow the chalk to the mantle.

Sailor's Delight B5.10
This is located up above the alcove on a prominent bulging roof. The spectacular position of the boulderer is sure to scare the wits out of any passing tourists on the road. FA: R. Candelaria 1974.

Crack Allegro B5.10
Below Sailor's Delight, on a north facing wall in the alcove, is this right-leaning crack. FA: R. Candelaria 1974.

Allegro Bulge B,1 –
This climbs the bulge right of Crack Allegro to a mantle on the top.

Other boulders located to the northwest of the Cloud Shadow proper offer some challenging problems.

THE GOLF CLUB BOULDER
On the south side of the far east end of Cloud Shadow there is a prominent blob that looks like a golf club when looking at it from the west.

The Angler B5.10
This is a strenuous hand and finger traverse from the east side of the blob to the far south side.

The Roof B5.10
On the west side there is an overhang which is surmounted via a heel hook.

Flagstaff Mountain – Mid-Range Areas

A CORWIN SIMMONS' ROCK
1. North Face

B CAPSTAN
1. Road Face B.1−
2. West Face B5.10
3. Sarabande B5.10+
4. South Crack B.1−
5. South Overhang B.1
6. Just Right B.1+
7. The Trough B5.9
8. East Face B.1−

C ROAD SIGN ROCK
1. South Face B.1−
2. Bucket B.1−

D BROWN GLASS WALL
1. Briggs' Bridges B.1
2. V-Crack B5.9
3. Crack Slot B5.10
4. Back Extension B5.10+

E NOTLIM BOULDER
1. Hollow's Way B.2

F NOOK'S ROCK
1. Northeast Undercut B5.10+
2. Butt Slammer B.2
3. That Flakes It B5.10
4. Wimpie's Revenge B5.9

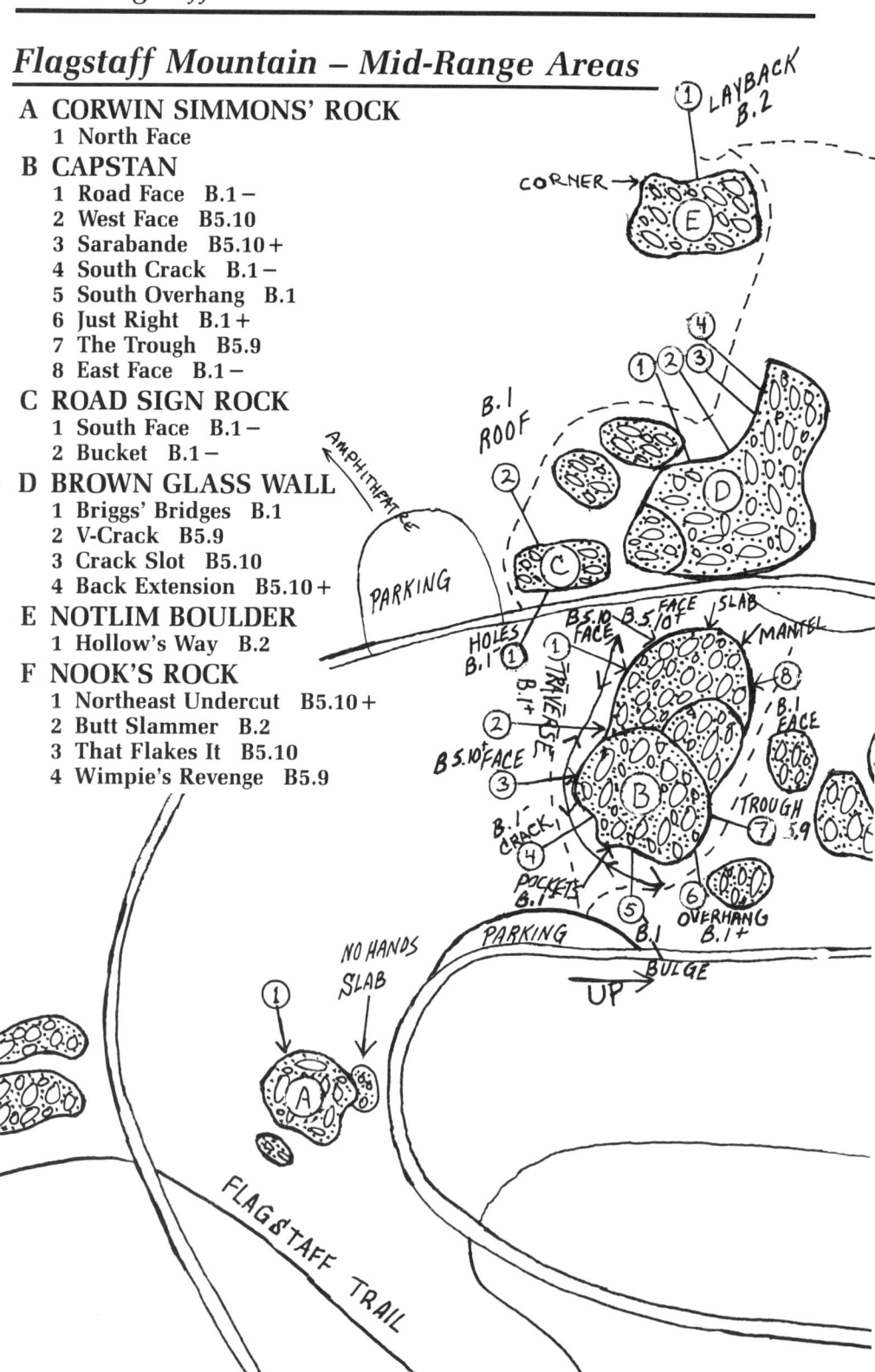

Flagstaff Mountain — 99

G CLOUD SHADOW
1. East Overhang B5.10+
2. Sailor's Delight B5.10
3. Crack Allegro B5.10
4. Bulge Allegro B.1−
5. Launching Pad B.1
6. Dandy Line B.1
7. Hagan's Wall B.1
8. Williams' Pull B.1
9. Contemplation B.1−
10. Consideration B.1−
11. East Inside Corner B5.9
12. The Bulge B.1

H REAR END ROCK
1. Left Bulge B.1−
2. Crack Crack B.1−

I GOLF CLUB ROCK
1. The Angler B5.10
2. The Roof B5.10

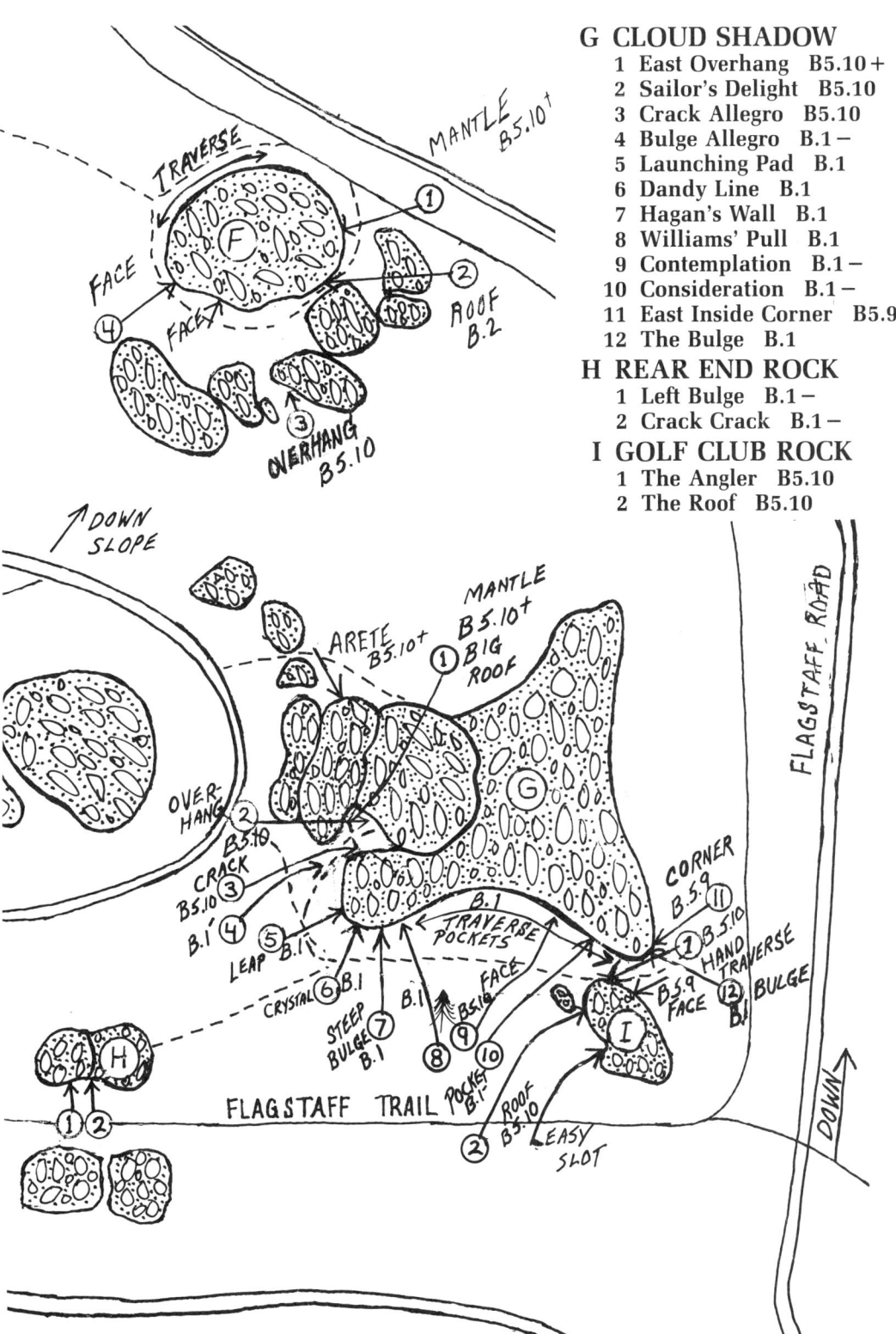

ONE ARM ROCKS
These two boulders sit together just off the road on the south side after a sharp curve 1.6 miles up Flagstaff road. Many variations ascend these fun boulders which are mostly known for their steep one-arm problems.

Right Hand Mantle B.1—
This one-arm problem climbs the north face of the west rock using a small crystal as a foothold while pressing into a one-arm mantle off a small edge. FA: P. Ament 1966.

One Arm Overhang B.1—
On the east rock's west-facing overhang, is another one-arm problem which climbs into the small dihedral above the overhang. FA: P. Ament 1966.

One Arm Arete B.1—
Left of the overhang route is an arete with a flake; climb this one-armed. FA: P. Ament 1966.

Smith's Face B.1
On the north face of the east boulder, is this one-arm thin slab with a hard start. FA: Richard Smith 1967.

Many two-handed routes also ascend these boulders, and are all good challenges. Also, behind the One Arm Rocks to the south are some short flat-looking boulders with some fun mantles.

CROWN ROCK
This large formation is located on the west side of the road just before the One Arm Rocks, 1.6 miles up Flagstaff Road. This is a low angle flatiron-like mass which is great for beginners. Other challenging problem can be found as one walks around its base.

PRATT'S OVERHANG AREA
From the One Arm Rocks, 1.6 miles up Flagstaff Mountain, walk a few hundred feet along a path leading south from the parking area and you will soon discover this west-facing, overhanging formation with several classic problems. This area was named after Chuck Pratt in recognition of his difficult Yosemite problems.

Far Left Side B5.9
This ascends the bulge to a slab on the far left hand side of the west face. An obvious mantle problem can be seen immediately to the right.

Pratt's Mantle B5.9
This is most directly done as a straightforward mantle, although many variations using small edges have also been accomplished.

Aerial Burial B.1—
From some small holds below the shelf on Pratt's Mantle is this double lunge problem which shoots for the shelf. FA: Rick Accomazzo 1980s.

Pratt's Overhang B5.10
To the right of the mantle shelf there is a right-slanting slot. Climb this via some awkward moves. Many variations exist. FA: B. Culp 1960.

Stone Ground B.1—
This climbs the face between Pratt's Overhang and Smith's Overhang. FA: D. Stone 1979.

Flagstaff Mountain

Smith's Overhang B.1+
To the right of Pratt's Overhang is a severely thin overhanging face with a prominent layback flake. This is usually done with a cheater stone start, but a few boulderers have done it without the stone. The problem was less difficult until a major part of the flake broke away. Pull onto the face and reach up for a thin edge, then slap for the sloping top and mantle. FA: R. Smith 1967.

Gill Swing B.1+
This is a super-dynamic move that goes off a small layback hold right of Smith's Overhang and shoots for the top. FA: John Gill 1960s.

Crystal Corner B5.10+
Just right of Smith's Overhang is a small overhanging arete with a prominent crystal on it. Layback the corner to the crystal, then move up to the top via a high step. FA: B. Culp 1960s.

Horandous B.1
This climbs the crystal corner with a strenuous layback move off the ground and avoids the crystal with one long reach to the top. FA: B. Horan 1982.

Gully B5.9
To the right of Crystal Corner is a gully which can be mantled or face climbed.

The Stretcher B.2
This impressive traverse starts left of Pratt's Mantle and moves across Smith's Overhang then through the Crystal Corner into the gully. FA: J. Holloway 1973.

MONKEY TRAVERSE AREA

Further down the trail, south of Pratt's Overhang Area is a nice, sunny, west-facing, overhanging outcropping with a variety of traverses and roof exit problems. This has to be the most crowded area of all of the Flagstaff Boulders. When first arriving at Flagstaff, this is a good place to start becoming familiar with the rock and to perhaps meet a climbing partner.

Monkey Traverse
This is the obvious chalked-up traverse which goes from right to left and back again. Your endurance will grow the more that you apply yourself to this routine. Many other contrived variations on this traverse exist, some very hard.

Million Dollar Spider B.1−
On the far south end of the traverse there are a few overhanging problems. This is the overhanging wall on the left side of the south end. Grab for a pinch in the overhang and reach for the top. FA: P. Ament 1960s.

Shallow Slot B.1−
On the far right end of the traverse there is a right angling slot in the overhang. Layaway its edge to the top. FA: P. Ament 1960s.

West Overhang B5.9
Just slightly left of the Monkey Traverse middle section is an obvious roof problem.

West Overhang Left B.?
This climbs the roof just left of the previous problem. FA: R. Candelaria.

West Lunge B.1+ (TR)
Just a few feet to the right of West Overhang there is a lunge problem out the roof. FA: C. Griffith 1980s.

SOUTH END COVE
Just above the south end of the Monkey Traverse, up a slab leading to the east, is a west facing overhanging wall with two leaning cracks on its right end.
Left Hand Crack B.1−
This climbs the left crack out the overhang. FA: R. Candelaria 1974.
Right Hand Crack B5.10
This is the right crack that starts with an awkward layback. FA: unknown
South End Traverse
This is a traverse on the wall a few feet uphill to the north from the cracks. FA: Mike Brooks 1980s.

LITTLE SPUR ROCK
Across (south) from South End Cove is a boulder with a tree growing against its west face.
Little Spur B5.10
This ascends the short face to the right of the tree.
Little Face B5.9
Around the corner to the right of the Little Spur is another good face problem.

STURDY TREE WALL
Follow the ledge from Little Spur Rock about one hundred feet to the south until you come to an overhanging west-facing wall. A good traverse and some overhanging face problems can be found here.

AID CRACK WALL
Farther right from Sturdy Tree Wall is another large west-facing wall with a reddish tint to it. Good top-rope problems can be found all over this wall.
Aid Crack B.1−
This ascends the leaning thin crack on the left side of the wall.
The Face
A few feet right of the aid crack is a slab leading to a corner and a steep face.
The Corner
Farther to the right along the wall is an easy corner.
Shane's Traverse B.1−
On the far right side of the wall is a sloping set of holds and small knobs offering a nice traverse.
William's Mantle B.1
Below the Aid Crack Wall, or about fifty yards downhill to the south along the path from the Monkey Traverse, is a difficult mantle problem on a very sloping shelf. FA: B. Williams 1969.
Ament's Bulge B.1−
Around the corner to the south of William's Mantle, and just left of a crack, is a bulge with a flake. FA: P. Ament 1964.
Bulge Boulder
Several feet left of William's Mantle, on a separate boulder, is this serious bulge problem. FA: B. Horan 1988.

THE ALAMO ROCK AREA
South of Crown Rock, and east of Pratt's Overhang area is a foot path leading to the southeast shoulder of Flagstaff Mountain. After about a hundred yards the large Alamo Rock formation can be found, with its rounded summit and overhanging west side. The east face resembles a Flatiron-like slab, offering moderate access to its summit.

Remember the Alamo B5.10+
The southwest-facing overhanging crack of the Alamo formation offers some technical jamming varieties. This makes an excellent lead or top-rope.
Diamond Face B.1
Below the overhanging crack is a vertical south-facing wall with small edges. Many variations to this face have been done. FA: Mike Sherman 1974.
Faint Crack B5.10+
This thin line can be seen on the south face of the Alamo, just around to the right of Remember the Alamo. FA: R. Candelaria 1974.
Navajo Crack B5.10
Just a few feet south of Alamo Rock are some blocky formations with an obvious off-width crack splitting the first blocks. Jam your way to the top.
Tear-Drop B5.10
To the left of Navajo Crack is a teardrop-shaped hueco in the upper wall of the block. Get hold of the hueco and head for the top. FA: P. Ament 1960s.

THE RIB BOULDER
Below and slightly northwest from Alamo Rock is a small cubical boulder with some fun routes on several sides.
The Crease B5.7
This climbs a flakey crease on the west end of the boulder.
Arete It B5.10
Climb the arete on the southwest corner.
Face It B5.10
This climbs the face to the right of the arete.

BULGING WALL
This sits below Alamo Rock and is somewhat connected to its lower northwest face. Just east of the Rib Boulder is a bulging wall with a prominent finger crack in it.
Dalke Finger Crack B5.10+
Climb the finger and hand crack in the wall. It is most difficult to do when just using the crack. FA: L. Dalke 1960s.
Bulging Face B5.10
Left of the finger crack is a bulging face route. FA: R. Candelaria 1974.
Rib Right B5.9
Right of the finger crack is a nice face with good holds.
Arrows Traverse B.1
Go back and forth along the lower potion of the Bulging Wall for a good pump.

Other delights such as dihedrals can be found south below Navajo Crack spire. A classic thin slot below and to the right offers excellent bouldering.

PUMP ROCK
This is a large block just north of Alamo Rock; it has some difficult top-rope problems on it.
Expotential Pump B.1−
On the northwest corner is a slanting, overhanging dihedral. FA: Gray Ringsby 1983.
Dinky of Doom
The right-leaning arete, just right of the slanting dihedral offers some exciting positions. FA: Jay Hartman 1983.
Ethiopia Blues
This is the overhanging face on the wall right of the arete. FA: Gray Ringsby.

Flagstaff Mountain – Long Traverse Area

A ONE ARM ROCKS
1. Right Hand Mantle   B.1–
2. One Arm Overhang   B.1–
3. One Arm Arete   B.1–
4. Smith's Face   B.1

B CROWN ROCK

C PRATT'S OVERHANG AREA
1. Far Left Side   B5.9
2. Pratt's Mantle   B5.9
3. Aerial Burial   B.1–
4. Pratt's Overhang   B5.10
5. Stone Ground   B.1–
6. Smith Overhang   B.1+
7. Gill Swing   B.1+
8. Crystal Corner   B5.10+
9. Horandous   B.1
10. Gully   B5.9

Flagstaff Mountain — 105

D MONKEY TRAVERSE WALL
1 West Overhang B5.9
2 West Lunge B.1+
3 Million Dollar Spider B.1−
4 Shallow Slot B.1−

E SOUTH END COVE
1 Left Hand Crack B.1−
2 Right Hand Crack B5.10

F LITTLE SPUR ROCK
1 Little Spur B5.10

G PAC MAN ROCK
1 West Slab B5.9

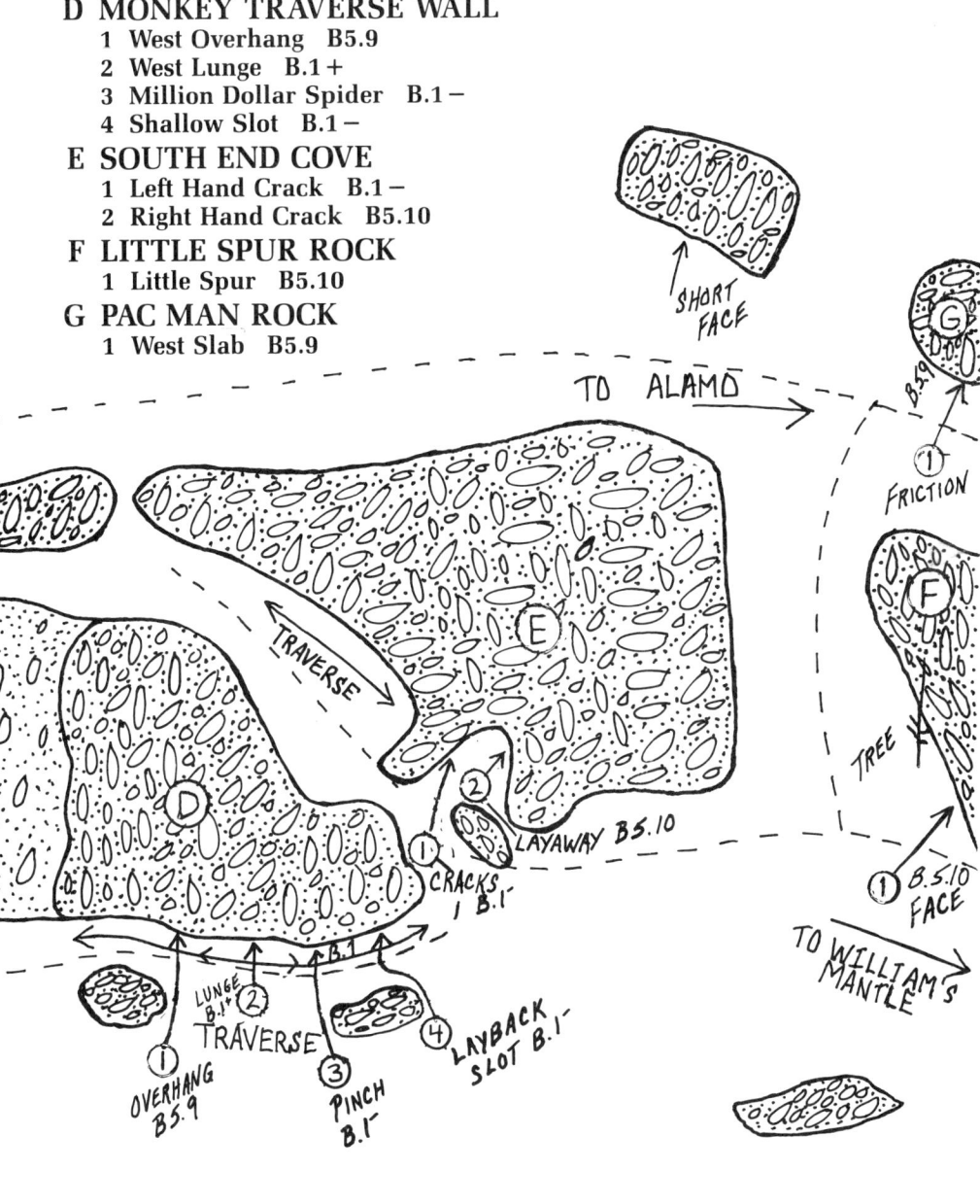

Alamo Rock Area

A PAC MAN ROCK
 1 West Slab B5.9

B LITTLE SPUR ROCK
 1 Little Spur B5.10
 2 Little Face B5.9
 3 Sturdy Tree Traverse

C WILLIAMS' MANTLE ROCK
 1 Williams' Mantle B.1

D AID CRACK WALL
 1 Aid Crack B.1−
 2 The Face
 3 The Corner
 4 Shane's Traverse B.1−

E PUMP ROCK
 1 Expotential Pump B.1−
 2 Dinky of Doom
 3 Ethiopia Blues

F THE RIB BOULDER
 1 The Crease B5.7
 2 Arete It B5.10
 3 Face It B5.10
 4 Corner It B5.9

G BULGING WALL
 1 Bulging Face B5.10
 2 Dalke Finger Crack B5.10+
 3 Rib Right B5.9

H ALAMO ROCK
 1 Diamond Face B.1
 2 Remember The Alamo B5.10+
 3 Faint Crack B5.10+
 4 Teardrop B5.10
 5 Navajo Crack B5.10
 6 Down There B5.9

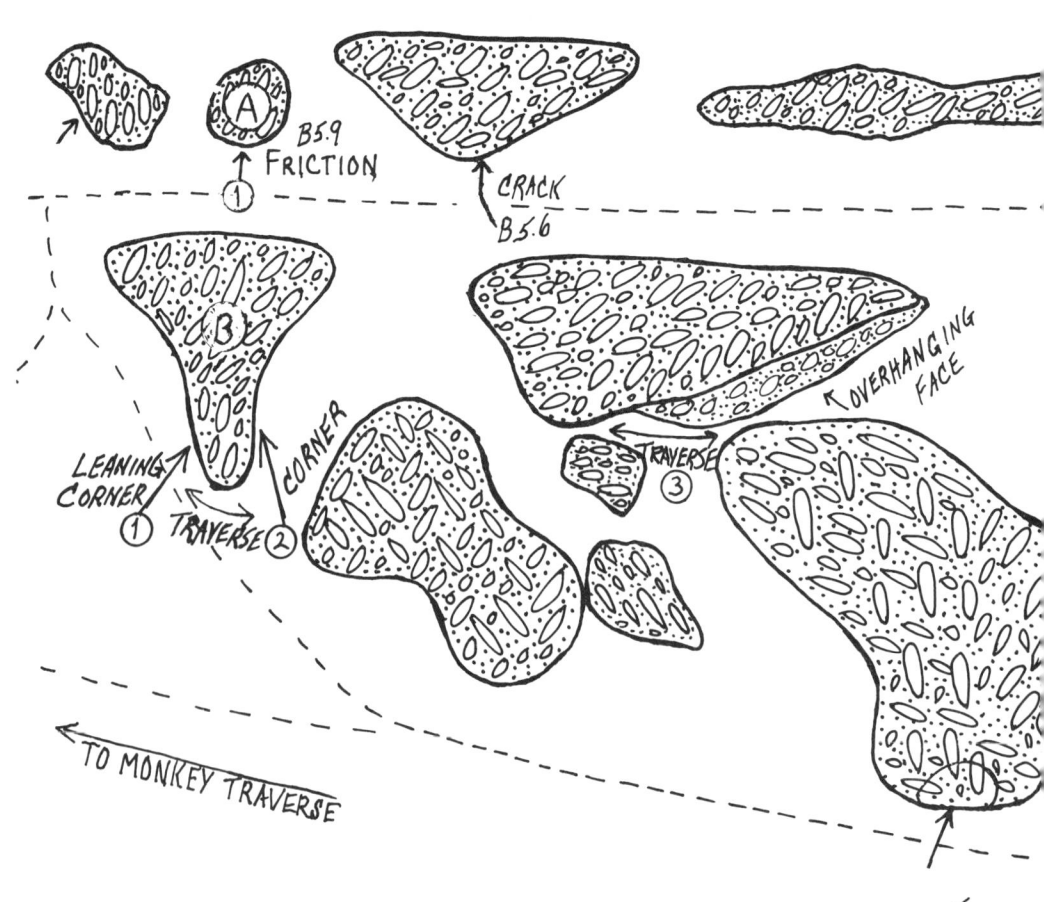

Flagstaff Mountain — 107

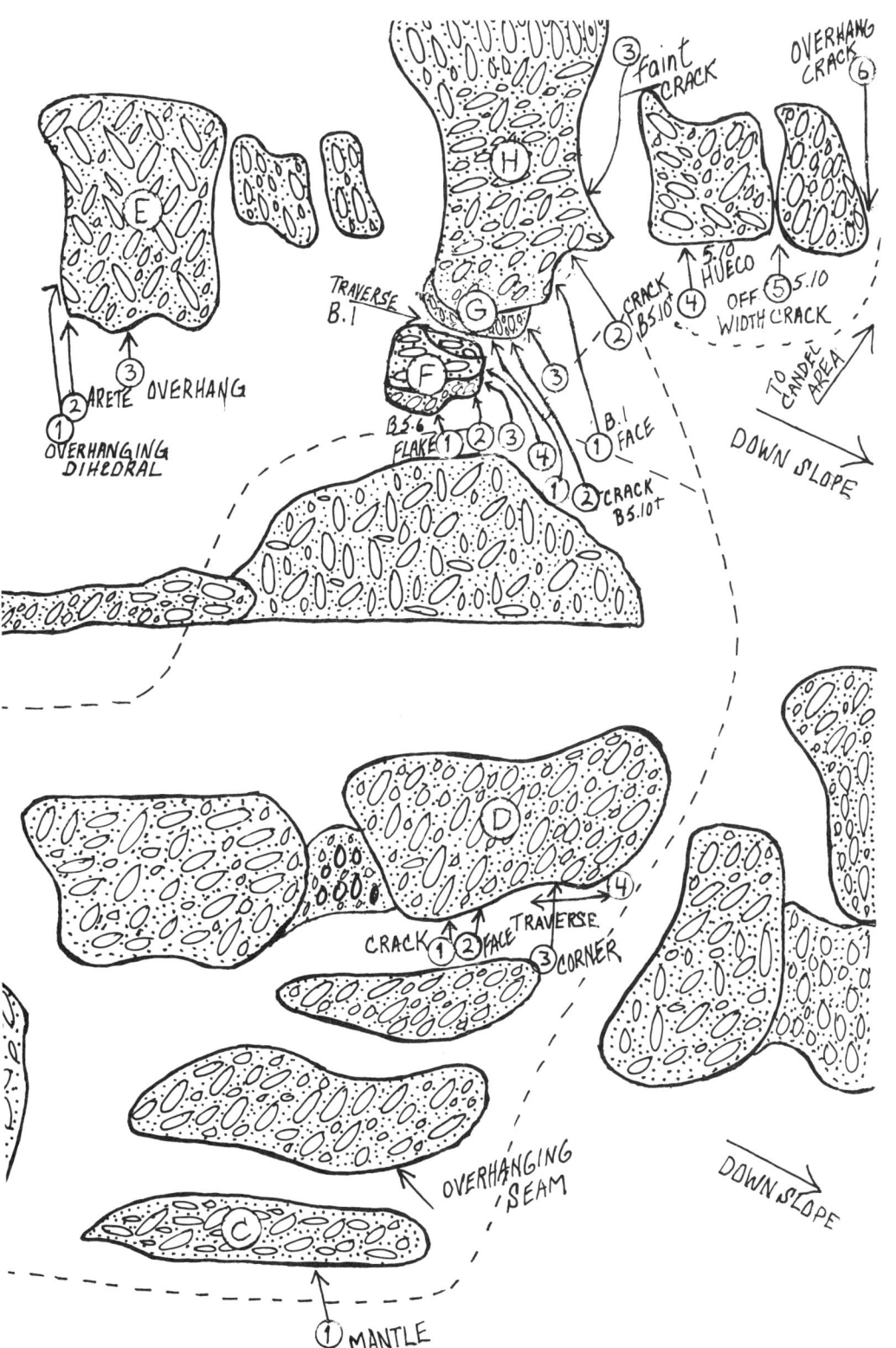

THE CANDEL AREA
This can be described as a ridge of broken boulders and slabs just to the southeast of Alamo Rock. This amazing ridge contains many bouldering classics extending far to the south. Just behind Alamo Rock and a bit south is a small boulder with some good holds on its northwest face.

Fingers Fingers B5.10+
Follow a faint trail to the south along the ridge until you come across a dead tree. To the right of the dead tree is a perfect bouldering-sized formation with an obvious finger crack on its west side. Start from a sitting position for added challenge.

Right Finger B.1
Climb the overhanging wall right of the finger crack. FA: R. Candelaria 1974.

Finger Arete B.1
This climbs the arete left of the finger crack.

THE RAMP
This southwest-facing narrow gray slab can be found just south around the corner from Fingers Fingers. A scary pebbled face makes this a real feat. FA: R. Candelaria 1974.

OVERHANG PEBBLE WALL
Just to the left of The Ramp is a long, overhanging wall with many excellent pebble moves on it.

HUECO ROOFS
Behind and uphill from The Ramp is an overhanging cove with various eliminates out the pocketed roof.

THE JUG
To the right of The Ramp is a prominent rock with some exciting problems on it.

Red Streak B5.9
On the west face of The Jug is a red-streaked wall topped by a small groove/corner. Exit through the groove, dig. FA: R. Candelaria 1974.

Legacy of a Kid B.1−
By taking the overhang on the northwest face of the Red Streak, a technical aerial problem is encountered. FA: R. Candelaria 1974.

Right Red
This is a moderate face climb up the wall to the right of Red Streak. FA: R. Candelaria 1974.

Southwest Face B5.10
Around the corner to the right of Red Streak is a delicate face that takes one fairly high off the ground. FA: R. Candelaria 1974.

MUFFET ROCK
Southeast of The Jug is an obvious overhanging wall with some great pockets in it. Many variations can be found on this roof.

SUNSHINE SLAB
Just to the right and farther downhill is a large southwest-facing slabby wall.
Bush Route B5.9
This climbs a slab above a bush. Minute holds are soon encountered.
Aerial Ballet B5.9
A few feet left of a tree is this challenging face. FA: R. Candelaria 1974.
Difficult Route B.1 –
About a foot left of the tree is a fun problem. FA: R. Candelaria 1974.
Michael's Face
Directly behind the tree is a thin face. FA: Jim Michael 1975.
Right Tree B5.9
This climbs the face immediately right of the tree. FA: P. Ament 1975.
Nubbin Wall B5.9
This is an apt description for the pebbled wall to the right of the tree on Sunshine Slab. Many variations exist on this delicate slab.
The Inner Earth Traverse B.1
This crosses Sunshine Slab via delicate moves. FA: R. Candelaria 1975.
Cave Hang B5.7
Slightly behind and to the south of Sunshine Slab is a cove-like overhanging wall with some excellent holds up a flake.
Overhanging Prow B.1
Just to the west, slightly below Sunshine Slab there is a prow requiring several pinch-type moves. FA: R. Candelaria 1975.
The Arete Prow B5.10
Across, and just south from the small overhanging prow is a high arete climb up the west face of a spire.

Candel Area

A THE RIB BOULDER
1. The Crease   B5.7
2. Arete It   B5.10
3. Corner It   B5.9

B ALAMO ROCK
1. Bulging Face   B5.10
2. Dalke Finger Crack   B5.10+
3. Diamond Face   B.1
4. Remember The Alamo   B5.10+
5. Teardrop   B5.10
6. Navajo Crack   B5.10

C FINGER ROCK
1. Finger Arete   B.1
2. Fingers Fingers   B5.10+
3. Right Finger   B.1

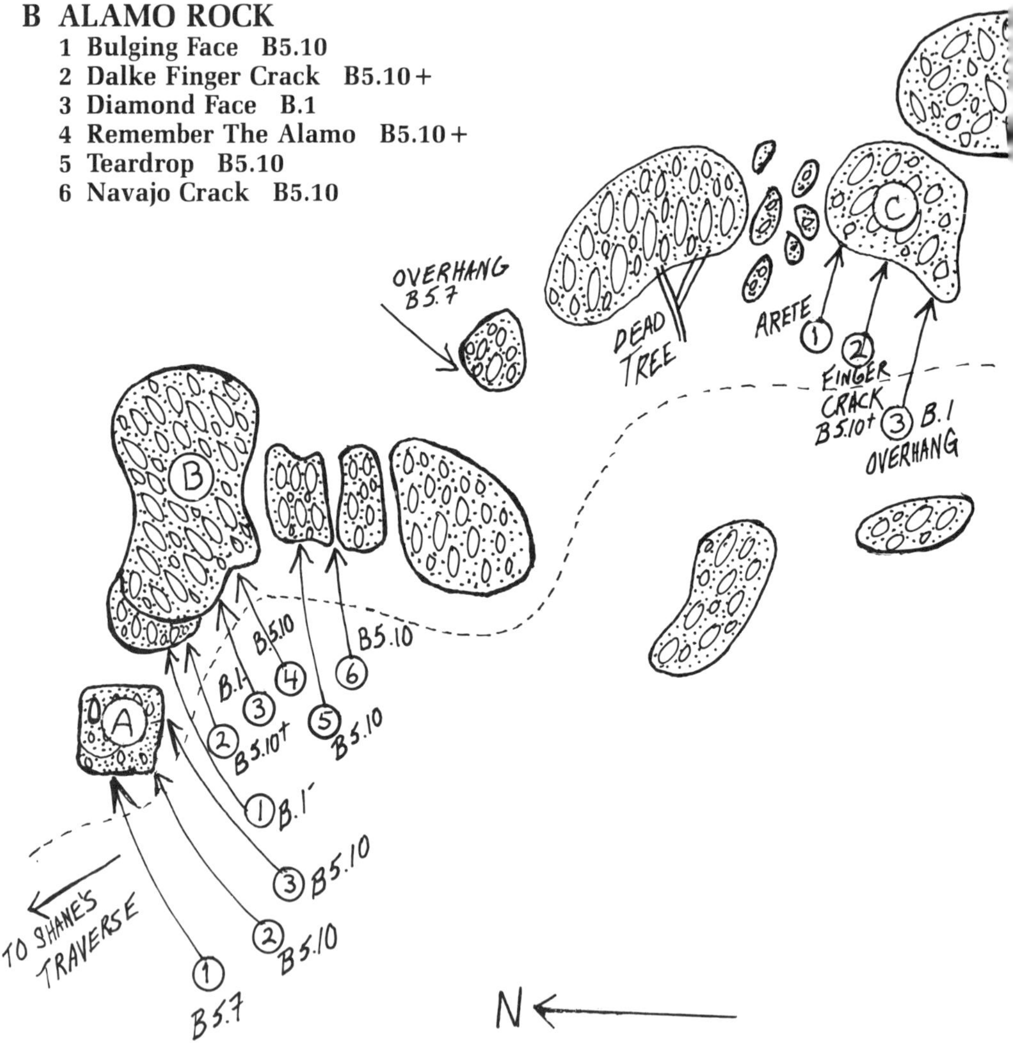

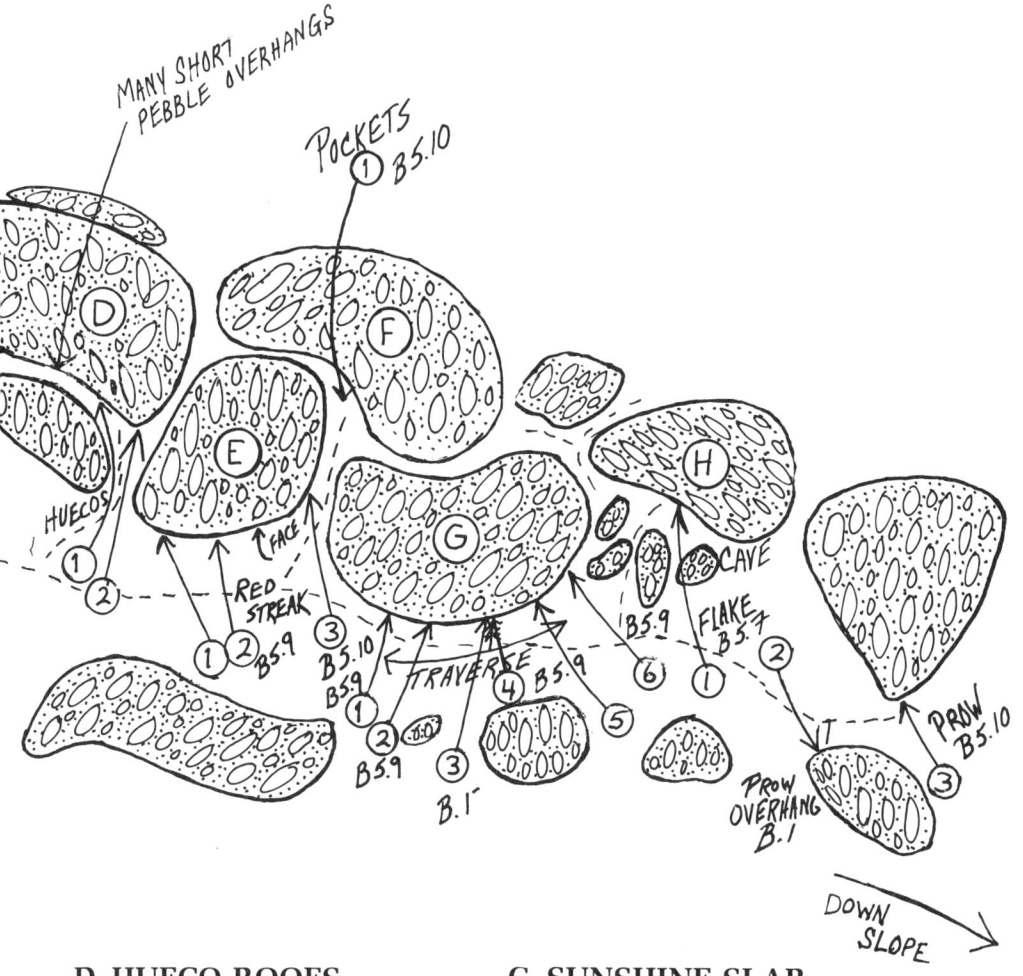

D HUECO ROOFS
   1 Hueco Hang   B5.9
   2 The Ramp   B5.10

E THE JUG
   1 Legacy of a Kid   B.1−
   2 Red Streak   B5.9
   3 Southwest Face   B5.10

F MUFFET ROCK
   1 Pockets   B5.10

G SUNSHINE SLAB
   1 Bush Route   B5.9
   2 Aerial Ballet   B5.9
   3 Difficult Route   B.1−
   4 Michael's Face
   5 Right Tree   B5.9
   6 Nubbin Wall

H CAVE HANG ROCK
   1 Cave Hang   B5.7
   2 The Prow   B.1
   3 The Arete Prow   B5.10

BEER BARREL ROCK

From the Parking area 1.6 miles up Flagstaff Road, where the trail that leads to Pratt's Overhang Area goes straight, drop down to the southwest until you see a picnic table. Just west of this table is the Beer Barrel formation. Many incredible problems and rock formations lie beyond.

East Slab
This has a large number of no hands problems and is also a fun beginner's boulder.

Poling Pebble Route B.1 −
This climbs the bulge on the southeast corner of the formation via some very small pebble pinches leading to a slap for a small edge over the bulge. FA: Bob Poling 1968. Several other bulge variations have been done on the southeast corner by M. Brooks.

Pinch Pebble B.1 +
This climbs to the left of the Poling Pebble route using only two pebbles with a semi-dynamic move to the top.

South Face B5.9
Climb the good edges up the south face to a overhanging bulge crack. Several other variations on the south face of the rock can be done.

Southwest Corner B5.9
This classic layback system is a very enjoyable problem.

Hritz Overhang
This climbs the wall just left of the classic southwest corner avoiding the good layback on the southwest corner route. FA: Bob Hritz 1972.

West Traverse B.1 −
On the west face of the Beer Barrel there is a great overhanging flake system. Traverse this back and forth for a good pump.

Double Clutch B.1 +
This is at the left end of the West Traverse, and can be done either static, via a thin edge layaway or a full out dyno with two hands to the small jug. FA: B. Williams 1972.

North Face
This climbs the bulging wall just left of Double Clutch. FA: P. Ament 1967.

DISTANT DANCER PINNACLE

This is the pointy spire just southwest of the Beer Barrel. Easy access to its summit can be found on its north face. A summit crack with a tree make for good top-rope anchors, bring a couple of 2½ Friends for the south face top-rope problem.

Distant Dancer B.1 +
This exciting problem ascends the south face of the spire via laybacks, underclings and long reaches with a swing. The route was first top-roped and then later soloed by Bob Horan in 1982.

Red Horn Overhang B5.10
On the southwest side of the spire is an overhanging corner. Layback this up to summit.

West Overhang B5.10
Many variations on the west side of the pinnacle can be done. Start as low as possible.

TREE SLAB
Down the hill to the south of Distant Dancer Pinnacle is a smooth west-facing wall/slab with many great problems up it. The moderate face problems makes this an area favorite.
Layback Crack B5.7
Right of the tree is a fun layback crack with a small challenge.
Classic Line B5.7
Behind the tree is an obvious face. This was done one-handed in the 1960s.
Slab Traverse 5.10
Move across this traverse of the slab one-handed for an excellent challenge. It is hardest if the climber stays close to the ground.

MISCELLANEOUS VALLEY
This is the group of rock formations below and to the north from the Tree Slab. The west-facing rocks have many good problems.
Phantom Face B.1 –
Below the Tree Slab and to the north is a short formation with a trough splitting it. To the right of the trough is a thin face problem. Delicate moves on small edges make this a scary climb.
Short O B5.10
To the left of the trough is an overhanging wall with some hard moves.
Indirect B5.9
This is a variation just to the left of the main overhang.

On the rock to the north is a delicate face problem up its right side and an obvious left-angling crack out a bulge on the far left.

Leaning Jam B5.9
This is the excellent crack that goes out the bulge on the left side of the wall.
Left Bulge B5.10
To the left of the crack is this enjoyable bulge problem.
Right Bulge B.1 +
To the right of the crack is an impropable-looking bulge route. FA: R. Candelaria 1970s.

LITTLE ROCK
Further north from Leaning Jam is a small spire-like formation with some fun moderate challenges.
Fun Lieback B5.8
A thin seam on the pointy spire creates a fun balance problem.

114 — Flagstaff Mountain

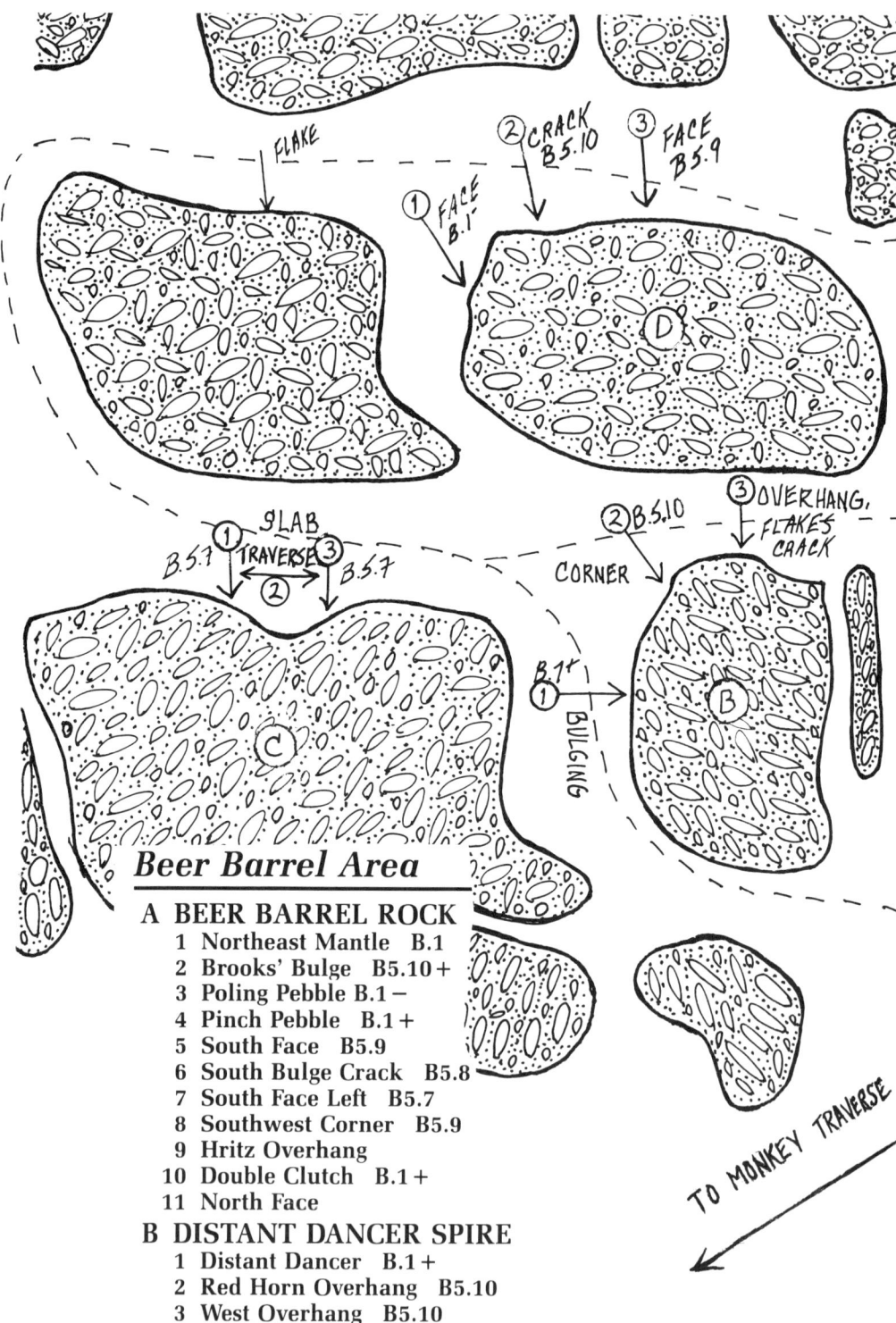

Beer Barrel Area

A BEER BARREL ROCK
1. Northeast Mantle B.1
2. Brooks' Bulge B.5.10+
3. Poling Pebble B.1−
4. Pinch Pebble B.1+
5. South Face B5.9
6. South Bulge Crack B5.8
7. South Face Left B5.7
8. Southwest Corner B5.9
9. Hritz Overhang
10. Double Clutch B.1+
11. North Face

B DISTANT DANCER SPIRE
1. Distant Dancer B.1+
2. Red Horn Overhang B5.10
3. West Overhang B5.10

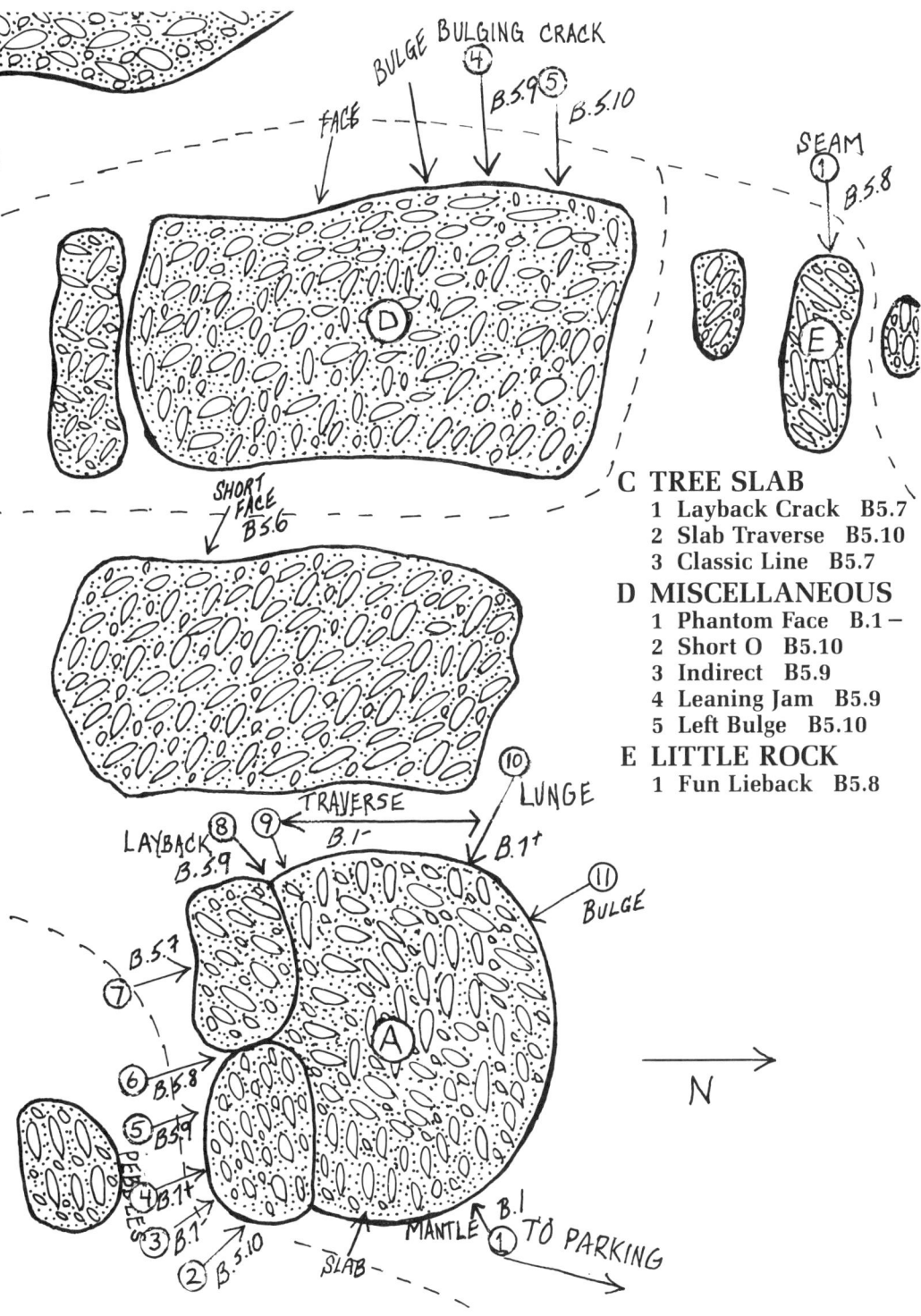

THE PEBBLE WALL

From the parking area around the curve from Crown Rock, 1.6 miles up Flagstaff Road, walk uphill to the north on the Flagstaff Trail for a few hundred feet. In the trees on the right you will find this incredible well-rounded boulder. Many pebbles and crystals lace the walls of the rock.

Original Route B5.7
On the southest corner of the boulder there is a face ending with an undercling. Start near the small boulder.

Crystal Mantle B5.10
There are several ways to mantle this obvious large crystal on the left from the Original Route, the right one being the easiest. FA: P. Ament 1960s. Jim Holloway did the mantle straight-on in the 1970s.

Direct South Face B.1
Left of the mantle crystal is a steep pebbly face that starts off a root. After the high-step smear, reach from crystals to a small knob. Balance on the pebbles to the top. FA: P. Ament 1960s.

High Step B5.10+
Farther left from the direct is another pebbly face. FA: Bob Poling 1960s.

Southwest Face B.1−
Left of the High Step there is another delicate face with a little more exposure than most of the problems. FA: B. Horan 1980s.

Southwest Corner B5.9
This scary reach problem laybacks the rounded corner up from the Southwest Face. FA: P. Ament 1960s.

West Overhang B.1−
On the west edge, just left of the Southwest Corner, is this climb up a prow. FA: R. Smith 1960s.

North Overhang B.1−
On the north side of the boulder is a prominent overhang with many pebbles. The scary lip moves will keep you on your toes. FA: P. Ament 1967.

North Face B5.9
This problem skirts left of the North Overhang, avoiding its crux moves.

NORTH ROCKS

Just east of the Pebble Wall are two boulders with an unlimited variety of good problems. Walk around the blocks and choose a line.

THE RED WALL

Just behind and to the east of the North Rocks is an interesting, smooth, south-facing vertical wall with very small edges on it. Some of Flagstaff's hardest problems lie on this wall.

Left Side B5.10
This short problem is found on the far left side and passes a small finger pocket.

Center Left B.1−
This tight move reaches up for an obvious hole with your right hand and then extends for a pinch crystal.

Standard Route B.1
Instead of reaching the hole with your right hand, try it with your left. FA: B. Culp 1960s.

Flagstaff Mountain — 117

Eric Varney Direct B.1+
Just right of the Standard Route there is a difficult problem that starts with a small pebble with your left and a dish or cup hold with your right. Reach up to a good edge then a small finger niche. FA: Eric Varney 1968.

Right Side B.1
On the right side of the wall, near a tree, is this classic hard problem that goes off a cup with your left hand to a long reach to a crystal niche with your right. FA: P. Ament 1967.

Far Right Side B.1−
Just behind the tree there is a face problem that reaches over from the right to the holds atop the Right Side route.

Many other variations exsist on this wall. By eliminating any one hold a new challenge can be encountered. Christian Griffith, Skip Guerin, and Jerry Moffat have all created some difficult direct starts to many of these routes. The east overhang of Red Wall also has a few problems that the boulderer may find interesting.

THE FLAGSTAFF AMPHITHEATRE

This enclosed outcropping can be found just to the north of the Pebble Wall and is packed with many splendid problems.

Wasp Nest B5.10
On the far right side of the right wall of the Ampitheatre, and just around the corner to the east, is this scooped wall leading over a small bulge. FA: R. Candelaria 1970.

South Corner B5.10
On the right wall of the Amphitheatre is a short overhanging corner on the farthest right side. FA: B. Culp 1960s.

South Bulge B5.10
Just left of South Corner is a tricky bulge.

Direct Route B.1−
Left of South Bulge is an overhanging problem with some sloping shelves. FA: P. Ament 1967.

Aerial Shoot B.1
From the sloping shelves of the Direct Route, lunge up to the upper holds. FA: D. Stone 1979.

Gill Direct B.1
From some small edges just left of Direct Route, ascend up and slightly right to some good holes at the lip of the boulder. FA: J. Gill 1969.

The Overhanging Hand Traverse B5.9
Left of the Gill Direct is a right-angling system of holds leading to the lip of the boulder. FA: P. Ament 1967.

Left of the Overhanging Traverse is another overhanging problem with a slightly rotten route up small edges. The crack just left of this, separating the right hand wall from the left, is very enjoyable to play on.

Crystal Swing B.1−
Just left of the crack on the left Ampitheatre wall is a leap to a large pebble on the right side. FA: B. Horan 1980s.

Direct South Face B.1
From a slab up and under the base of the left wall climb up the small pebbles. FA: P. Ament 1967.

Briggs Route B.1
To the left of the Direct South Face is another thin pebbled face which starts up a leaning corner. FA: Roger Briggs 1970s.
Finger Trip B.1+?
This difficult mantle problem is located just left of the Briggs Route and has changed due to a broken key mantle hold. FA: R. Candelaria 1974.
South Face Left Side B.1+
Left of Finger Trip is an obvious corner/arete with some small edges leading up. A large slab used to help one get started, but is now gone making for a much harder pull onto the corner. FA: P. Ament 1967.
High Overhang B5.9
Up the slot from the Left Side there is a scary reach problem off a high boulder, which finishes by mantling the airy lip. FA: P. Ament 1967.

OVERHANG WALL
When leaving the Amphitheatre heading southwest, if you continue up the hill to the north, you will find a long wall of overhanging problems.
South Undercling B5.10
At the lower south end of this formation, just outside the Ampitheatre,is a narrow south-facing wall with a steep face to an undercling.
Southwest Face B.1 (TR)
Just around the corner from South Undercling and slightly uphill is a vertical face with some shakey flakes.
Short Crack B5.10
Just left of the Southwest Face there is an obvious line starting close to the ground. Ascend the bulge.
Cove Crack B5.10+
Uphill even farther is this short, overhanging crack that climbs out of a cove on a boulder-like section of the wall.
Big Overhang B5.10+
This is the true gem of this wall. The problem climbs the large overhanging block at the top, on the north end of the formation. One may climb out the right or left side. FA: unknown
Balance Overhang B5.10
On a separate overhanging block just north of Big Overhang is another shorter, more delicate overhanging problem out the west face.

Flagstaff Mountain — 119

Pinching away at the small pebbles of the Direct South Face (B.1) of the Pebble Wall.   photo: Jim Sanders

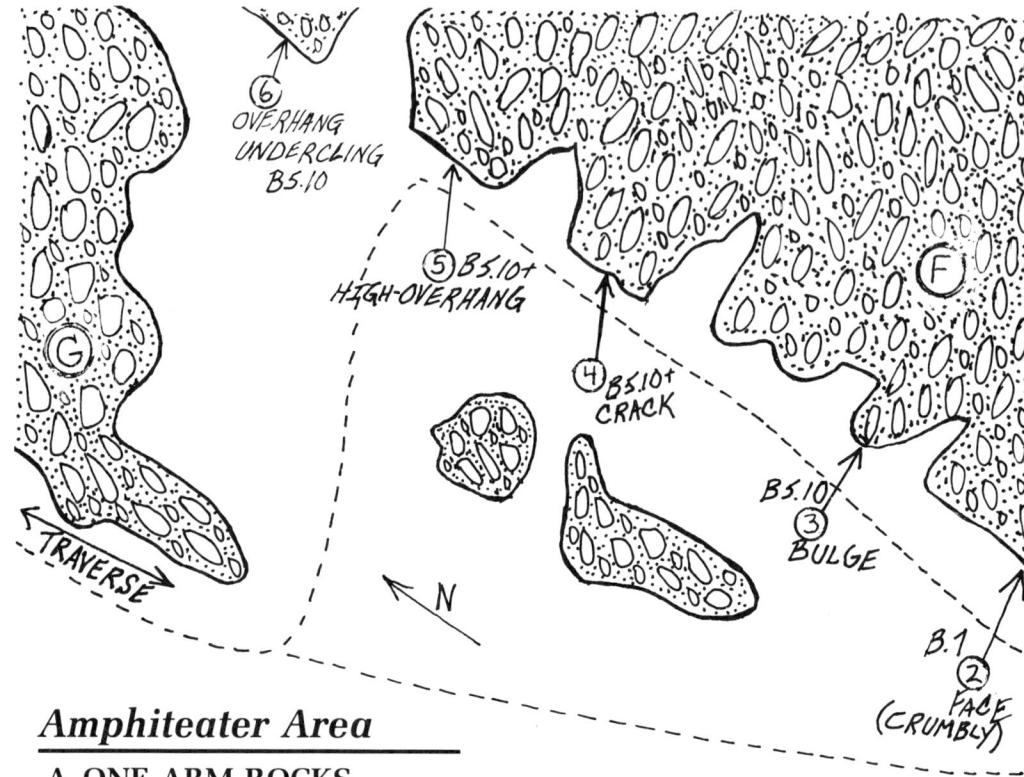

Amphiteater Area

A ONE ARM ROCKS
B PEBBLE WALL
1. Original Route B5.7
2. Crystal Mantles B5.10
3. Direct South Face B.1
4. High Step B5.10+
5. Southwest Face B.1−
6. Southwest Corner B5.9
7. West Overhang B.1−
8. North Overhang B.1−
9. North Face B5.9

C NORTH ROCK
1. Southeast Corner B5.8
2. Slipper Crystal B5.9
3. Arete B5.9

D RED WALL
1. Left Side B5.10
2. Center Left B.1−
3. Standard B.1
4. Eric Varney Direct B.1+
5. Right Side B.1
6. Far Right Side B.1−

E AMPHITHEATER ROCKS
1. High Overhang B5.9
2. South Face Left B.1+
3. Direct South Face B.1
4. Crystal Swing B.1−
5. Overhanging Hand Traverse B5.9
6. Gill Direct B.1
7. Direct Route B.1−
8. South Corner B5.10
9. Wasp Nest B5.10

F OVERHANG WALL
1. South Undercling B5.10
2. Southwest Face B.1 (TR)
3. Short Crack B5.10
4. Cove Crack B5.10+
5. Big Overhang B5.10+
6. Balance Overhang B5.10

Flagstaff Mountain — 121

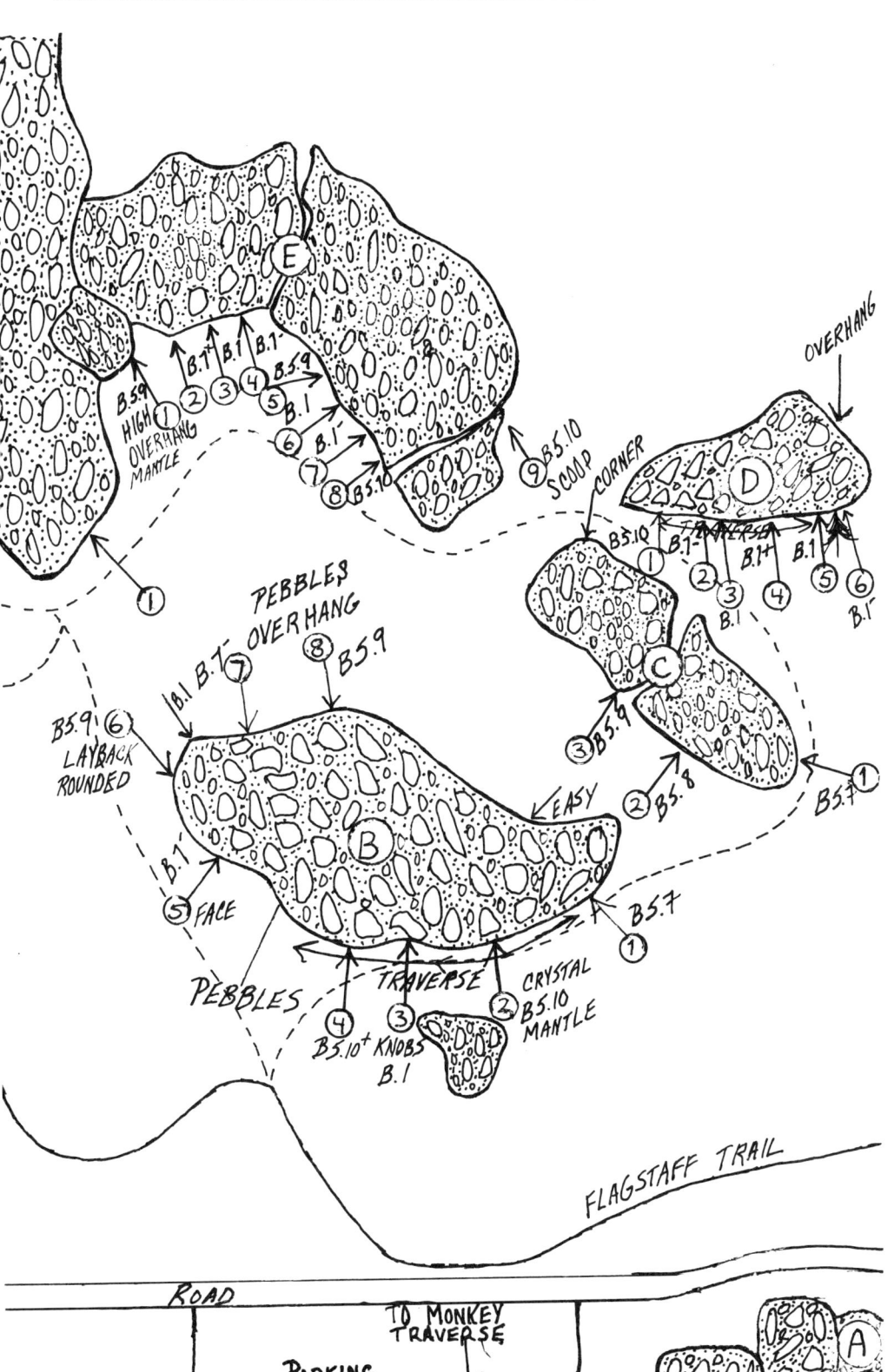

THE GREAT RIDGE
This is a series of west-facing overhanging walls and spires uphill to the northwest of the Overhang Wall and Pebble Wall. Many classic problems can be found as well as some excellent traverses.

THREE OF A KIND WALL
This is the first formation at the lower south end of the Great Ridge. Three serious face problems and a low traverse can be played on here.

Bulging Slab B.1 –
At the start of the Great Ridge, on the far right side of Three of a Kind Wall, is a sloping traverse that leads to a groove. This problem climbs up the sloping slab at the start of the traverse.

The Groove B5.7
To the left of the slab with sloping ledges is an obvious groove with a fun challenge.

High Flake B.1 –
On the right side of the wall, just to the left of a groove/trough, is a prominent flake extending up and to the left. From the top of the flake reach up for a small crystal. The exposure can be terrifying.

Round Pebble B.1 –
To the left of High Flake is another problem ascending a thin seam via laybacks on small edges to a good edge and pebble and ending in a slot. FA: B. Culp 1960s.

The Face B.1 –
Just a bit up to the left of the Round Pebble Wall there is a soft, high-quality sandstone face. Be careful of the loose flakes.

Sitting by itself just west of The Face is a short slab with a very balancey no-hands problem (B5.9).

Reaching for the small pebble on High Flake (B.1−), Three of a Kind Wall.
photo: Jim Sanders

The Great Ridge

A AMPHITHEATER ROCKS
 1 Gill Direct   B.1
 2 Overhanging Hand Traverse   B5.9
 3 Direct South Face   B.1
 4 High Overhang   B5.9

B OVERHANG WALL
 1 South Undercling   B5.10
 2 Cove Crack   B5.10+
 3 Big Overhang   B5.10+

C THREE OF A KIND WALL
 1 High Flake   B.1−
 2 Round Pebble Wall   B.1−
 3 The Face   B.1−
 4 No Hands Slab   B5.9

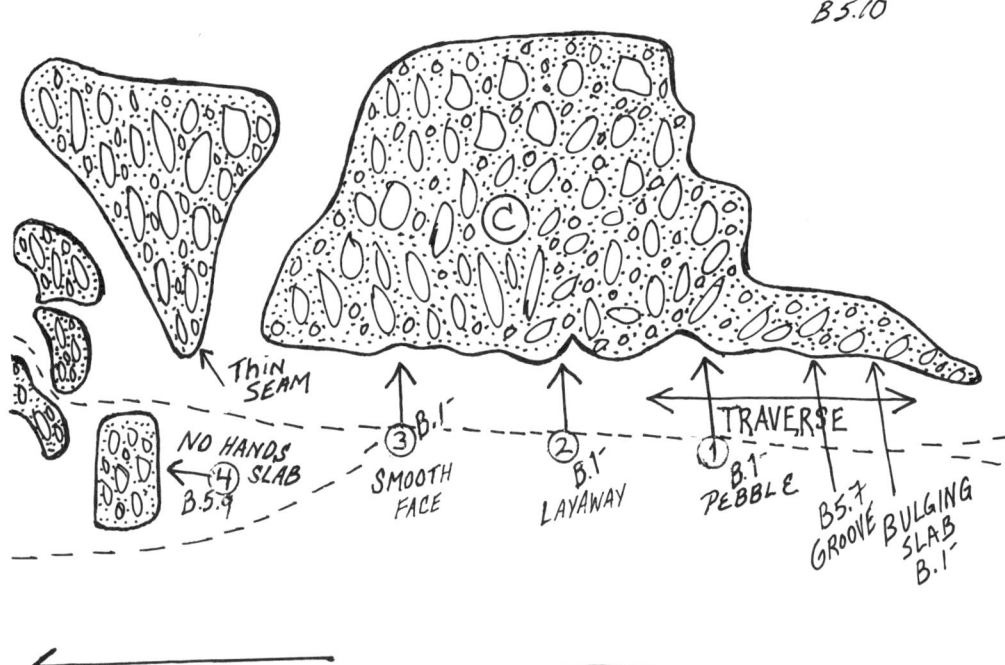

Flagstaff Mountain — 125

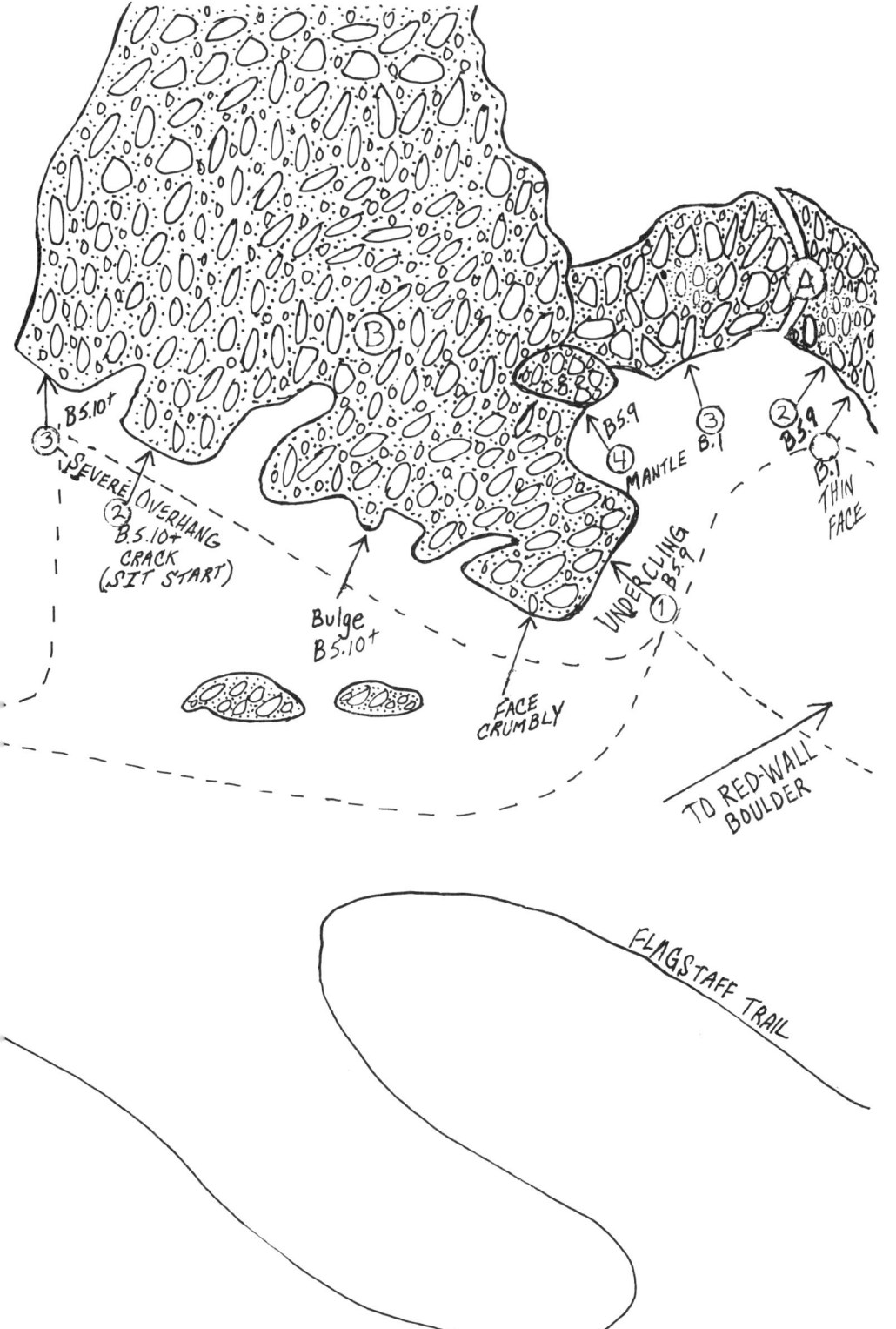

UPPER Y TRAVERSE
Uphill from the no-hands slab and Three of a Kind wall is another large outcropping with an overhanging west wall and a chalky traverse skirting its base. A Y-shaped crack can be seen in a gap in the wall.

Pinch Bulge B.1 —
At the far right end of the wall is a good finger flake in the overhang. From this flake reach up with your left hand to a pinch layback on the arete, then reach for the top. FA: unknown

Direct Mantle B.1
Left of the pinch problem there is an obvious mantle shelf. FA: unknown

Y-Right B5.8
Left of the mantle shelf and just right of the Y-Crack is a slightly overhanging face with good finger jugs. For an extra challenge try this without feet.

Many other routes can be done on the west face of this outcropping, especially the Y-crack gully which has two moderate variations up its right and left. The traverse of this wall is considered one of the best on Flagstaff Mountain. A good pump is sure to result. Just north and slightly up hill from the Y-Wall is a cave-like formation with a few good problems climbing out of it.

SHARK'S ROCK
Just east of the cave, up from the Upper Y Traverse, is a prominent spire with a vertical corner on its southwest face. When looking straight up at it, it looks like a shark popping out of the water. A picture in Edlinger's *Rock Games* shows Patrick turning the lip of the corner problem.

West Arete B5.10
This climbs the obvious corner with edges. FA: P. Ament 1964.

Leap of Faith B.1
On the rectangular formation just north of the Shark is a scary lunge out the west overhang of the rock. A spotter is very handy for this bold undertaking. FA: R. Accomazzo 1983.

Northern Arete B5.10
On the left corner from Leap of Faith is a leaning arete with small edges up it.

LITTLE FLATIRON
This describes the small spire just uphill to the north of Shark's Rock.

Leany Face B5.10
This ascends the left overhanging face of the spire.

Right Arete B.1
This difficult problem takes the overhanging arete on the southwest corner of the spire.

KING CONQUER ROCK
This is the large blocky formation at the top of the Great Ridge loaded with many excellent problems, including a classic overhanging jam crack.

Southwest Layback B5.9
On the far right side of the formation is an overhanging layback system with some long reaches.

Face Out B.1
Just left of the layback is a smooth overhanging face with some very small, sharp edges up it. FA: R. Candelaria 1974.

Flagstaff Mountain — 127

King Conquer Overhang B5.10+
This is the obvious overhanging crack that splits the block. FA: P. Ament 1960s.

Right Slot B5.9
This is the right of the two slots and is somewhat awkward.

Left Slot B5.9
This is the left of the two slots.

Direct West Slot B5.10+
Left of the Left Slot is an overhanging face with small edges.

Conquer Traverse B.1+
This is a low traverse along the King Conquer formation and has been done back and forth, and in conjunction with other problems on the rock. FA: S. Guerin 1980s.

A sloping mantle can be found on the far left side near some large drill holes.

FIRST OVERHANG AREA

At the second hairpin, uphill past the Crown Rock Parking area, you will see a classic boulder sitting at the northeast edge of a parking area. This boulder, and several other west-facing pinnacles just west of the Great Ridge offer some of the best bouldering on Flagstaff.

First Overhang B.1
This is a great problem on the southwest face of the boulder on the edge of the parking area. FA: P. Ament 1968.

Masochism Tango B.1+
Just left of the First Overhang, on the overhanging bulging arete, is a difficult problem. FA: B. Horan 1985.

PINNACLE COLADA

This is the first prominent rectangular pinnacle uphill to the north of the First Overhang boulder. A top-rope may be useful for some problems.

South Face B5.6
On the south face of the pinnacle is a short face problem with a good flake on top.

Southwest Corner B.1−
On the southwest corner of the formation is a vertical arete with some long reaches from a small hole. FA: unknown

Pebble Reach B.1
On the west face of the pinnacle there is a steep face on the right side with a pebble just below the top. Hopefully the good pebble will remain in place when pulling through to the top. FA: R. Candelaria 1974.

Standard Route B5.9
On the left side of the west face is a right-leaning corner under a bulge. Climb this to a good finger lock on the face above. FA: R. Candelaria 1974.

On the lower west face of the pinnacle is a large pocket that can be used in various ways to mount the face.

Colada Traverse B.1
From the far left or right, traverse across the overhang on the bottom of the pinnacle. FA: B. Horan 1980s.

TOMBSTONE SPIRE
Just to the north of Pinnacle Colada is another smaller rectangular pinnacle with good routes on its sides. A peculiar broken tombstone or mile marker can be seen on the foot path just in front of the west face.

Southwest Bulge B5.10
On the southwest corner of the spire is a bulging reach problem, using a kind of pinch to gain the summit. FA: B. Horan 1984.

West Side B5.7
On the west face of the pinnacle is a good route with large holds.

Triple Bulge B5.10+
On the northwest corner of the pinnacle is an obvious bulging arete with some good moves out it. Reach for the pothole on the summit from the last bulge. FA: B. Horan 1984.

North Face Slab B.1−
To the left of Triple Bulge is a steep slab with thin edges. FA: B. Horan 1984.

LOOSE FLAKE SPIRE
Just north of the Tombstone is yet another spire with a scary route on its south face.

South Face B.1−
On the south face of the spire there is a right-angling face with a loose flake in the middle. From here one has to reach for the lip and mantle the leaning edge. A fall from here could be serious. FA: B. Horan 1984.

FACE WALL
Just north of Loose Flake Spire is an incredible bouldering wall with some trees very close to its south face. Many problems can be found on its south and west faces.

Right Side B.1−
Just behind the east-most tree is a thin edged face on the south wall. FA: B. Horan 1983.

Center B.1
On the south face of the wall is a delicate face going up the middle. The top is a little scary without a rope. FA: P. Ament 1967.

Left Side B.1−
On the left side of the south face is another delicate face problem that ascends some pebbles up and slightly left. FA: unknown

West Roof B5.10
On the west side of the formation is an obvious overhang with little edges. Many eliminates can be thought of on the overhang to make it harder.

Mantle B5.10
Left of West Roof is a sloping mantle shelf with some fun challenges. Try a one arm mantle also.

Southwest Block B.1−
Slightly north of the Face Wall is a little formation with a thin face going up its southwest face. FA: unknown

Flagstaff Mountain — 129

Spread out on the overhanging face of First Overhang (B.1), Upper Area.
photo: Jim Sanders

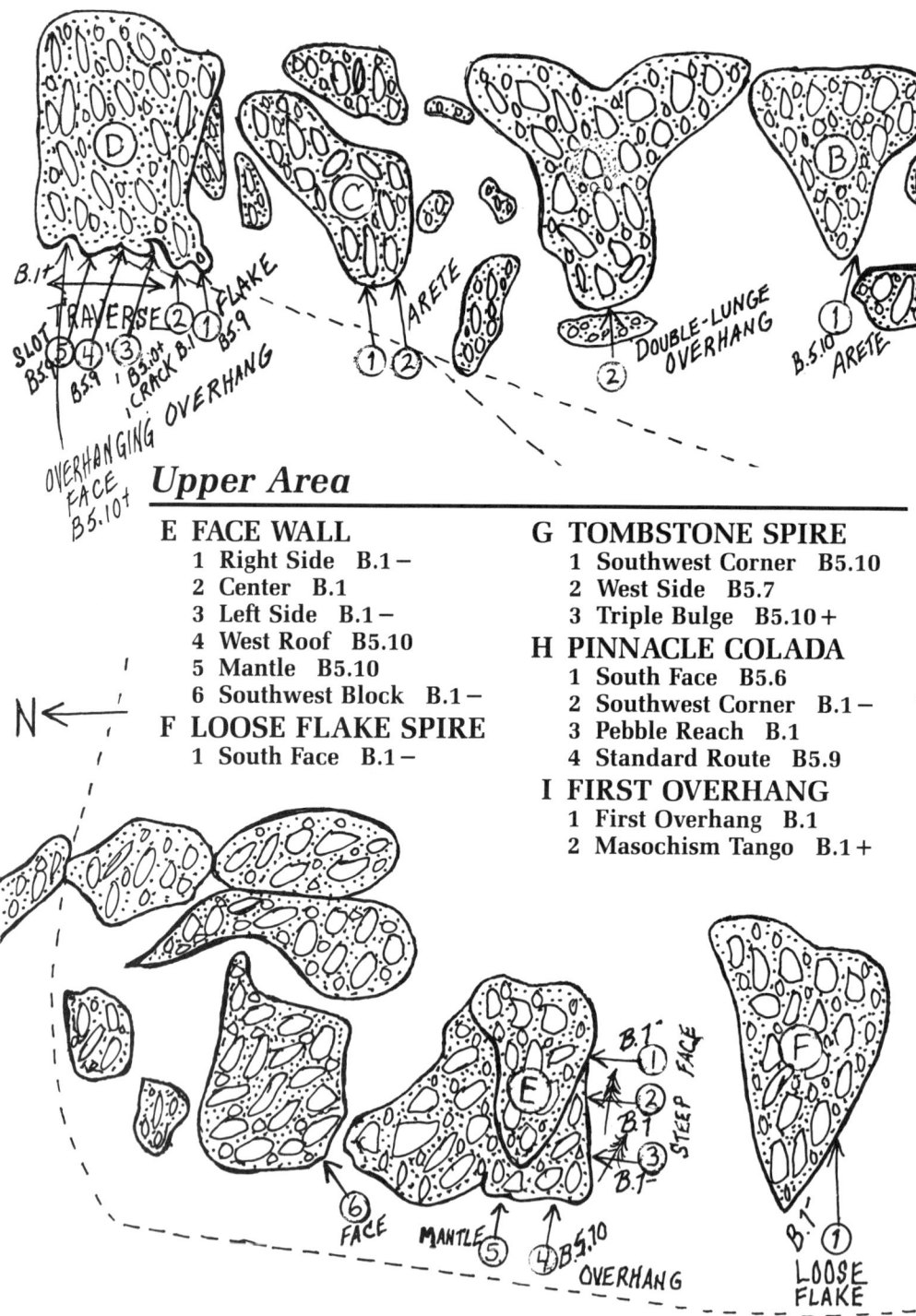

Upper Area

E FACE WALL
1 Right Side B.1−
2 Center B.1
3 Left Side B.1−
4 West Roof B5.10
5 Mantle B5.10
6 Southwest Block B.1−

F LOOSE FLAKE SPIRE
1 South Face B.1−

G TOMBSTONE SPIRE
1 Southwest Corner B5.10
2 West Side B5.7
3 Triple Bulge B5.10+

H PINNACLE COLADA
1 South Face B5.6
2 Southwest Corner B.1−
3 Pebble Reach B.1
4 Standard Route B5.9

I FIRST OVERHANG
1 First Overhang B.1
2 Masochism Tango B.1+

Flagstaff Mountain — 131

The Great Ridge

A UPPER TRAVERSE
1. Pinch Bulge   B.1 −
2. Direct Mantle   B.1
3. Y Left   B5.8
4. Y Right   B5.10

B SHARK'S ROCK
1. West Arete   B5.10
2. Leap of Faith   B.1

C LITTLE FLATIRON
1. Leany Face   B5.10
2. Right Arete   B.1

D KING CONQUER ROCK
1. Southwest Layback   B5.9
2. Face Out   B.1
3. King Conquer   B5.10+
4. Right Slot   B5.9
5. Left Slot   B5.9

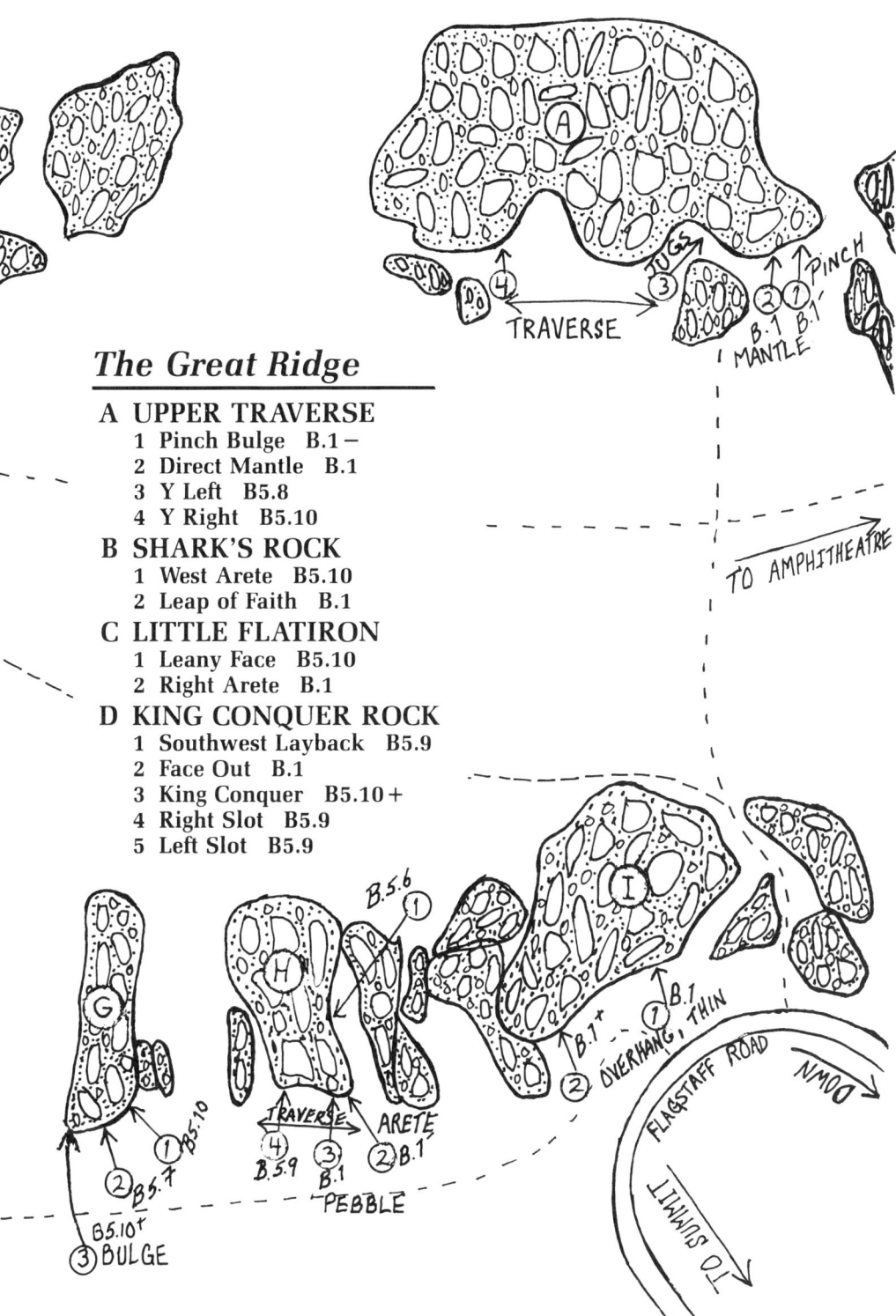

Eldorado Canyon

Located just eight miles south of Boulder, Colorado at the south end of the Flatirons, this climber's paradise is filled with colorful walls and boulders. Many excellent boulder problems are found on the bases of the walls and along the Eldorado Creek bed. The creek over the years has polished the lower rocks of the canyon to create a truely unique type of bouldering, one that is extremely enjoyable for all levels of ability.

To locate this beautiful canyon from Boulder drive south out of town on Highway 93 (Broadway) several miles until you reach a stop light. About eight miles from Boulder the state park signs will point you towards the west and the town of Eldorado Springs. Eldorado Canyon State Park is just to the west. There is a kiosk at the bridge that will list current regulations and fees, and will often house someone to take your money. A large parking lot is up the road another couple hundred yards, though when the park is open you may drive to the picnic ground at the west end of the park.

Eldorado Canyon — 133

The Eastern Priest (B.1−) on the River Block.

Eldorado Canyon

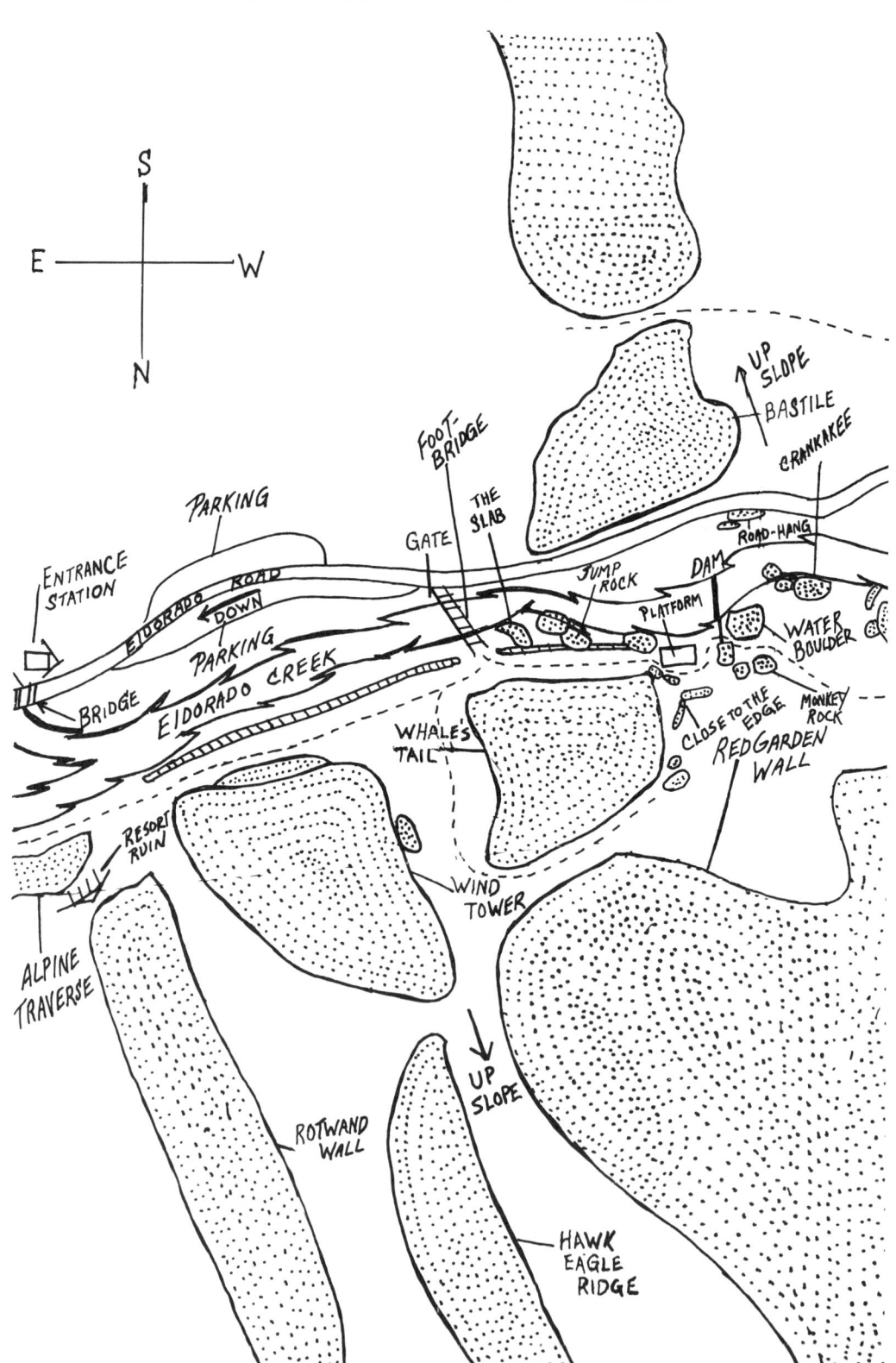

Eldorado Canyon — 135

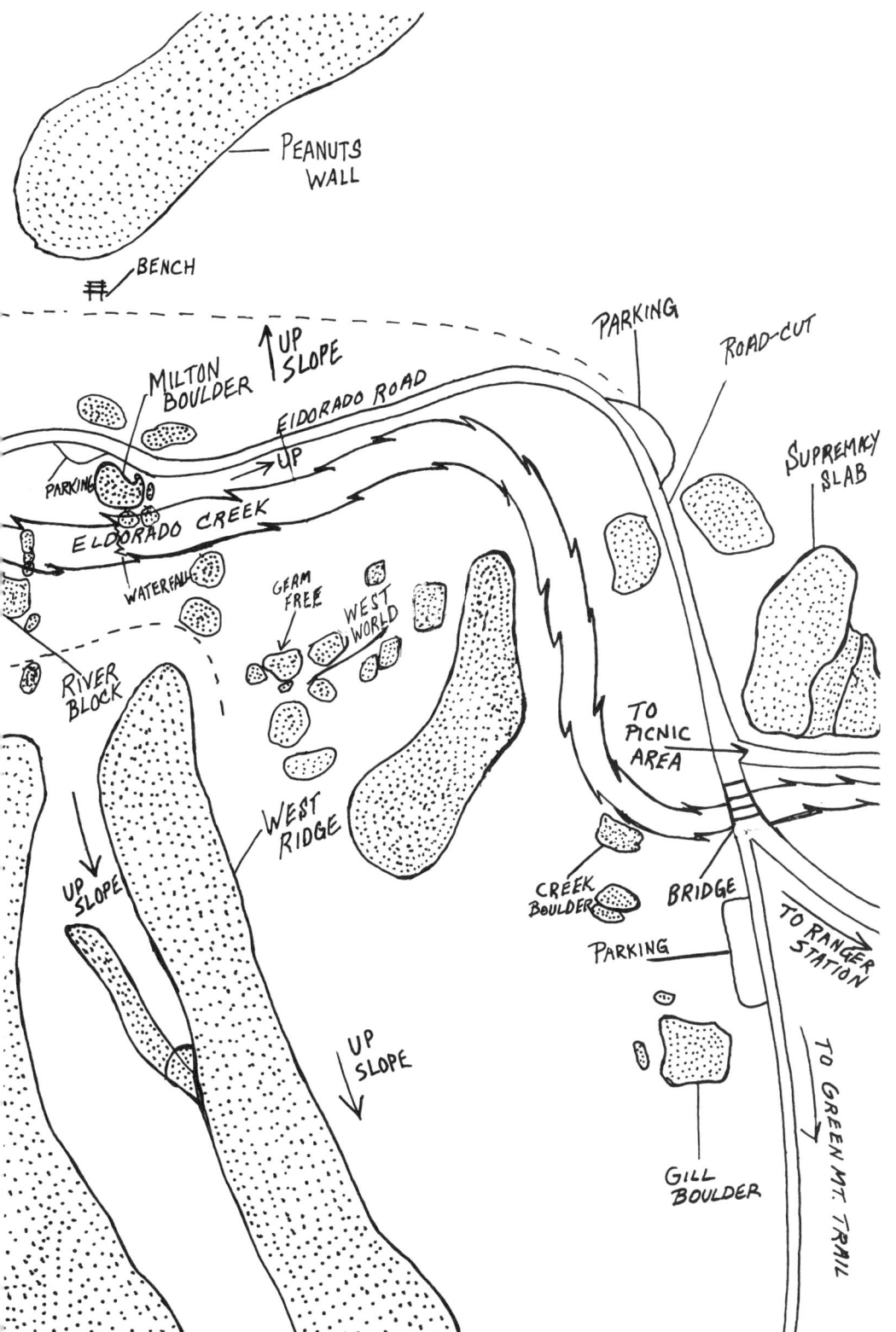

THE BASTILLE
Just up the road from the main parking area in the front of the canyon, sits the towering Bastille on the south side of the road. In prime season you will see groups of people standing along the side of the road watching and pointing up at the entertaining boulderers and climbers. The base of The Bastille has some of the best bouldering in the whole canyon and is best known for its long traverse that skirts its base from east to west.

The Shield B.1
From the start of the wall on the east end walk up the road about twenty-five feet or so and you will notice a smooth vertical face with small layback edges on it. Crank your way up the twenty-foot face. FA: Dave Breashears 1970s.

Shield Traverse B.1 –
At the base of the Shield face there is a delicate traverse with a stretchy move. This is probably the single hardest part of the lower Bastille Traverse. FA: unknown

Micro Traverse B.1 +
To the right of the Shield Traverse there is a delicate little edge traverse problem that skirts the ground. FA: S. Guerin 1980s.

March of Dimes Direct B5.10 +
Another twenty-feet or so from the Shield there is an obvious crack with a small undercling reach in it. Make the reach and proceed to the prominent left-angling finger crack up high.

Zorro Crack B.1
Just to the left of the March of Dimes Direct is a very thin right angling crack that intersects the upper finger crack from the latter route. FA: unknown

Flake Left B.1 –
To the right of March of Dimes Direct, after the traverse breaks up a little, is a short left-leaning flake with a thin crack parallelling it on the left. Avoiding the flake on the right, ascend this delicate crack. FA: unknown

Slope Face B.1 –
Just right of Flake Left is a small, right-angling ramp system with some bolt holes off the start of the flake. Without getting too off balance or tangled up, try to mantle your way across this. FA: unknown

Lower Bastille Traverse B.1
From the far left side of the north facing wall, traverse across the base to the scree field on the far right side and then back again. This is an area favorite. FA: unknown

THE WIND TOWER
From the main parking walk west past a steel gate. On the right a few feet past the gate you will see a foot brige that leads across the creek to the north side. The Wind Tower can be seen to the northeast from the bridge. Take a right down the trail to the east to find excellent problems on the base of this large tower of rock.

Swoopy B5.9
Just before a prominent laid-back dihedral leading off the ground on the south face, there is a nice face with some interesting flakes. FA: B. Horan 1985.

Access Corner B5.7
This is the aforementioned laid-back corner/dihedral you will see along the lower south face.

Crystal Lift B.1 –
To the right and around the corner from the Access Corner there is a polished arete with a small hollow flake at the start and a small crystal part way up. The balancy reach for the top is a real thrill. FA: Duncan Ferguson.

South Wall B5.10
There are many variations on this polished wall just left of the Crystal Lift. The easiest is found up a sort of groove on the left side, the middle is nice and the right side is also a good challenge. As you walk further to the right you will find an enormous amount of short problems with a wide range of difficulty.

Round-up B.1 –
On the right end of the bouldering wall, where the wall breaks into a left upward angling ramp system, there is a well rounded boulder with a short overhang that leads up to a mantle.

Gold Rush B.1
Across the gap from Round-Up there is a goldish, smooth vertical wall with some small edges. Crank away. FA: B. Horan 1985.

Wind Tower Lower Traverse B.1
This mostly moderate traverse starts on the far west side of the south face just below the Uplift and traverses the entire south face.

The Bastille

1. The Shield   B.1
2. Shield Traverse   B.1−
3. Micro Traverse   B.1+
4. Zorro   B.1
5. March of Dimes Direct   B.1−
6. Slope Face   B.1−
7. Northcutt Direct
8. Bastille Crack
9. X-M
10. Northwest Corner

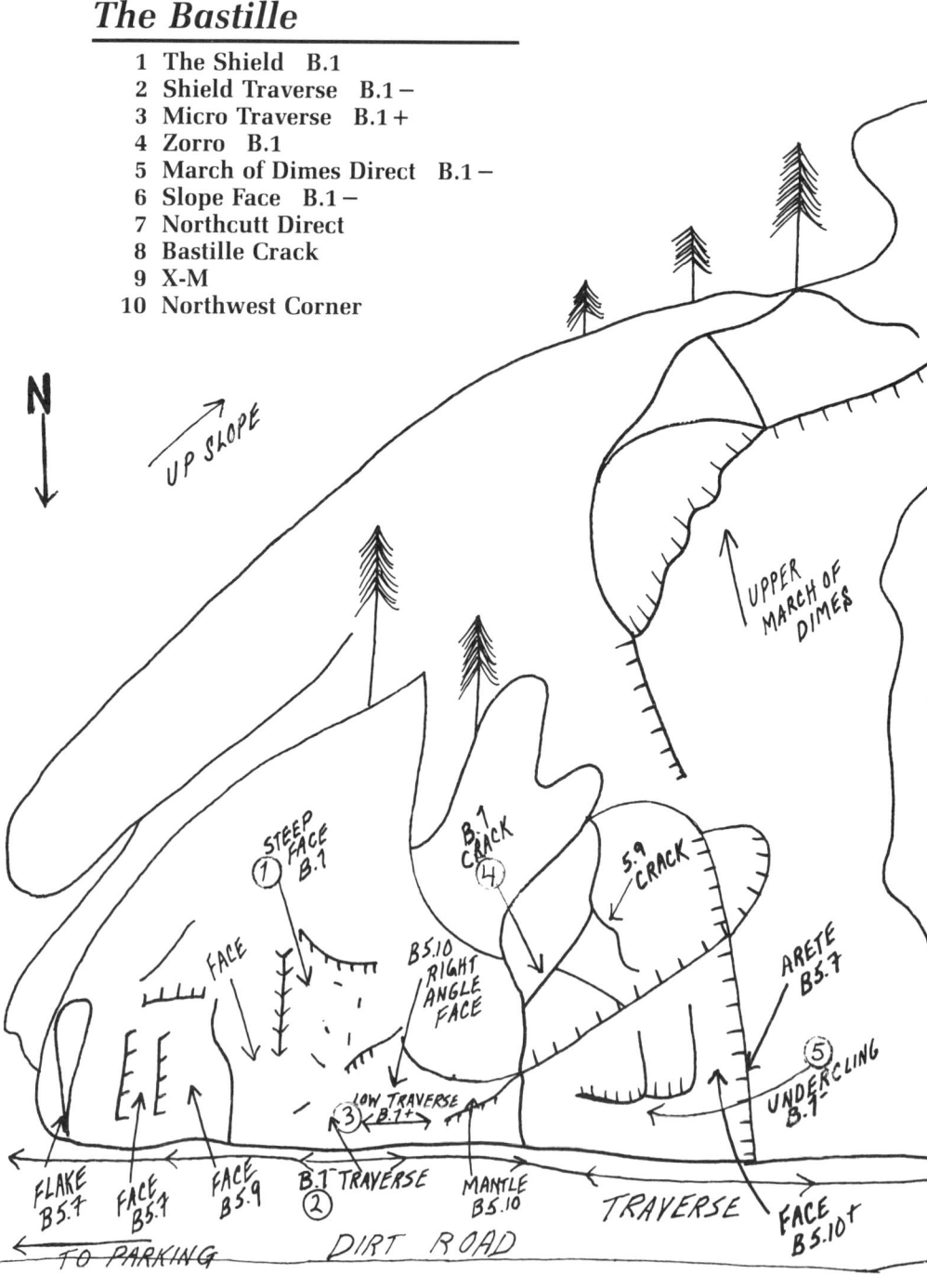

Eldorado Canyon — 139

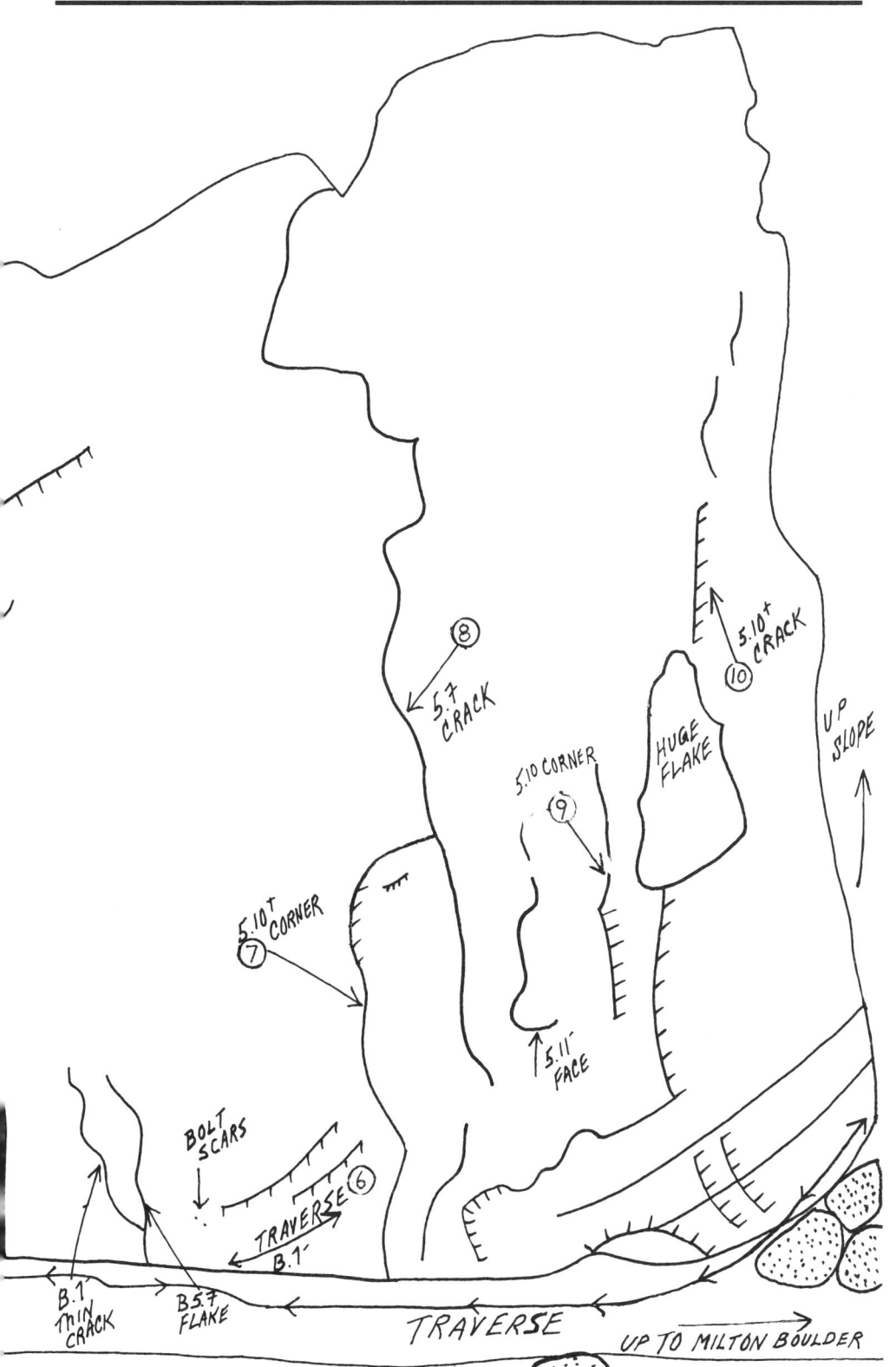

Wind Tower

1. Muscle Up
2. King's X
3. Swoopy   B5.9
4. Access Corner   B5.7
5. Rainbow Wall
6. Crystal Lift   B.1−
7. South Wall   B5.10
8. Round-Up   B.1−
9. Gold Rush   B.1

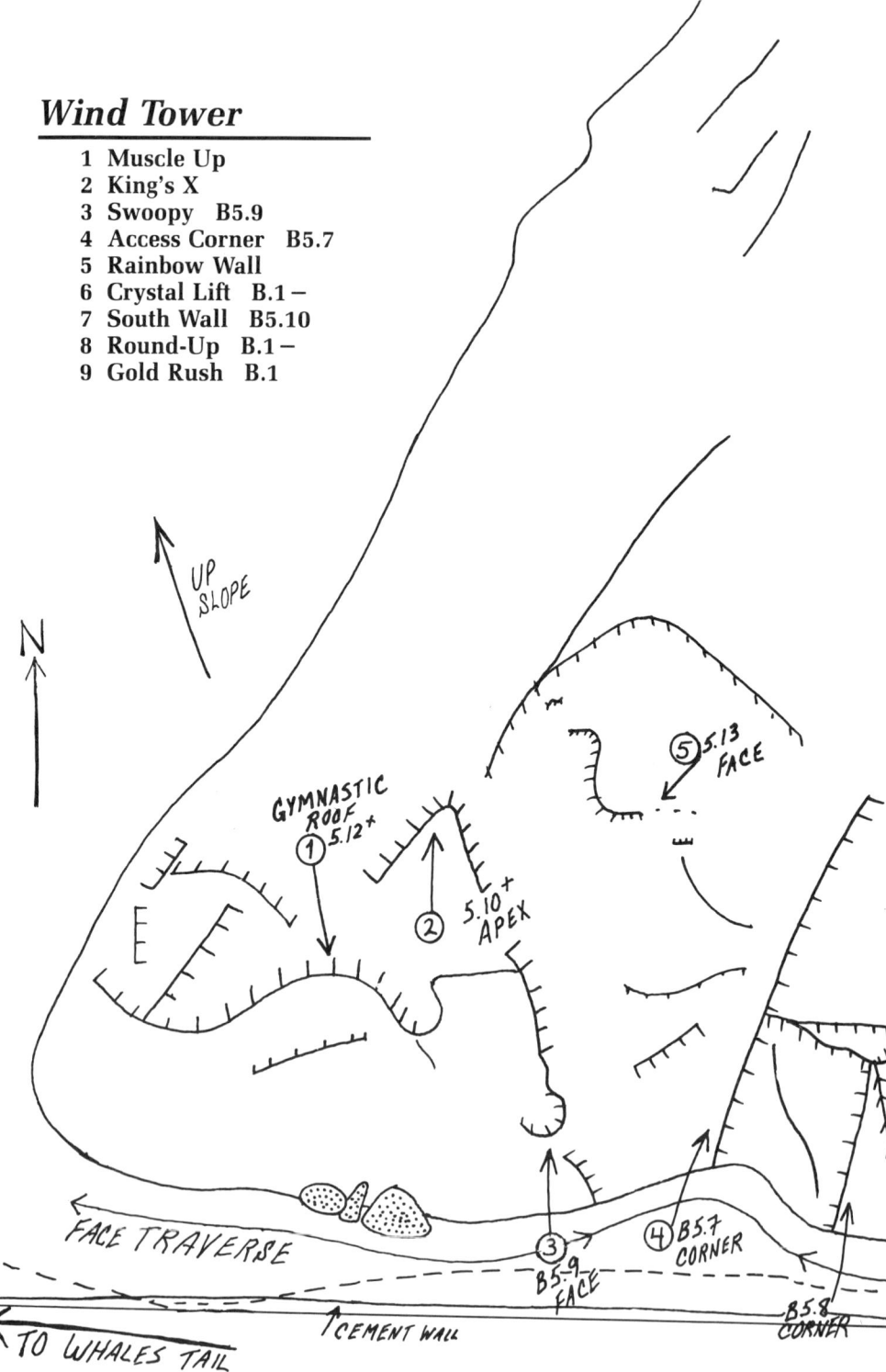

Eldorado Canyon — 141

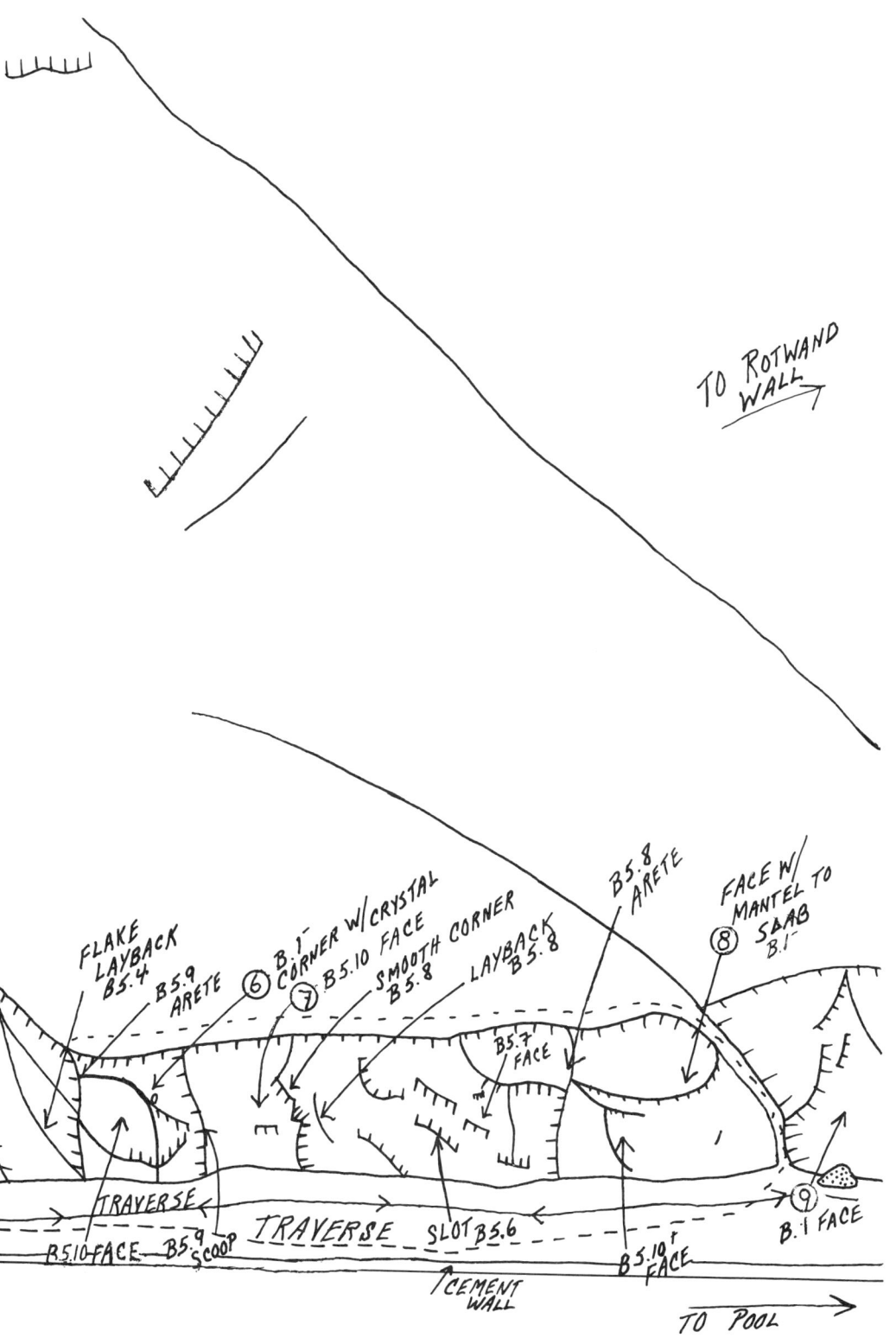

WHALE'S TAIL

From the north side of the foot bridge across Eldorado Creek take a left and you will be at the base of this large spire. Off the well-worn trail leading west you will find an awesome variety of problems. The Whale's Tail is most famous for its large cave at the base of its west end; some of the best bouldering comes out from the inside.

Mantle Man B.1
As you walk west for a few feet along the eastern base of the Whales Tail you will come across a polished sloping mantle shelf, which can be done in various ways. One way uses an undercling and a one-arm mantle and the other uses a straight-on, two-handed push. FA: unknown

Slipper Face B5.10+
Just to the left of the strenuous Mantle Man there is a vertical face with an undercling start to a down-sloping ledge. FA: unknown

Dihedral 1 B5.10+
Just left of Slipper Face is a small corner with some barndoor moves. You can go left or right. FA: unknown

Slick Traverse B.1+
Just above the ground, from Dihedral 1 to Mantle Man there is a very delicate traverse. FA: S. Guerin 1980s.

Throw Back B.1−
Just to the left of Dihedral 1 there is an overhanging face that ascends the arete of the left wall of a prominent diheral.

Scary Cling B.1
Just left of Throw Back there is a vertical wall with an interesting move somewhat high up. FA: K. Donald 1970s.

Dihedral 2 B5.8
This is the classic dihedral with a block overhang in it just left of Scary Cling. FA: unknown

Just Left B5.9
Just to the left of Dihedral 2 there is an overhanging face with good holds all the way up. FA: unknown

Pocket Bulge B5.10+
Left of the preceding route is a bulging wall with an obvious hole or pocket about ten feet up. FA: unknown

Amputee Love 5.12+
This is the severely bulging face just left of Pocket Bulge and was first done as a top-rope by Harrison Dekker and later bouldered out ropeless by Darius Azar 1987.

Horangutan 5.12
This is a severly overhanging route just above the cave. It takes the left-angling line to the slab above. This was first top-roped by Richard Ciley and then led by Bob Horan. Horan then bouldered it out ropeless in 85'.

The Monument 5.12+ (TR)
This is a very strenuous top-rope problem that starts inside the cave and underclings out the roof to the lip. FA: Woodruff?

Cave Traverse B.2
From the back of the cave traverse out towards the opening via laybacks, underclings, knee locks and iron cross moves. FA: D. Stone?

Eldorado Canyon — 143

Around the World B.1+
On the east side of the cave at the opening there is a very polished bulging and scooping wall that is the right most section of the Cave Traverse. Try to traverse in a circular motion around this section of the wall. FA: unknown

Vertical Polish B.1−
In the middle of the Around the World problem there is a face with some small edges that can be ascended with a tricky mantle. FA: unknown

N.E.D. 5.12−
This is the roof problem just left of the cave. A short sling can be seen hanging from a pin in the overhang. This was first top-roped by Alan Carrier and Adam Grosowsky and then led by Charlie Fowler. Bob Horan committed to bouldering this dynamic problem without a rope in 1985.

Off the Couch B5.9
Below and slighty left of the N.E.D. roof there is a slightly overhanging face with some nice little jugs in it.

Clementine Direct B5.9
Just left of Off the Couch is an obvious crack line that fades left onto some polished ledges. FA: unknown

Lunge Break B.1−
Just left of Clementine Direct, across from the northeast corner of the cement platform is a bulging, sloping ledge system. There are many different eliminates to gain the sloping ledges, including a double lunge.

Uphill from the Lunge Break on the west wall of the Whales Tail there is a rounded polished bulge with some fun challenges.

The Arete B.1−
Just left and slightly south, almost touching the Lunge Break problem there is a short arete with a tricky heel hook.

Micro Pull B.1+
To the immediate left of the Arete there is a short bulging wall. Feel up for the micro edges if you can reach them and pull to the top. FA: S. Guerin 1980s.

The Layback B5.9
From a sitting position left of Micro pull there is a short layback problem. FA: B. Horan 1980s.

CREEK SLAB
Across the trail from the Mantle Man on the Whale's Tail there is an excellent boulder with a smooth northeast-facing slab. Many problems exist on this slab as well as many little edges.

CREEK BOULDER
Just west of the Creek Slab there is a nice rounded boulder with a difficult east-facing bulge off the sandy beach below. In the summer you may witness many overheated climbers or hikers taking leaps from the top of this boulder into a hole in the raging Eldorado Creek.

East Bulge B.1+
From the sandy beach below the retaining wall you will notice a slick east-facing bulge with some delicate layback edges. Although this problem has been done from the right, the first ascent of the direct mantle was done by Patrick Edlinger in 1985.

144 — *Eldorado Canyon*

Whale's Tail

A WHALE'S TAIL
1. Mondo Man Traverse B.1+
2. The Arete B.1−
3. Clementine Direct B5.9
4. Lunge Break B.1−
5. N.E.D.
6. Around the World B.1+
7. Horangutan
8. Urban Gorilla
9. Spoof
10. Andrea's Bulge
11. Amputee Love
12. Pocket Bulge B5.10+
13. Dihedral 2 B5.8+
14. Dihedral 1 B5.10+
15. Mantle Man B.1

B CREEK BOULDER
1. East Bulge B.1+

C CREEK SLAB

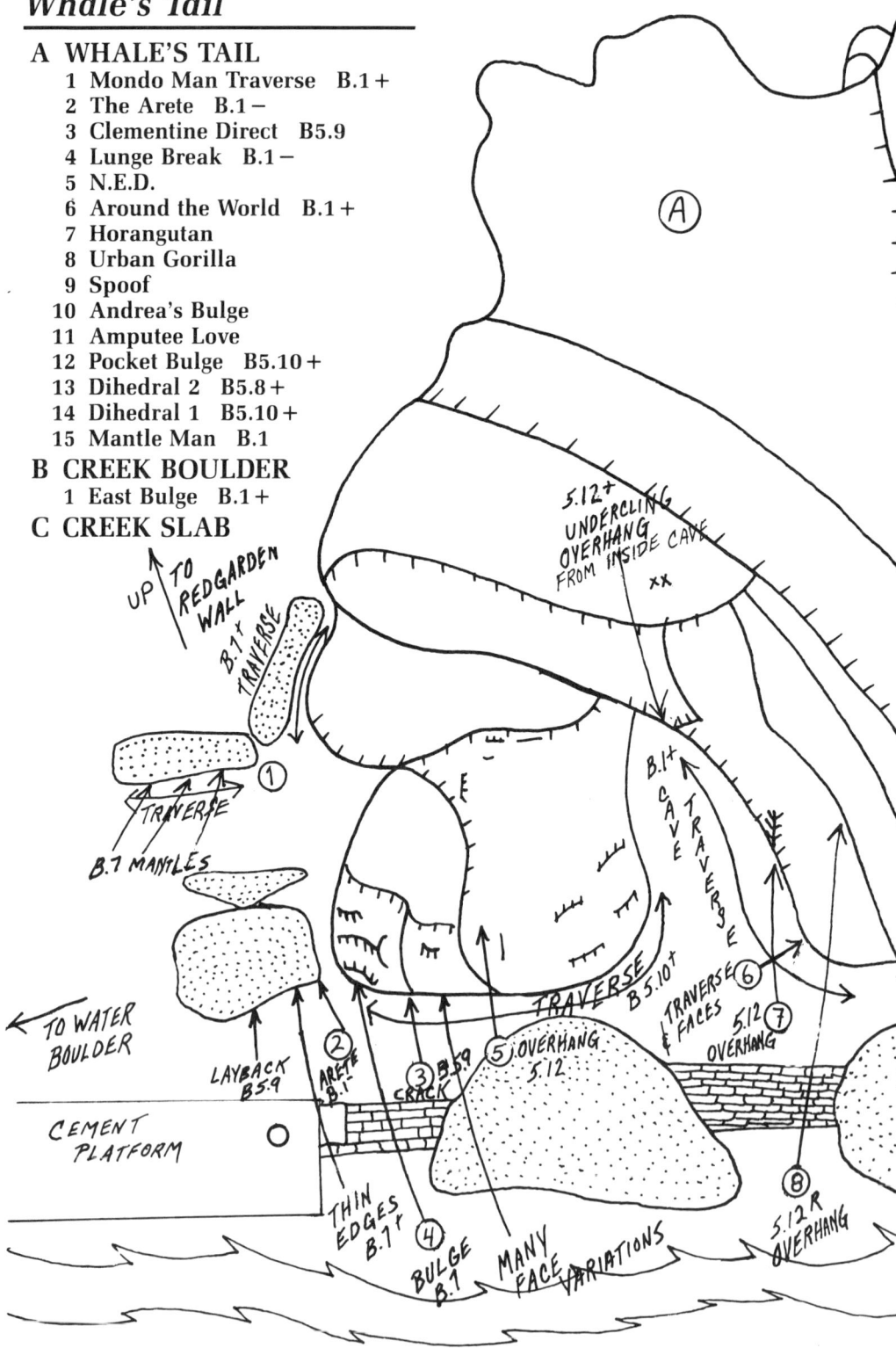

Eldorado Canyon — 145

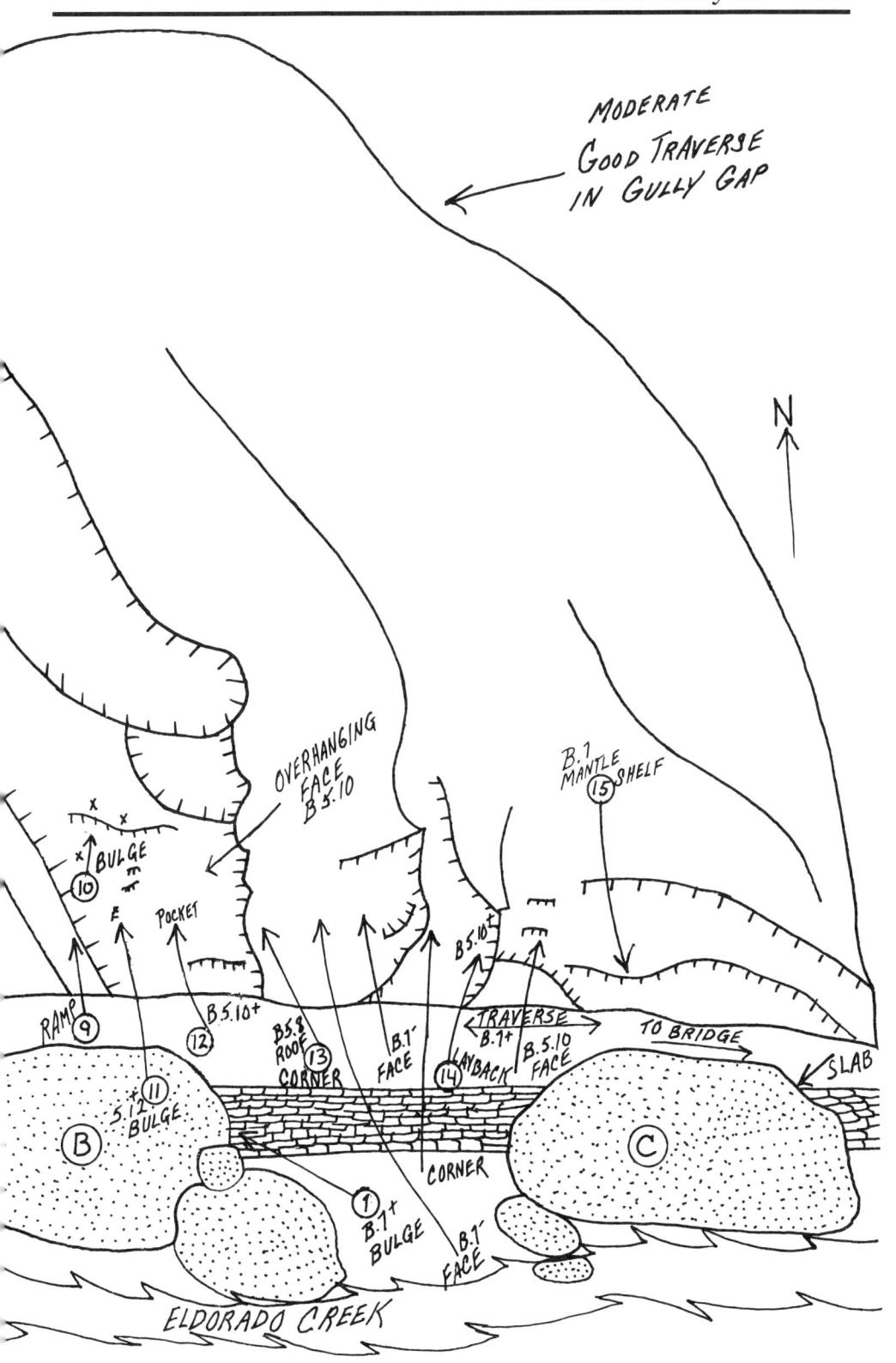

CLOSE TO THE EDGE SLABS
Just to the west of the west face of the Whale's Tail, uphill from Lunge Break, are two long slabby boulders sitting in the talus. These offer some incredible traverses.

Close to the Edge B.1
This upward, right-leaning edge traverse frictions its way up the upper boulder to the top. FA: S. Guerin 1980s.

Mondo Man Traverse B.1+
From the far west edge of the lower rock, traverse across and then link upward with the Close to the Edge Problem. FA: B. Horan 1985.

Many difficult mantles can be found on the lower rock. Each one is unique from the other.

WATER BOULDER
From the cement platform at the southwest corner of the Whales Tail, the trail continues west along the creek. After about fifty feet, near a cement dam, you will discover this nice block with a sheer northwest face. Many problems exist all around this, including an exciting traverse over the water.

East Arete B5.10
On the east corner of the boulder is a right-leaning face up the edge.

Center Route B.1
This is a tricky layaway problem up the center.

West Side B.1−
Just right of the Center Route is another small-edged challenge. Footwork is always the key on these problems.

Undercling Face B5.10
On the far right side of the boulder is a fun undercling route that consists of a high step with a long reach to a good edge.

Water Boulder Traverse B.1
This is a traverse of the lower northwest face of the boulder. Little edges and foot holds make this a great challenge. FA: S. Guerin 1980s.

On the west side of the rock there is a fun low angle slab with some good friction. This is also the easiest descent from the top.

Over Water Traverse B5.10
On the south face of the boulder, over the water there is a nice set of holds that can be traversed or ascended via a small layback system.

BARREL BLOCK
Just to the east of the Water Boulder there is a barrel-shaped polished block with some thin problems on it. The rock that has fallen against its north end also has some great roof moves.

MONKEY BOULDER
This is the boulder in the hillside above, just north of the Barrel Block. The west overhang has an incredible swinging move (B5.10+) to gain the summit. FA: C. Ruckgaber 1980s.

Eldorado Canyon — 147

Charlie Fowler (above) goes for the Monkey Swing (B5.10+) as Nancy Prichard traverses the Water Boulder (B5.10).

148 — Eldorado Canyon

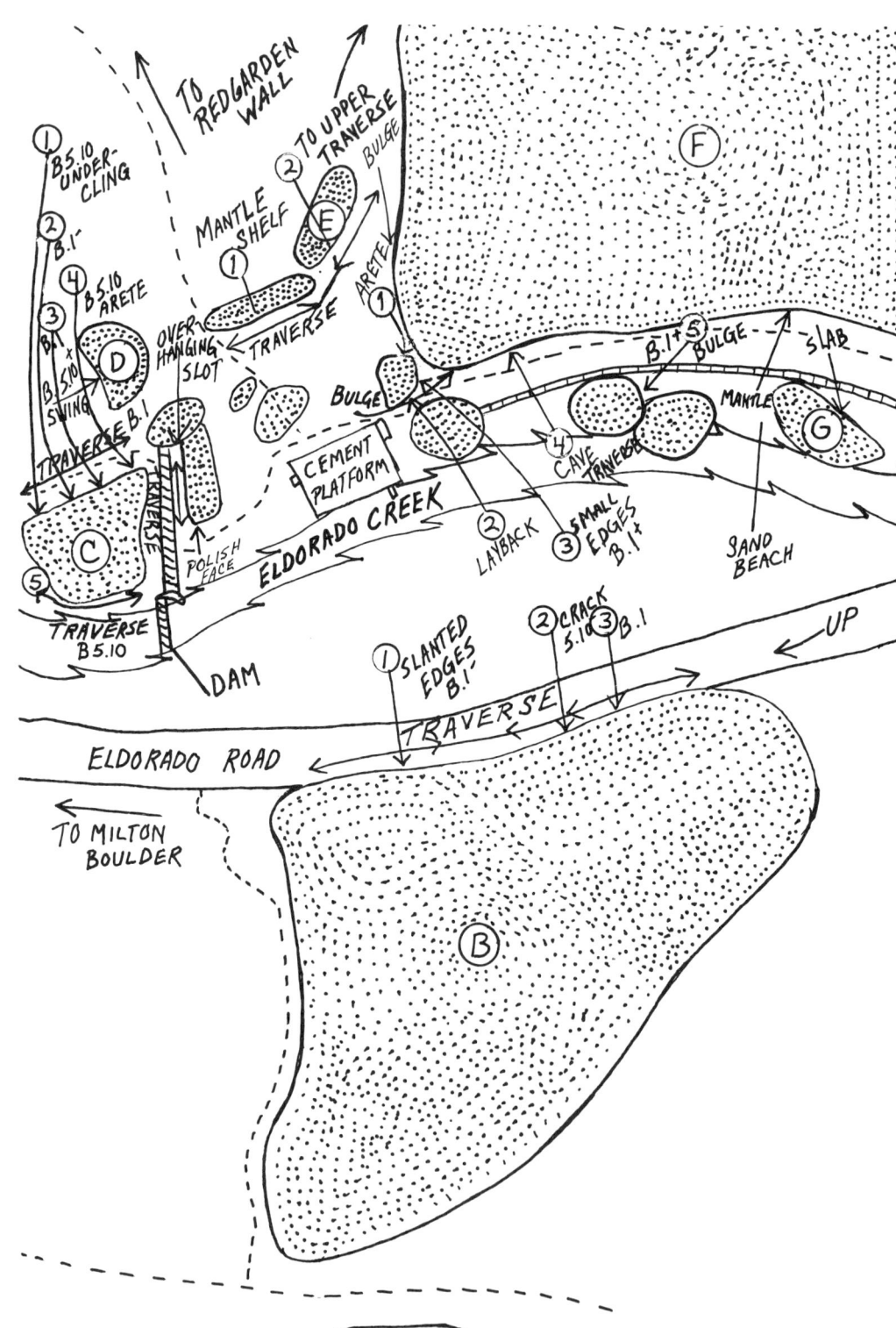

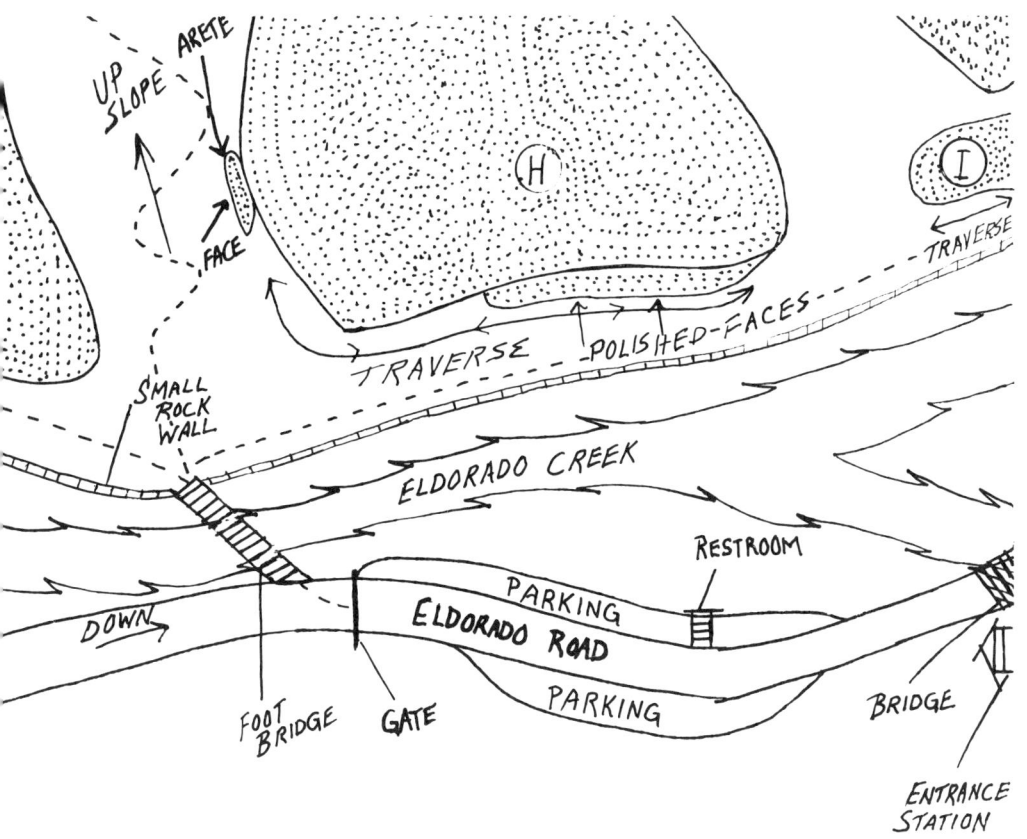

Eldorado Canyon – East End

A **LITTLE BASTILLE**
B **THE BASTILLE**
  1 Slope Face B.1−
  2 March of Dimes Direct B5.10+
  3 The Shield B.1
C **WATER BOULDER**
  1 Undercling Face B5.10
  2 West Side B.1−
  3 Center Route B.1
  4 East Arete B5.10
  5 Water Boulder Traverse B5.10
D **MONKEY BOULDER**
E **CLOSE TO THE EDGE ROCK**
  1 Mondo Man Traverse B.1+
  2 Close to the Edge B.1
F **WHALE'S TAIL**
  1 The Arete B.1−
  2 Layaway Edges B5.9
  3 The Thin Bulge B.1+
  4 Around the World B.1+
  5 Creek Bulge B.1+
G **CREEK SLAB**
H **WIND TOWER**
I **ALPINE WALL**

ROADSIDE OVERHANG
From the Water Boulder and across Eldorado Creek to the southwest there is a hidden overhang sitting just below the top of the road.
Standard B5.10+
This is the easiest way out the overhang and finishes over the lip to the left in some good pockets. FA: B. Horan 1980s.
Psychit B.1
This is a direct roof problem with counter pulls to gain the lip. FA: B. Horan 1980s.

CRANK ROCK
This is a smooth, overhanging wall just upcreek from the Water Boulder and on the same side. Follow the trail slightly up hill and cut across a faint path leading towards the creek. The south-facing wall sits right next to the water. Although the routes were bouldered out onsight by Horan, another climbing team placed a bolt on the top of the boulder for a top rope. Not a bad idea considering the free solo danger of these problems.
Crankakee B.1+
On the south face of the rock there is an overhanging face with sloping holds. FA: B. Horan 1986.
Direct B.1
This is an extra move that comes in from the right side. FA: B. Horan 1986.

Across to the southeast from the Crank Rock there is a small boulder with a classic west facing moderate scoop up it.

RIVER BLOCK
Getting back to the main trail on the north side of Eldorado Creek, follow it west past the lower south end tail of the Red Garden Wall for about three hundred feet. From here drop down towards the creek and you will soon discover this massive block which sits in the creek bed. A few very serious problems can be found on its south and east faces.
Gunk Roof B5.10+
On the upper slope of the east side of the block, hidden in the bush somewhat, there is an incredible set of good holds leading out right to the dicey lip. The ground is close enough for comfort. FA: B. Horan 1986.
Kiss of Life B.2
This is a very serious problem that was top-roped, led and then bouldered ropeless by Bob Horan in 1986. On the east lower side of the block is a large roof with a little jam in it. From here one must reach up to the sloping ledge and mantle to a stance. The rest is airy but moderate.
Eastern Priest B.1−
On the south face of the boulder, just out of the creek there is an overhanging face with some scary reaches. FA: B. Horan 1986.
Fall Line B5.7
Left of Eastern Priest there is a classic crack. Laybacking this line is a true delight.

MILTON BOULDER
This is one of the true prizes of the Eldorado Boulders and is located up the road from the Bastille a couple hundred yards. The boulder sits next to the north side of the road and is very hard to miss with its blank looking southwest face. Many incredible routes can be found all around this gem. Eldorado's most difficult face problems can be found on this boulder.

Ridge Face B5.9
On the far left side of the west face there is a thin slab with some delicate moves.

Layaway B5.8
This is probably the easiest way to ascend the west face and starts out with several side clings and works its way to the right.

Micro Slab B.1+
To the right of Layaway there is a thin slab with no foot holds and hard to use edges. FA: S. Guerin 1980s.

Standard B5.10
To the right of Micro Slab there is a thin face with some very minute polished toeholds. The trick is to get into a layback on the good handholds.

Undercling Route B.1−
To the right of the Standard Route there is a conspicuous little undercling which can be used to gain the upper slopes of the boulder.

Smeary Thing B.1+
Immediately right of the undercling there is a strenous friction problem that ascends the scoop. Start by pinching the arete, throw a smeary stem out right, reach a small layaway just inches right of the undercling, reach for the sloping shelf above and mantle. FA: B. Horan 1987.

Donna B.1
This was named after the graffetti below its face. To the right of the smear route there is another thin finger problem that uses a two finger left hand nitch with a high step. Reaching the top and mantling is the true test. FA: Jim Erickson 1970s.

Milton B.1
This is the center problem on the southwest face and was named after the writing on the southwest wall. Pull on the face with a good layback and reach up for an obvious crystal with your right hand. Go for the top and mantle. FA: P. Ament 1968.

Layreach B.1
Immediately right of the Milton there is a right-hand layback hold. Smear up to this and launch for the top. FA: B. Horan 1980s.

Never Say Never B.2
This is the blank looking scooping face to the right of the Milton problem. This problem had been unsuccessfully tried for years and was written up in an *Outside* magazine as an impossible face. Steve Mammen was able to do it from the ground up via a dynamic start off the ground in 1987. Bob Horan repeated this problem with a static start in 1988.

Micro Sheer B.2
On the south face of the boulder there is an improbable-looking face that was climbed in 1986 by Bob Horan. One of the key holds for the left hand was broken off and the problem has been unrepeated ever since.

Leaning Arete B5.7
On the south side of the boulder, just right of Micro Sheer is a left-leaning arete. Keep the body on the left side and traverse up to the top.
Milton Upper Traverse B.1 −
On the top edge of the southwest face one can traverse back and forth until totally pumped. FA: B. Horan 1980s.

On the east side of the Milton Boulder there is an excellent beginners slab that can be done in many ways, including no hands for a good challenge.

WEST WORLD BOULDERS
Across the creek from the Milton Boulder and uphill several hundred feet to the northwest there is a fantasy world for the hard-core boulderer. Several overhanging boulders exist in this hidden playground.

GERM FREE BOULDER
Uphill a few hundred feet from the creek and about the same distance to the west from the West Ridge, one will discover this obvious overhanging south face with a good flake system going out to the lip.
Germ-Free Adolescence B.1+
On the lower eastern boulder of the slope there is an extreme south facing roof with a tree close by. Yard on the flake system to the edges in the roof. The scary part is turning the lip. FA: John Sherman 1980s. Start from a sitting position for an extra pump.
The Day the World Turned Day-Glo B.1
Just to the left of Germ-Free there is a bulging wall with a delicate move to gain the top. FA: H. Dekker 1980s.
Genetic Engineering B.1
This is another bulge problem just to the left of the Day Glo bulge. FA: H. Dekker 1980s.

ROOFUS ROCK
Just to the left of the Germ Free boulder there is an overhanging rock with many good problems on its sides. Two roof problems go out its southeast overhang.
John's Scoop B5.9
On the west side of Roofus Rock you will find an obvious scoop with good moves. FA: J. Sherman 1980s.
Sheep Thrills B.1
On the west side of Roofus Rock just up to the left from the scoop you will find this thin vertical face. FA: J. Sherman 1980s.

THE HIGH SPIRE
Just behind to the northeast of the Germ Free Boulder you will discover this twenty-five foot spire. An obvious crack system starts on its southwest corner and then angles up to the right.
Lost Generation B.1 −
From the start of the obvious crack line, continue straight up to the top of the spire, rather than traversing along the crack to the right. FA: J. Sherman 1980s.
High Spire Crack B5.10
This very committing problem takes the obvious crack system on the south face of the spire. FA: J. Sherman 1980s.

Eldorado Canyon — 153

Angel Dust (TR)
Where the crack on the south face of the spire tops out on the right, follow a line of holds straight down the arete. Ascend these to the top. FA: J. Sherman 1980s.

Klingon B5.9
On the east side of the spire is a nice face route leading up to the summit. FA: J. Sherman 1980s.

Squeeler B.1
On the north side of the spire is a thin very steep face that reaches up to a good finger edge. FA: J. Sherman 1980s.

MIND BOGGLE BLOCK
Just to the northwest, almost connected to the High Spire, is this large block with an incredibly overhanging southwest face.

Bulge Roof B.1− (TR)
On the far right side of the overhanging southwest face there is a bulge problem with strenuous moves to gain the lip. FA: J. Sherman 1980s.

Studebaker Hawk B.1
Left of the bulge problem on the right there is an obvious set of holds going out the roof to a kind of flake. FA: J. Sherman 1980s.

Around the corner to the left of the overhanging side of the block, on the west side there are some delicate face problems that use crystals and small pockets. The landings are marginal. Several of these problems where done by B. Horan in the 1980s.

SPOTLESS BOULDER
This fun boulder sits due west from Roofus Rock. Another smaller boulder sits on its east side to form a gully between the two. Problems can be found all over this boulder.

Venus and the Razorblades B.1
On the east side of the Spotless Boulder there is a gully with some incredible face routes climbing out it. This route is found on the far right side of the east face. FA: J. Sherman 1980s.

Don't Touch I-Man Locks B.1−
Just to the left of the Venus problem there is another good face route. FA: J. Sherman 1980s.

Punky Reggae Party B5.10+
To the left of the I-Man problem there is yet another good face. FA: J. Sherman 1980s.

Follow the boulder around to the left or west side for some more fun problems including a classic V-slot dihedral. Just below the Spotless boulder you will spot a small boulder. A very fun sit-down overhang problem can be found on its south side.

WEST END ROCK
Moving even further to the west from the Spotless Boulder you will find a large rock with some challenging faces on its southeast face.

154 — Eldorado Canyon

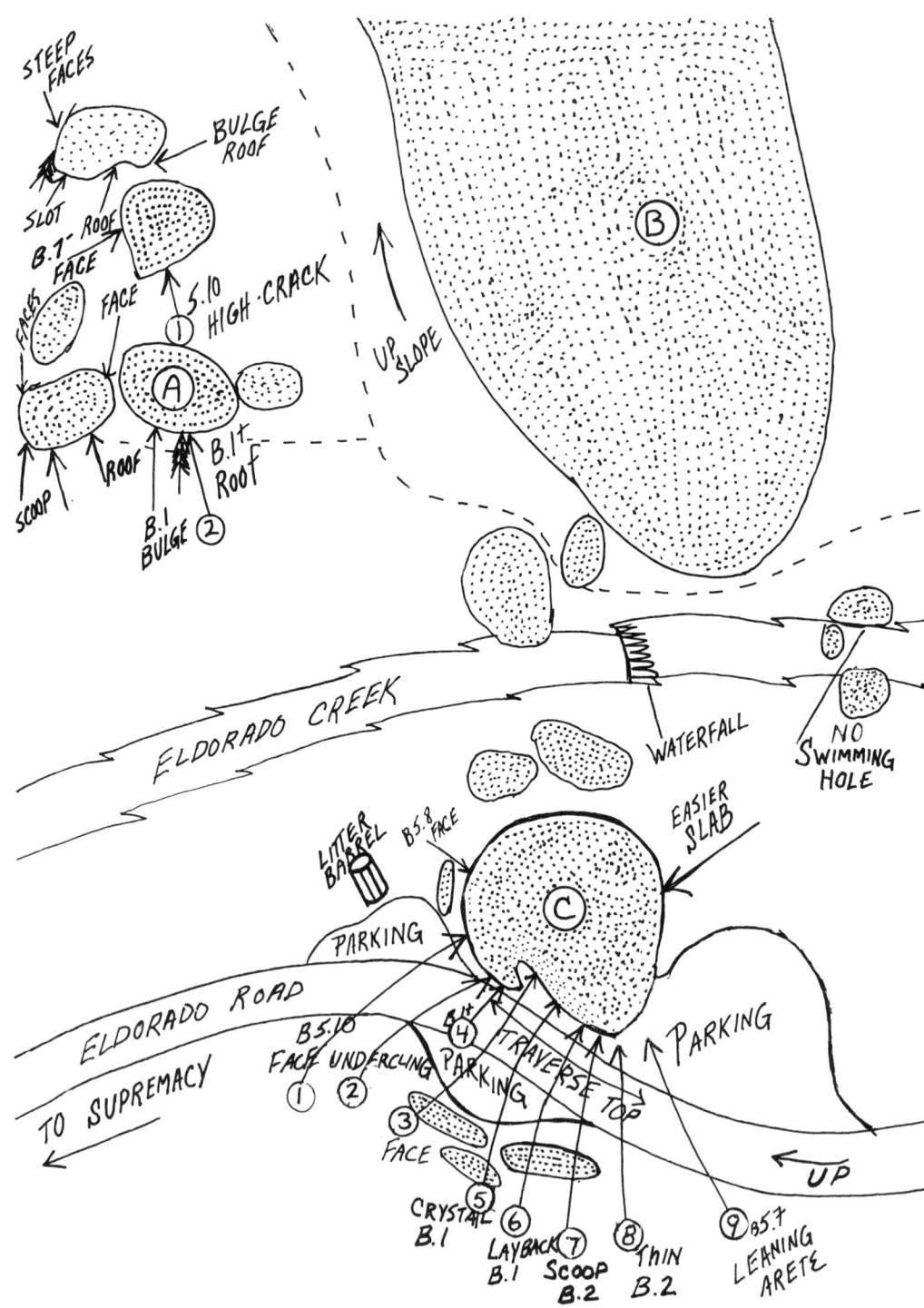

Eldorado Canyon — 155

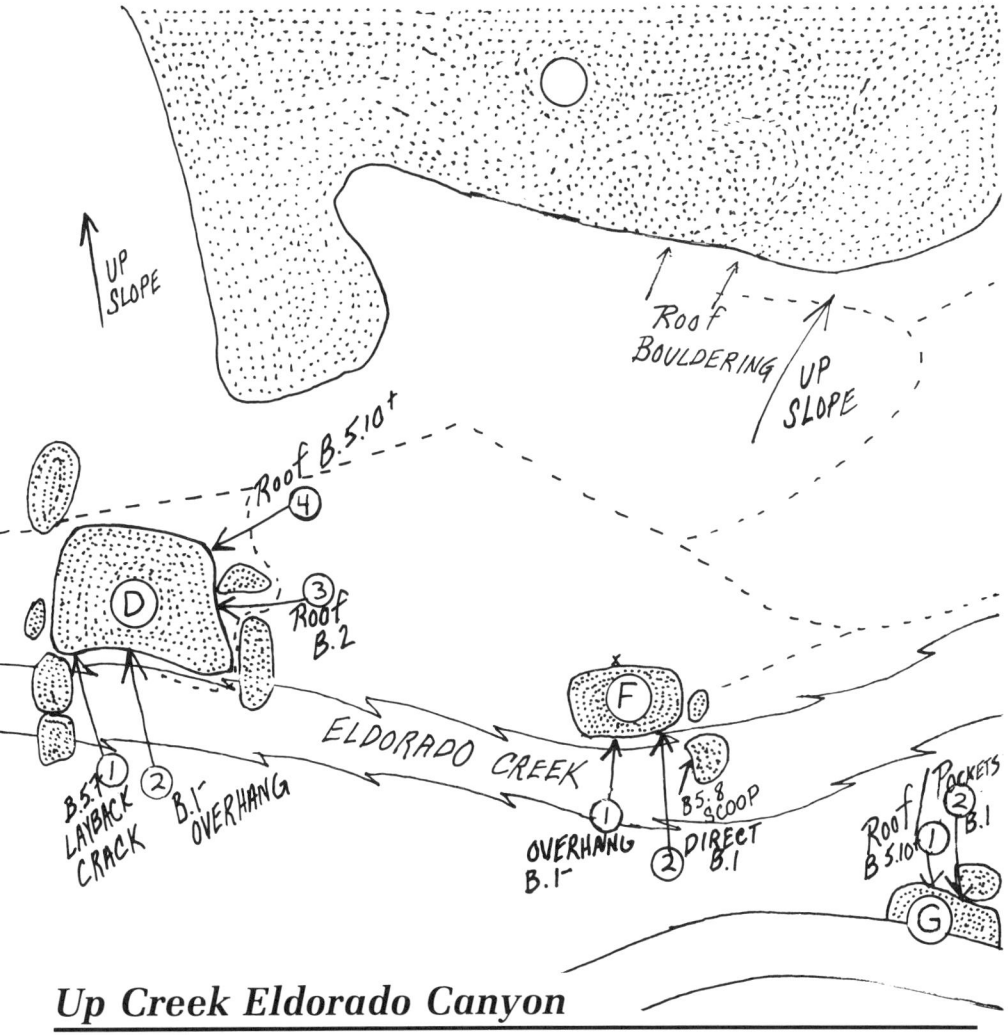

Up Creek Eldorado Canyon

A WEST WORLD BOULDERS
  1 High Spire Crack B5.10+
  2 Germ Free Adolescence B.1+

B WEST RIDGE

C MILTON BOULDER
  1 Standard Route B5.10
  2 Undercling Route B.1−
  3 Donna B.1
  4 Smeary Thing B.1+
  5 Milton B.1
  6 Layreach B.1
  7 Never Say Never B.2
  8 Micro Sheer B.2
  9 Leaning Arete B5.7

D RIVER BLOCK
  1 Classic Layback B5.7
  2 Eastern Priest B.1−
  3 Kiss of Life B.2
  4 Gunk Roof B5.10+

E RED GARDEN WALL

F CRANK ROCK
  1 Crankakee B.1−
  2 Direct B.1

G ROADSIDE OVERHANG
  1 Standard B5.10+
  2 Psychit B.1

Ascending the extremely delicate Never Say Never (B.2) on the Milton Boulder.   photo: John Baldwin

Yarding for the lip on Germ-Free Adolescence (B.1+), West World Boulder.
photo: Jim Baldwin

West World Boulders

A MILTON BOULDER
1. Never Say Never B.2
2. Milton B.1
3. Standard Route

B WEST RIDGE

C GERM FREE BOULDER
1. Germ Free Adolescence B.1+
2. The Day the World Turned Day-Glo B.1
3. Genetic Engineering B.1

D ROOFUS ROCK
1. John's Scoop B5.9
2. Sheep Thrills B.1

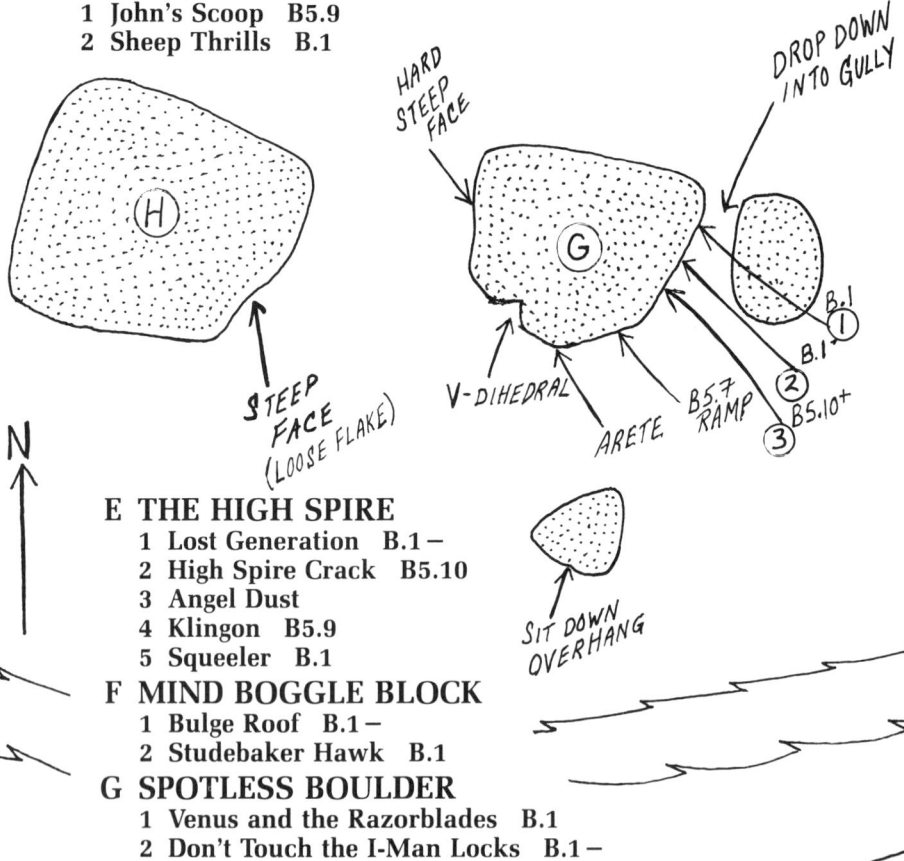

E THE HIGH SPIRE
1. Lost Generation B.1−
2. High Spire Crack B5.10
3. Angel Dust
4. Klingon B5.9
5. Squeeler B.1

F MIND BOGGLE BLOCK
1. Bulge Roof B.1−
2. Studebaker Hawk B.1

G SPOTLESS BOULDER
1. Venus and the Razorblades B.1
2. Don't Touch the I-Man Locks B.1−
3. Punky Reggae Party B5.10+

H WEST END ROCK

Eldorado Canyon — 159

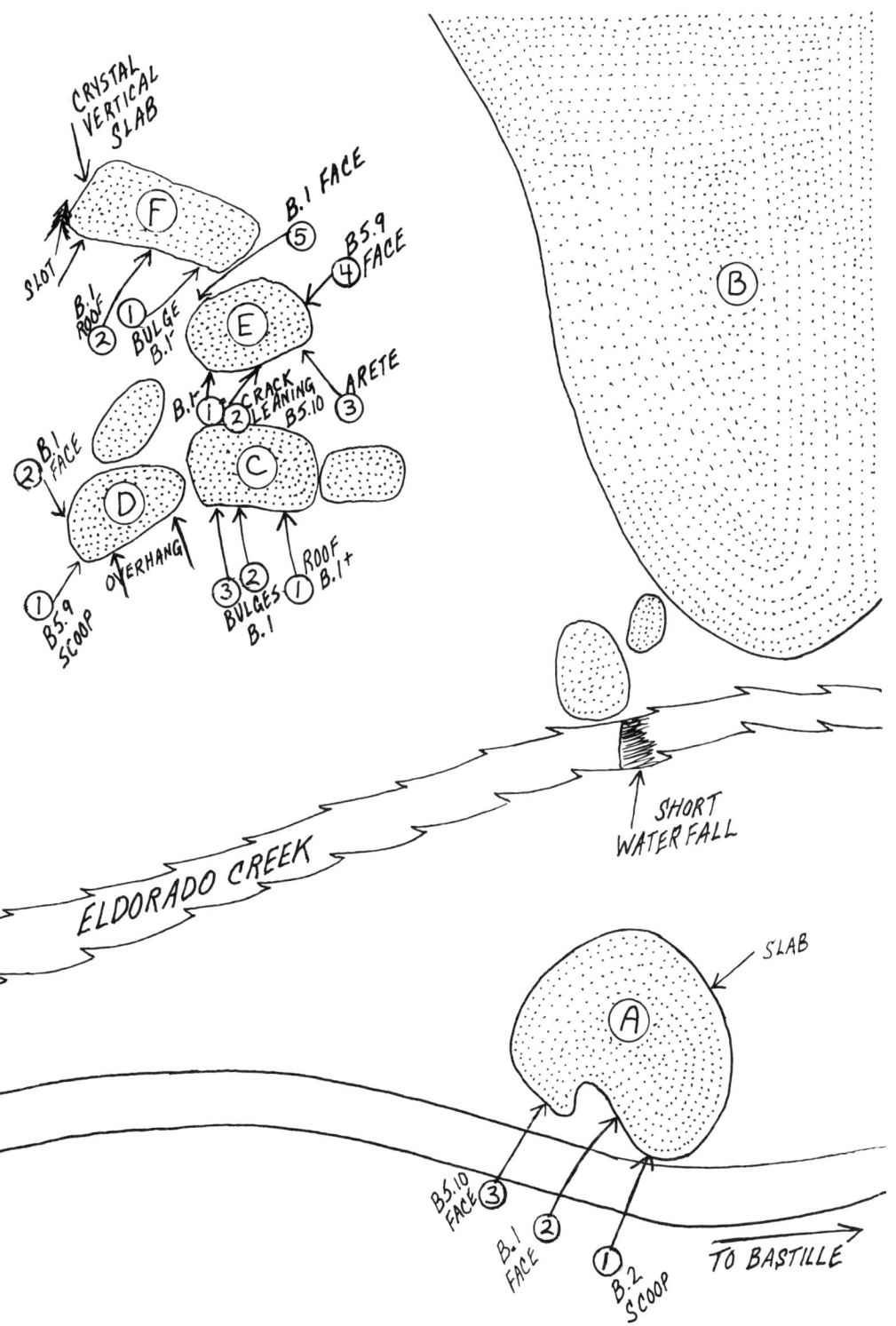

SUPREMACY ROCK
From the Milton Boulder continue up the road past a curve heading north through a road cut and down to a intersection in the road right near a bridge over Eldorado Creek. Supremacy Rock can be seen along the side of the road on the left, where the road takes a left before the bridge. A fun traverse right off the road can be played on.

WATER ROCK
From the bridge near Supremacy Rock, look to the southwest and you will see this rock sitting on the east side of the creek with its oval-shaped west face.
West Scoop B5.8
This is the obvious west face with a crystal jug halfway up the problem. Many other variations can be done on this large rock.

BLOCKS ROCKS
To the north of Water Rock is a blocky boulder sitting on top of a slab. Good problems exist on all sides.
South Face B5.9
On the south face of the block there is a classic face with great edges.
West Arete B5.9
Left of the South Face there is an arete with some tricky moves.

THE GILL BOULDER
This challenging, very diverse boulder is located just northeast of the bridge by Supremacy Rock, hidden in the trees. The south face has a vertical thin edged slab with a variety of difficult problems. The north face has a very steep wall with hard problems. The other sides have more moderate walls with a wide variety of good classic bouldering. Gill was pictured in *Master of Rock* on a challenging problem on the west side of the north face.
Western Slab B5.10
On the southwest corner of the boulder is a narrow slab leading to the top.
West Face B.1–
Just to the left of the Western Slab and right of the prominent descent tree is a vertical wall with a hard move off some small edges. FA: P. Ament 1960s.
Gill Face B.1–
Around the corner to the left of the West Face is a smooth vertical wall immediately left of the northwest corner of the north face. This is the problem on which Gill was pictured in *Master of Rock*. FA: J. Gill 1960s.
Baldwin Face B.1
Left of the Gill Face about fifteen feet is a thin-edged face that moves up and right. FA: J. Baldwin 1988.
Standard Face B.1
This is the obvious vertical face up the center of the sheer north face. A semi-dynamic move is used to gain the finger jug up top.
Horan Face B.1
Just left of the Standard Route is a set of little edges that make their way to the top of the Standard Route. FA: B. Horan 1986.
Northeast Reach B5.9
On the northeast corner of the boulder is an exciting route that starts out with some great edges and makes a long reach to the top.

Eldorado Canyon — 161

East Dihedral B5.9
On the east side of the boulder is an obvious dihedral leading up to the top.
Southeast Corner B5.7
This short but fun route climbs the southeast corner via some laybacks.
East Side Traverse B5.10
This is a good traverse that skirts the east face of the boulder, the most difficult section being at the north end.
South Right B.1
On the far right side of the thin south-facing slab is a delicate face requiring a thumbs-down push with a small step.
South Center B.1
This is a very difficult thin edges face up the center of the south slab.
South Left B.1 −
On the left side of the south facing slab there is a thin face that is gained by a small toe pocket to a high step.

Many other variations can be played on. The Gill Boulder offers routes every few feet. The best descent is located on the west face by using a tree.

If you continue up the road to the north from the Gill Boulder and locate the Green Moutain Trail you will see some good looking boulders in the slopes to the north of the trail. Problems of all abilities can be had on these rocks.

Nancy Prichard enjoys a classic face on the West Scoop (B5.8) of the Water Rock.

Eldorado Canyon – West End

A SUPREMACY ROCK
  1 Supremacy Crack
  2 Supremacy Slab
  3 The Web

B WATER ROCK
  1 West Scoop   B5.8

C BLOCKS ROCK
  1 South Face   B5.9
  2 West Arete   B5.9

D THE GILL BOULDER
  1 Western Slab   B5.10
  2 West Face   B.1 –
  3 Gill Face   B.1 –
  4 Baldwin Face   B.1
  5 Standard Face   B.1
  6 Horan Face   B.1
  7 South Right   B.1
  8 South Center   B.1 +
  9 South Left   B.1 –

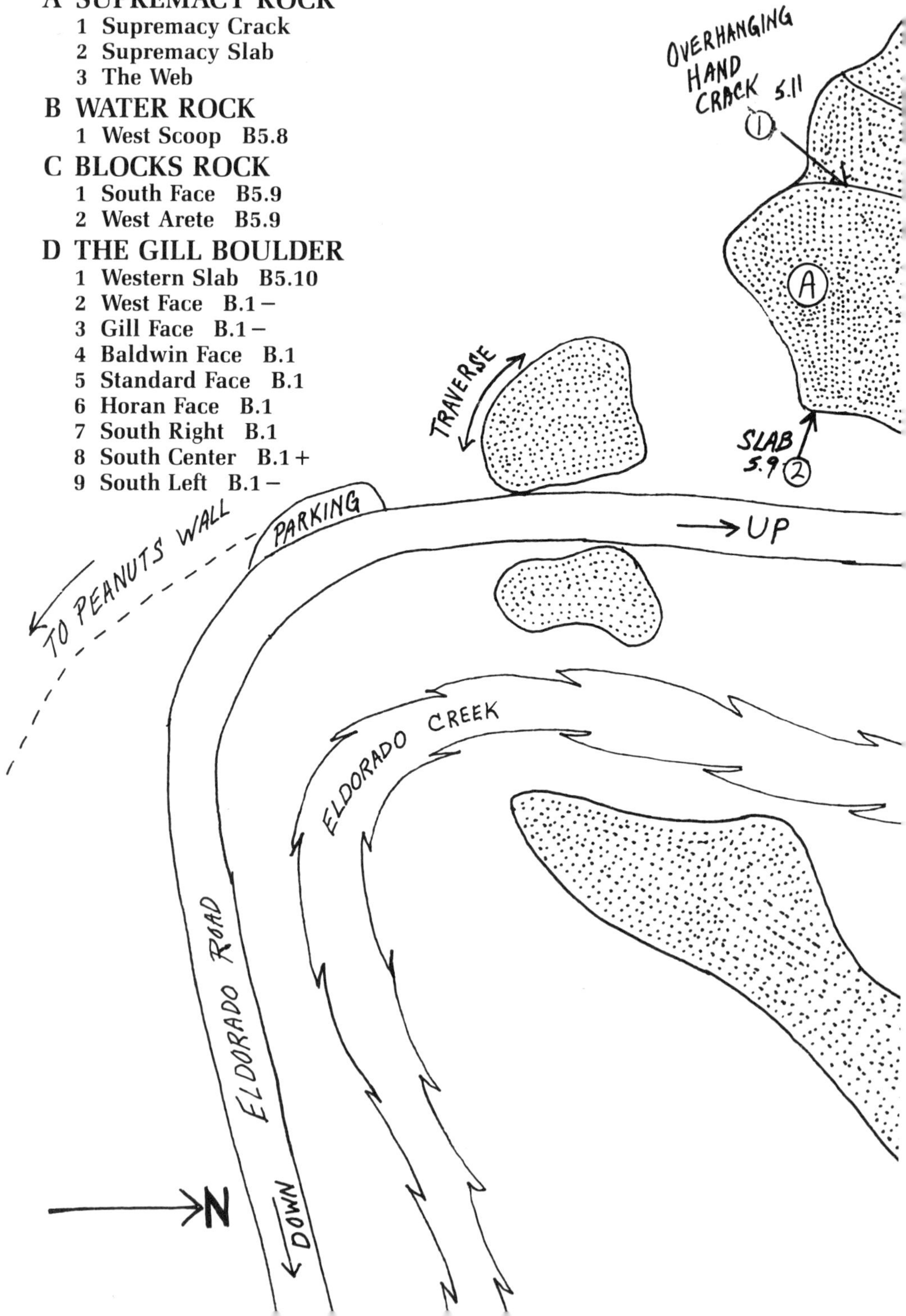

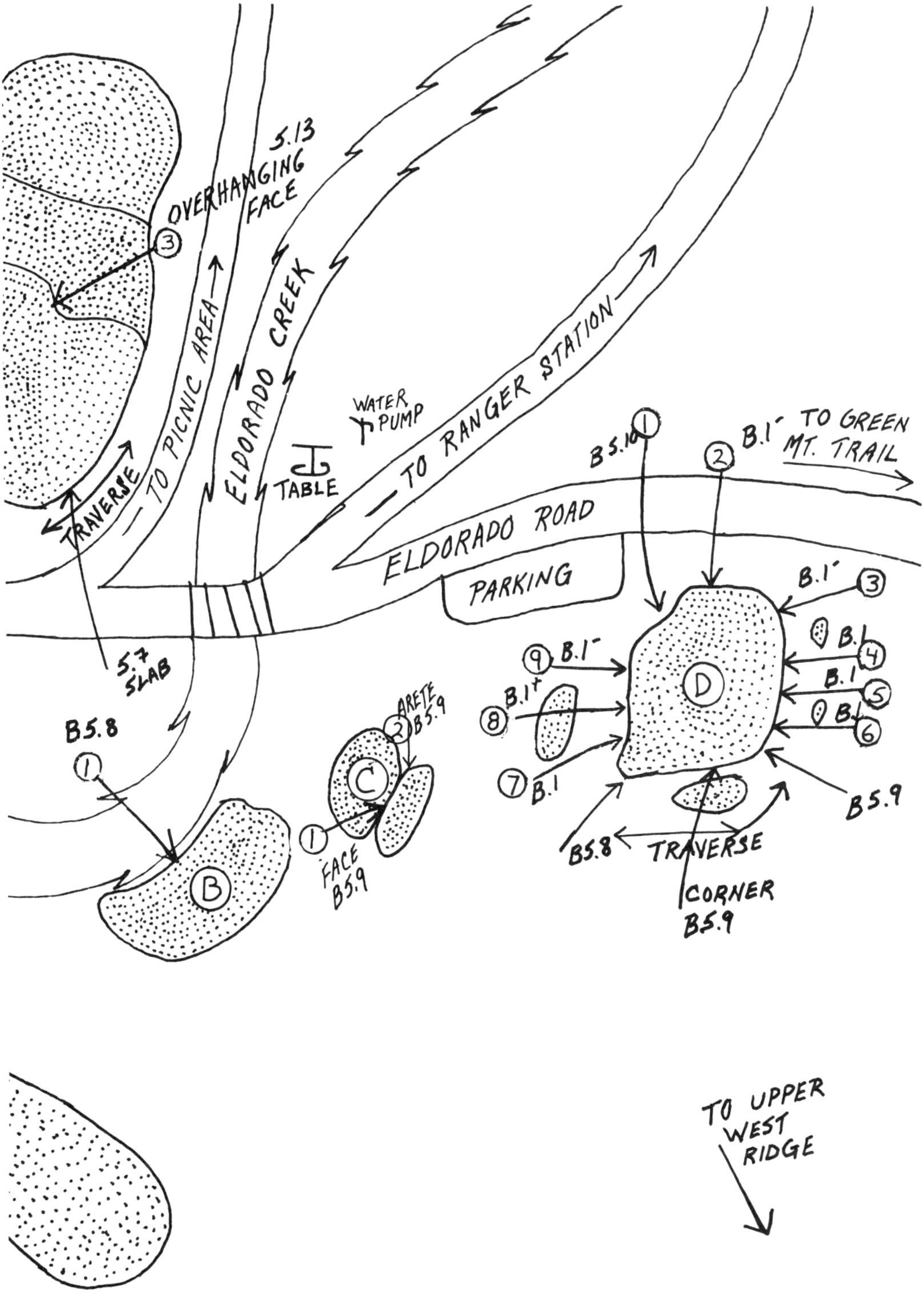
5.13
OVERHANGING
FACE
3
TO PICNIC AREA
ELDORADO CREEK
TRAVERSE
WATER
PUMP
TABLE
TO RANGER STATION
B5.10
1
2
B.1-
TO GREEN
MT. TRAIL
ELDORADO ROAD
PARKING
B.1-
3
B.1
4
B.1
5
B.1
6
9
B.1-
B.1+
8
D
7
B.1
B5.9
B5.8
TRAVERSE
CORNER
B5.9
5.7
SLAB
B5.8
1
B
ARETE
B5.9
2
C
1
FACE
B5.9
TO UPPER
WEST
RIDGE

Morrison Wall

For winter bouldering on the Front Range, the incredibly overhanging outcropping of Morrison Wall can not be beat. Its smooth south-facing sandstone rock walls have become a favorite for the year-round climber. The overhanging walls are filled with boulder problems, traverses and awesome top-ropes. Some of the longer top-rope routes overhang for over forty feet or more. This unique area has become a major training ground for all levels of ability and a good pump can be found every few feet.

To locate this amazing bouldering area follow Interstate 70 west from the Denver metro area to the Morrison/Red Rocks Park exit. Head south past Red Rocks Park until you come to a stop light in the town of Morrison, Colorado. From this light, hang a left (east), and if you look up to the northeast you will see the long ridge of overhanging rock. A parking area next to the creek sits opposite the upper section of the wall. It should be noted that this guide only covers the routes on the south-facing side of the canyon. The numerous rocks on the shady side are largely unexplored; a particularly steep hillside mandates frequent use of a rope.

For all top rope problems, bring a selection of nuts as anchor backups and plenty of long slings.

Morrison Wall — 165

Leaning up the Cocaine Corner of Spike Rock (B5.10), while the Hogback Mama looms overhead.

166 — *Morrison Wall*

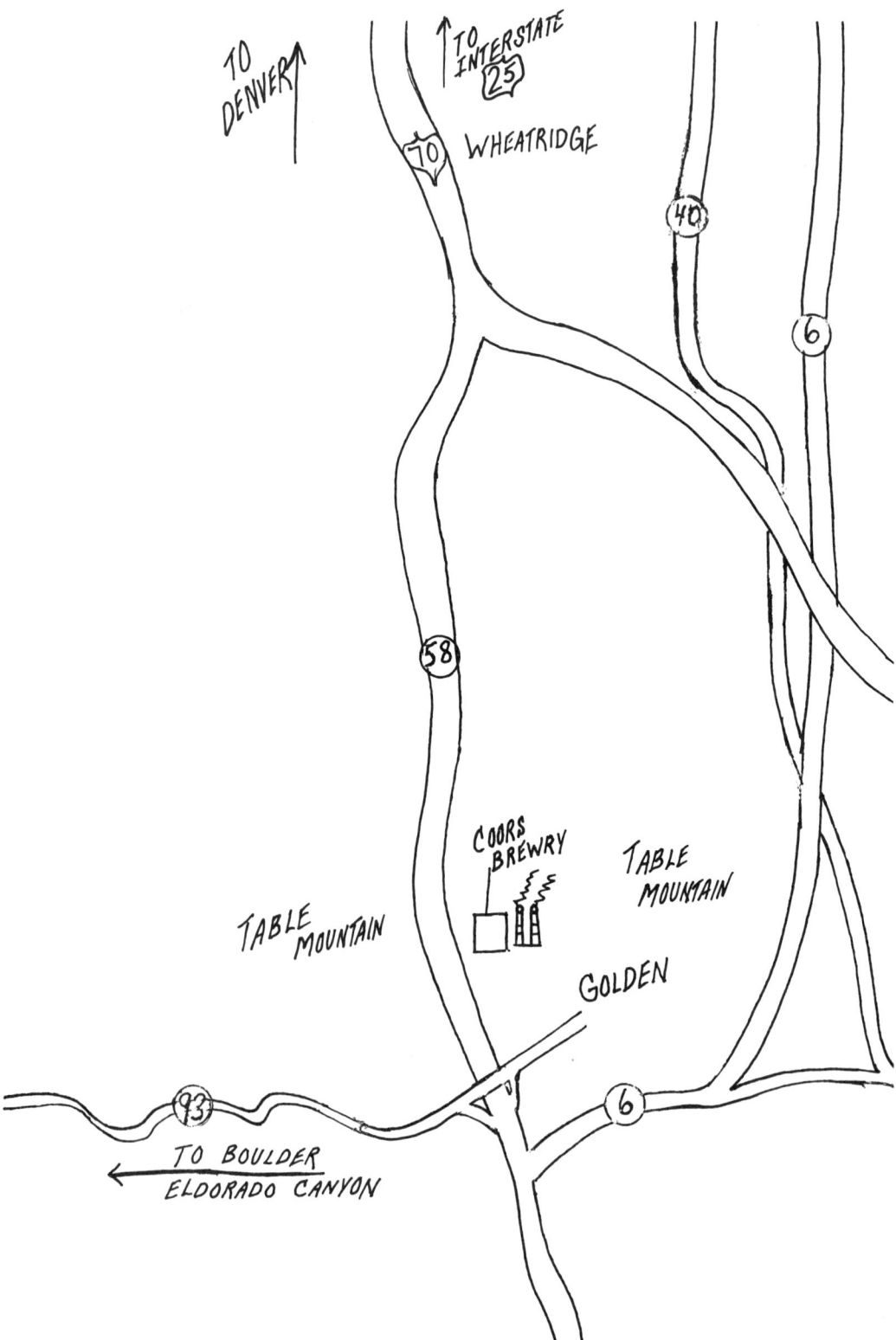

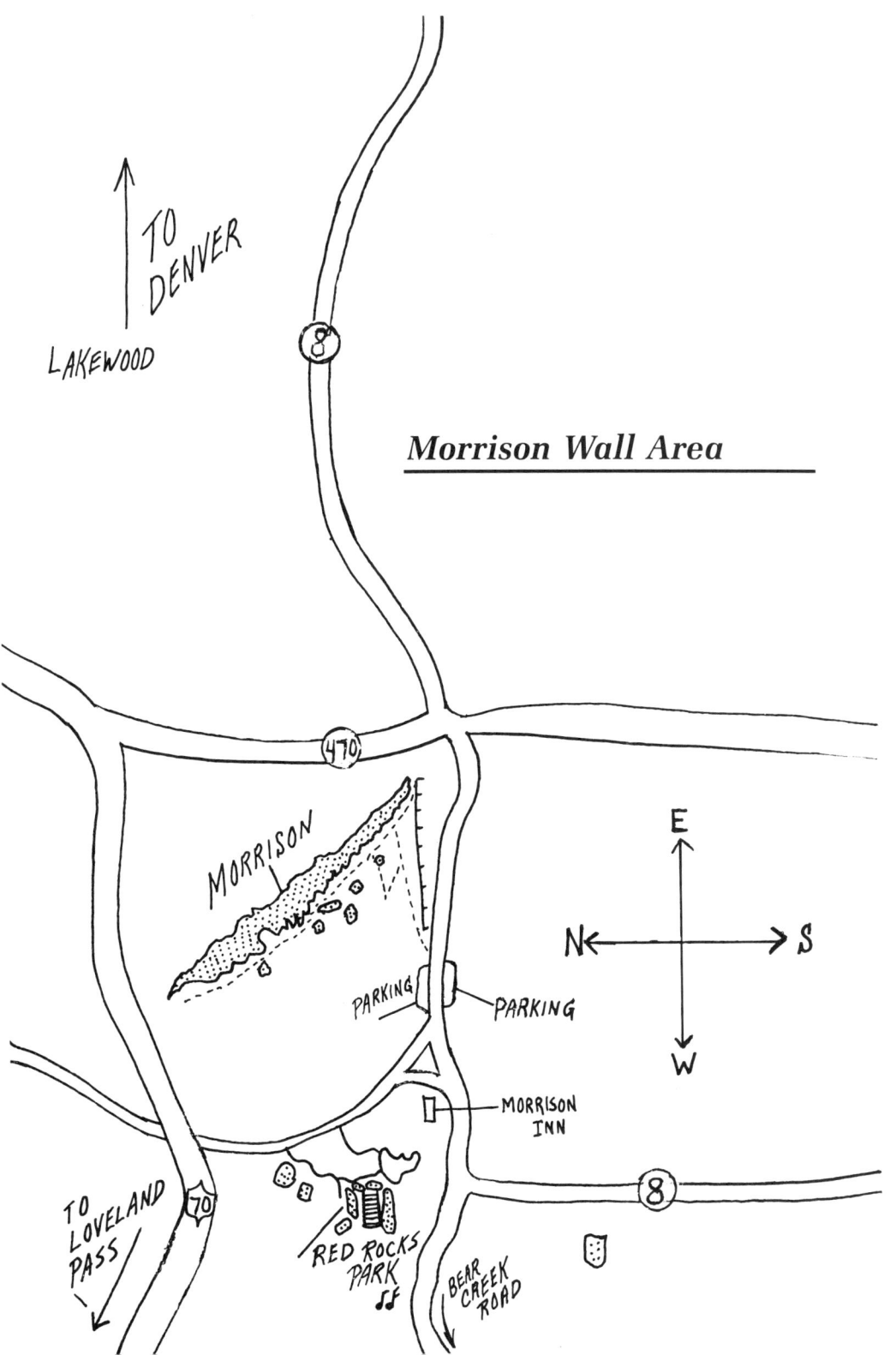

WIRELESS WALL
This contains the overhanging cracks out the roofs at the lower right hand side of the cliff band, just off the road. There are three obvious lines which where climbed by Rufus Miller.

DINOSAUR TRACKS WALL
To the right of the Wireless Wall is a series of small corners and slabs with many good problems. If you look along this wall really hard you will discover some fossilized dinosaur tracks in a small roof above.

Eric Weinstein Memorial Wall
This takes the obvious dihedral up the slab to the right of the Wireless Wall roofs. A bolt can be seen up on the face.

THE BLACK HOLE
Up the hill from the Wireless Wall several hundred feet is a cave/hole, blackened by years of campfires. Many strenous problems exist in here, including a desperate traverse.

MAIN HANGS
Just down and left, from the Black Hole is this long roof traverse that extends several hundred feet up hill. An unlimited variety of problems exist all along this section of the wall, including several top-ropes.

Psycho Simulator
This describes the traverse of the Main Hangs area. Many variations and eliminates can be done. This is a popular pumping ground and a waiting line is common.

HAIRY SCARY WALL
Up hill from the Main Hangs is another overhanging section of wall with some good traversing and short but difficult roofs and aretes.

Local Motions 5.12a (TR)
This is the main route out the overhang above Hairy Scary Wall. FA: R.Miller '80s.

SAILOR'S DELIGHT BLOCK
Up the hill from the Hairy Scary Wall, there is a prominent little pinnacle, blocked together with an overhanging flake problem on its south side.

Sailor's Delight B5.10+
On the south side of the block, undercling out the roof and make a long reach to a good edge for both hands. Swing out into the exposure.

Solid Illusion B.1−
Left and below the block there is a fun off-width slot that starts off the ground from a sitting position. Other problems can be found on the rocks surrounding the slot.

THE COCKPIT
Just behind the Sailor's Delight Block is a hidden hole with an interesting overhang and a few variations. The hole was cleared out by Olaf Mitchell to extend the overhang's length.

TREE SLAB
Left of the Cockpit about thirty feet you will see a short smooth slab just to the right of a tree.

Tree Slab Traverse B.1−
This delicate traverse moves across the Tree Slab without using the top edge.

MAGNUM WALL
Around the corner to the left of the Tree Slab there is a section of wall with overhanging starts to blank looking slabs.
Magnum Force B.1
This thin-edged problem is one of the most popular difficult problems at Morrison. On the west side of the overhanging block, just off the ground, there is a hard move that surmounts onto the thin slab above. FA: D. Stone.

Many other difficult problems exist on both sides of the Magnum Wall. Pick a line and go.
Hogback Mama 5.12a (TR)
This may be the most amazing overhang at Morrison. The climb follows a set of good holds up corners and flakes in the huge overhang above the Magnum Wall.
SUDDEN IMPACT AREA
Left of the Magnum Wall there is a gully leading up to a shelf just left of the Hog Back Mama overhang. Follow this gully up to the shelf where you will find some exposed overhangs with big holds.
BOWLING BALL WALL
Left of the gully that leads up to the Sudden Impact Wall there is a pocketed face. One large hole stands out on its left side. Many variations can be played with on this wall.
Standard Route B5.9-B5.11
The prow of this wall can be climbed; a 5.9 move up high leads to an easy choice left or more difficult ground up the right-leaning corner.
NAUTILUS WORKOUT AREA
This is the area left of the Bowling Ball Wall which has a large cave. Many routes ascend in all directions from the cave.
SHARP'S ARETE
Up hill from the Nautilus Wall you will discover a prominent arete with a 5.12 route up it. This was done by Alec Sharp in the '80s. Many other excellent routes can be found all over this wall.

If you where to continue up the ridge to the north you will find other problems spread out amoung the broken ridge. This ridge continues north for a long ways.

Morrison Wall – Right Section

A THE BLACK HOLE
1. Olaf's Roof 5.11 (TR)
2. Wisdom Simulator B5.11+ -B.2 (many variations)
3. Twist and Shout 5.12 lead
4. B.1– problem

5 Rollover B.2
6 Mantle Boulder B.1 –
7 Cheap Whine Overhang 5.11 (TR)
8 Helicopter B.1 (many variations)
9 Sidogrinder Wall B.1 – -B.2
10 Breashears Roof B5.11 –
11 Tendonitis Traverse B5.11 +
12 5.11 Overhang

B MAIN HANGS AREA
1 Bushwhacker 5.10-5.11
2 Inversion #1   5.11 (TR)
3 Traverse B5.10 +
4 Old 5.12 Ramp B5.12a
5 5.11 Face
6 5.10 + lead corner/overhang
7 Holloway's Route B.2 –
8 Inversion #2 5.11 + (TR)
9 numerous problems
10 Balance Mantle B5.10 +

C HAIRY SCARY WALL
1 Local Motions 5.12a (TR)
2 Museum Piece 5.12b (TR)
3 The Black Scoop 5.12 (TR)
4 Scary B5.10
5 Hairy B5.10

172 — *Morrison Wall*

Morrison Wall – Center Section

A HAIRY SCARY WALL
1. 5.10 Prow
2. The Prow B5.9
3. Shin Dig B5.10
4. The Stretcher B5.11
5. Local Motion B5.12a (TR)
6. Museum Piece B5.12b (TR)
7. The Black Scoop B5.12 (TR)
8. Scary B5.10
9. Hairy B5.10
10. Bushwhacker B5.10

B SAILOR'S DELIGHT BLOCK
1. Solid Illusion B.1– offwidth
2. Guter's Problem B5.10
3. Sailor's Delight B5.10+

C THE COCKPIT
1. Pit Overhang B5.9

D SPIKE ROCK
1. Cocaine Corner B5.10
2. Spike Overhang B.1
3. 5.8 Boulder

E TREE SLAB
1. Corner Overhang B5.10
2. B.1– route

Morrison Wall – Left Section

A MAGNUM AREA
1. 5.11 Death
2. Upper Magnum B.1− (TR)
3. Make My Day B.1−
4. Magnum Force B.1
5. Judo Magnum B.1
6. Power Punk B.1+
7. Hogback Mama 5.12a (TR)

Morrison Wall — 175

B SUDDEN IMPACT WALL
1 Sudden Impact B5.9
2 5.10 (TR)

C BOWLING BALL WALL
1 Standard Route 5.9- 5.11
2 Stone Face B5.11b
3 Jug Roof B5.8

D NAUTILUS AREA
1 Nemo B5.10
2 Leaque B5.10
3 5.10 Face
4 The Corners B5.9 (TR)
5 Reed's Solo B5.10+ (TR)
6 The Slot 5.12 (TR)

E SHARP'S ARETE
1 The Chimney Slot 5.10 (TR)
2 Sharp's Arete 5.12a (TR)
3 Middle Face 5.12+ (TR)
4 Mighty Arete 5.12 (TR)
5 Rufus Roof
6 Portable Handhold 5.10X (TR)

F THE OUTBACK AREA
1 The Outback Arete 5.12+ (TR)